DEDICATION

My father, Dr. Frank R. Stewart (1910-1964), served as a teacher, a coach, a high school principal, a county Superintendent of Education, Alabama's State Superintendent and a college president. He was a genial man who could interact with people better than anyone I ever knew, and his life was devoted to the cause of educating children. I dedicate this book to his memory.

FOREWORD

I was a professional player and, I thought, a rather better teacher when I began to write articles and books on bridge. In 1984 I became a co-editor of the ACBL's magazine, and I retired from competition and never un-retired; I found pounding away at a word processor easier and more rewarding than coping with a partner and two opponents. If you think this makes me a questionable counselor, I can't blame you. But in my twenty years as an author, editor, analyst and syndicated columnist, I've had plenty of chances to observe what factors make a winning player. A solid foundation, partnership trust, discipline, focus and judgment will make a winner of anyone, and those are the themes in this book. *Becoming a Bridge Expert* contains four main sections: constructive bidding, dummy play, competitive bidding and defense. Each section has fifteen tips, and most begin with a problem, proceed to illustrative deals and end with a problem so you can see if you have the idea. Assume IMP scoring (like party bridge or Chicago) unless otherwise shown. A fifth section deals with the more personal aspects of the game.

I hope you enjoy it all. May all your finesses be winners!

Frank Stewart
Fayette, AL
August, 2000

ACKNOWLEDGMENTS

Portions of the material originally appeared in the *OKbridge Spectator*, the *American Contract Bridge League Bulletin* and *The Bridge World* and are used with the kind permission of those publications. A few deals and their commentary are adapted from my earlier book *The Bidder's Bible* or from *Daily Bridge Club*, my syndicated column. *The Bridge World* and the ACBL's *World Championship* books were sources of some deals.

CONTENTS

I. Constructive Bidding

Tip 1	Know your basics cold	10
Tip 2	Is it forcing?	19
Tip 3	Choose a sensible system	25
Tip 4	Leave the exotic conventions to your opponents	31
Tip 5	When you suspect how the cards lie, be bold	38
Tip 6	Before you bid, visualize the play	42
Tip 7	Don't play your partner for perfect cards	45
Tip 8	Don't ignore the threat of bad breaks	49
Tip 9	Describe your hand	52
Tip 10	Support your partner	56
Tip 11	Don't be a slave to the point count	59
Tip 12	If it's a misfit, quit	62
Tip 13	Don't make ambiguous bids	66
Tip 14	A cuebid shows slam interest	69
Tip 15	Expert gambitry	74

II. Dummy Play

Tip 1	Know your card combinations	82
Tip 2	Plan before you play	88
Tip 3	Establish your side suit early	92
Tip 4	Assume your contract is makable	95
Tip 5	Consider what can go wrong	101
Tip 6	Find out what you need to know	105
Tip 7	Assume a logical opening lead	109
Tip 8	Assume the defenders' plays make sense to them	114
Tip 9	'Eight ever, nine never?' Don't believe it!	118
Tip 10	With extra trumps, look for an endplay	122
Tip 11	Look for the loser-on-loser	125
Tip 12	Run your long suit	129
Tip 13	Attack your weak suit!	132
Tip 14	Let your opponents make the mistakes	136
Tip 15	The discards have a message	141

III. Competitive Bidding

Tip 1	Know your basics cold	146
Tip 2	Is it forcing?	153
Tip 3	When your partner strains to compete, don't hang him	158
Tip 4	Don't let competition get your goat	162
Tip 5	In a competitive auction, put your partner in the picture	166
Tip 6	Make your bidding farsighted	172
Tip 7	Support your partner	176
Tip 8	When you overcall, weigh what you have to gain and to lose	179
Tip 9	Beware the 'death seat'	185
Tip 10	Preempt sensibly	187
Tip 11	Don't sell out too soon	192
Tip 12	See what your partner thinks	197
Tip 13	Don't be trigger-happy	201
Tip 14	Make inferential penalty doubles	206
Tip 15	Direct the defense	210

IV. Defense

Tip 1	Opening leads: let the bidding guide you	216
Tip 2	Opening leads: be willing to go against the book	219
Tip 3	Opening leads: when your partner is weak, all bets are off	222
Tip 4	Give yourself a chance	225
Tip 5	Preserve your options	229
Tip 6	Cherish the ace of trumps	233
Tip 7	Count, count, count!	236
Tip 8	Assume declarer is operating correctly	240
Tip 9	Assume your partner knows what he's doing	244
Tip 10	Make things easy for your partner	248
Tip 11	Don't give declarer an easy ride	252
Tip 12	Don't be a winner grabber	256
Tip 13	Don't get hung up on suit preference	260
Tip 14	Look for extra trump tricks	264
Tip 15	Conceal your holding	269

V. Personal Glimpses

Tip 1	Honor your partner	274
Tip 2	Don't be contentious with your opponents	281
Tip 3	Maintain your focus	282
Tip 4	Be all you can be	286
Tip 5	Cultivate your table presence	291
Tip 6	For bridge teachers: can bridge be taught?	295
Tip 7	Enjoy the post-mortem	298

CONSTRUCTIVE BIDDING

①

Constructive bidding is bidding with no interference. The term also describes a bid that is encouraging or suggests more values than one might expect. In Standard methods, for instance, a single raise promises six to nine points, but in some styles, `constructive' single raises promise more.

When I teach intermediate players, I stress the importance of a solid bidding foundation. If a player never errs in a textbook sequence, he'll have an edge over 95% of his competitors; and the best part of an expert's game is that he never fouls up a basic auction. Hence, my first tip ...

KNOW YOUR BASICS COLD

TIP 1

Here's a multiple-choice quiz. For each sequence, pick the hand East is most likely to hold using Standard bidding methods. Each answer appears under the problem — cover the page so you won't peek.

1)

	WEST	EAST
		1♠
	2◇	2♠
	2NT	3♡

a) ♠ A Q 9 7 4 3
♡ A J 10 4
◇ J 4
♣ 3

b) ♠ A Q 7 6 4 3
♡ A J 6 4 2
◇ J
♣ 3

c) ♠ A J 8 7 6
♡ A K Q
◇ J 2
♣ 4 3 2

d) ♠ A Q 7 6 5 4
♡ A K 4 3
◇ K 3
♣ 3

Since East's sequence suggests six spades, four hearts and minimum values, (a) is correct. Hand (b) would rebid 2♡; hand (c) would raise 2NT to 3NT; hand (d) would bid spades-hearts-spades, showing 6-4 in the majors with extra strength.

2)

	WEST	EAST
	1♡	1♠
	2♣	2♡

a) ♠ A 6 5 4
♡ K 5 4
◇ 5 4 3 2
♣ 7 5

b) ♠ A 7 6 5 3
♡ K Q
◇ 4 3 2
♣ Q 4 3

c) ♠ A 6 5 4
♡ K J 3
◇ 4 3 2
♣ Q 4 3

d) ♠ A 7 6 5 4
♡ Q 3
◇ 6 5 4 3
♣ Q 4

Hand (a), which is worth only one bid, would raise 1♡ to 2♡ at its first turn; hands (b) and (c) are too strong for a cheap preference — either hand might jump to 3♡ over 2♣. Hand (d) is correct: East will have only two hearts on this bidding.

3)

	WEST	EAST
		1♠
	2◇	2♡
	2NT	3♠

a) ♠ A Q 9 7 4 3
♡ A J 10 4
◇ J 4
♣ 3

b) ♠ A Q 7 6 4 3
♡ A J 6 4 2
◇ J
♣ 3

c) ♠ A Q 8 7 6
♡ A K 4 3
◇ Q 2
♣ 4 3

d) ♠ A Q 7 6 5 4
♡ A K 4 3
◇ K 3
♣ 3

Hand (d) is correct. Hand (a) would bid spades-spades-hearts; hand (b) would bid 3♡ or 4♡ over 2NT; hand (c) would raise 2NT to 3NT.

	WEST	EAST
④	1♠	2◇
	2♠	2NT
	3♡	3♠

a) ♠ Q 5 3
  ♡ 10 4 3
  ◇ A J 6 5
  ♣ A 10 4

b) ♠ Q 3
  ♡ K 7 6
  ◇ Q J 6 5 4
  ♣ K 4 3

c) ♠ Q 6
  ♡ A J 5
  ◇ Q 9 7 4 3
  ♣ A 10 4

d) ♠ Q 5
  ♡ A J 3
  ◇ A 7 6 5 4
  ♣ 6 5 4

Hand (b) is correct.   Hand (a) would raise 2♠ to 3♠; hand (c) would jump to 3NT over 2♠; hand (d), with all working cards, would jump to 4♠ over 3♡.

	WEST	EAST
⑤	1♠	2♣
	2♡	4♠

a) ♠ K 7 6
  ♡ 7 6
  ◇ A Q 6
  ♣ A J 4 3 2

b) ♠ K 7 6
  ♡ K 7
  ◇ A J 4
  ♣ A J 4 3 2

c) ♠ Q 6 5 4
  ♡ 6 5
  ◇ A 5
  ♣ A J 5 4 3

d) ♠ K Q 4 3
  ♡ 4 3
  ◇ 5 4
  ♣ A K Q 4 3

Hand (d) is correct: this sequence suggests strong spades, strong clubs and slam interest. Hands (a) and (b) would jump to 3♠ (forcing) over 2♡; hand (c) would do likewise but might just raise spades without introducing the clubs.

	WEST	EAST
⑥	1♡	1NT
	2♣	2♠

a) ♠ 9 8 7 6 5 3
  ♡ 5
  ◇ J 6 5
  ♣ A Q 3

b) ♠ A K Q
  ♡ 5 4
  ◇ J 6 5 4
  ♣ 10 5 4 3

c) ♠ A K 2
  ♡ 3
  ◇ 8 7 5
  ♣ Q 8 7 6 5 3

d) ♠ A 7
  ♡ 4 3
  ◇ J 8 6 5
  ♣ K 9 6 5 2

Hand (c) is correct: the 2♠ bid shows spade values in a hand greatly improved by West's 2♣ rebid.   Hand (a) would respond 1♠ over 1♡. Hand (b) would raise 2♣ to 3♣ or try 2NT; hand (d) would raise 2♣ to 3♣.

	WEST	EAST
7		1♣
	1♠	2♡

a) ♠ 5 4
   ♡ A K 4 3
   ◊ J 5 4
   ♣ A Q 5 4

b) ♠ 6
   ♡ Q 6 5 4 3
   ◊ A 4
   ♣ A K Q 5 4

c) ♠ A J
   ♡ A Q 5 4
   ◊ 5 4
   ♣ A K J 6 5

d) ♠ J 7
   ♡ A K 5 4
   ◊ K 4 3
   ♣ A K J 5

Hand (c) is correct: East has reversed and promises great strength and longer clubs than hearts. Hand (a) would rebid 1NT; hand (b) would open 1♡; hand (d) would jump to 2NT over 1♠.

	WEST	EAST
8		1♡
	2♣	2◊
	2NT	3♣

a) ♠ —
   ♡ A K 7 6 5
   ◊ A 7 6 5
   ♣ J 6 5 4

b) ♠ 6
   ♡ A K 7 6 5
   ◊ A 7 6 5
   ♣ J 5 4

c) ♠ 7
   ♡ A Q 7 6 5
   ◊ A J 7 6
   ♣ K Q 5

d) ♠ —
   ♡ A K 7 6 5
   ◊ Q J 9 7 6
   ♣ A J 6

Hand (b) is correct; this sequence should show a minimum hand that prefers not to play in notrump. Hand (a) would raise 2♣ to 3♣; hand (c) would jump to 4♣ over 2NT; example (d) is a hard hand to describe but might jump to 4♣ or 4◊ over 2NT.

These answers reflect my opinion, but many experts would bid as East did with hands (c) and (d) and perhaps even with (a), since they would treat East's sequence — a change of suit followed by a bid supporting partner — as strong and forcing. Presumably, they'd raise 2♣ to 3♣ or pass 2NT with (b). But without the change of suit, for example in this auction:

	WEST	EAST
		1♡
	2♣	2♡
	2NT	3♣

in which East limited his strength with the 2♡ rebid, his 3♣ would certainly not be forcing. Discuss both sequences with your regular partner.

	WEST	EAST
		1♠
	1NT	2♦
	3♦	3♡

⑨

a) ♠ A Q 8 6 5   b) ♠ A Q 6 5 4   c) ♠ A Q 6 5 4   d) ♠ A K 6 5 4 2
   ♡ A 7 6 5   ♡ A Q 5   ♡ A J 6   ♡ A J 6
   ◇ A J 5 4   ◇ K J 5 4   ◇ A K 5 4   ◇ K J 4 3
   ♣ —   ♣ 5   ♣ 3   ♣ —

Hand (b) is correct: East has enough strength to move toward game, and 3♡ is his most descriptive bid. Hand (a) would rebid 2♡ over 1NT; hand (c) would jump shift to 3◇ over 1NT; hand (d) would bid 3♠, forcing, over 3◇.

	WEST	EAST
	1♡	1♠
	1NT	2♡

⑩

a) ♠ A 7 6 5 4   b) ♠ A 7 6 5 4   c) ♠ A 9 6 4 3   d) ♠ A 9 6 5 3
   ♡ K Q   ♡ Q J 5   ♡ A Q 4   ♡ K J
   ◇ 6 5 4   ◇ 5 4   ◇ 4 3   ◇ K 5 4
   ♣ 5 4 3   ♣ 5 4 3   ♣ 5 4 3   ♣ 5 4 3

Hand (c) is correct. With heart support and a weak hand, East would have raised to 2♡ right away. Here he promises about ten points with real heart support. Hand (a) would pass 1NT; hand (b) would raise 1♡ to 2♡ initially; hand (d) would raise 1NT to 2NT.

	WEST	EAST
	1♠	2◇
	2♠	3♣
	3◇	3♠

⑪

a) ♠ Q 6 5   b) ♠ Q 5   c) ♠ Q 6 5   d) ♠ Q 5
   ♡ 5 4   ♡ 8 7   ♡ 7   ♡ 7 6
   ◇ A J 4 3   ◇ Q 8 7 6 3   ◇ A Q 6 5 4   ◇ A K 5 4 3
   ♣ K J 4 3   ♣ A K 5 4   ♣ A K 6 5   ♣ A J 5 4

Hand (d) is correct: East's sequence is forcing. Hand (a) would raise 2♠ to 3♠; hand (b) can't force to game and would probably risk raising 2♠ to 3♠; hand (c) would jump to 4♠ over 3◇.

	WEST	EAST
(12)	1♠	2◇
	2♡	3♣
	3NT	4♠

a) ♠ K 6 5
♡ 4
◇ A J 5 4 3
♣ K J 5 4

b) ♠ K 7 6
♡ 6 5
◇ A Q 7 6
♣ A K 5 4

c) ♠ Q 6 5
♡ —
◇ A Q 7 6 5 4
♣ K 4 3 2

d) ♠ K J 5
♡ 5
◇ A Q 5 4 3
♣ A J 5 4

Hand (d) is correct: East's sequence shows slam interest with good spade support and a singleton heart. If West has 'working' honors such as the ◇K, ♡A and good trumps, he should move toward slam. Hands (a) and (b) would jump to 3♠ (forcing) over 2♡, and (c) might also.

	WEST	EAST
(13)		1◇
	1♡	1♠
	1NT	2♡

a) ♠ A 7 6 5
♡ J 7 6 5
◇ A K 5 4
♣ 3

b) ♠ A 7 6 5
♡ K 6 5
◇ A Q 5 4
♣ 6 5

c) ♠ A 7 6 5
♡ K 7 6
◇ A K 6 5
♣ Q 6

d) ♠ A 9 6 5
♡ Q 7 6
◇ A K J 7 6
♣ 4

Hand (a) would raise 1♡ to 2♡; hand (b) can't bid a third time and would pass 1NT; hand (c) would open 1NT. Hand (d) is correct: East must have better than minimum values to bid again when West suggests weakness.

If East has

♠ J 5 4 3   ♡ K J 4   ◇ A K 5 4 3   ♣ 5

I believe he should let the spades go and raise 1♡ to 2♡. The direct raise is also barely possible on (b), but this is not as good a hand for hearts, so opener has more reason to look for alternative strains.

	WEST	EAST
(14)	1♡	1NT
	2♡	2♠

a) ♠ 9 8 7 6 5
♡ 3
◇ A 6 5 4
♣ Q 4 2

b) ♠ A K 4
♡ K 6
◇ 7 6 5 4
♣ 6 5 4 3

c) ♠ A 6
♡ —
◇ J 10 7 6 4
♣ Q 9 7 6 5 4

d) ♠ 8 7 6 5
♡ —
◇ K 9 7 6 4
♣ K 8 7 5

This is a tricky one. Hands (a) and (d) would respond 1♠ over 1♡; hand (b) would raise 2♡ to 3♡ or try 2NT. Hand (c) is correct: East's odd sequence says, "Pick a minor."

	WEST	EAST
		1♣
15	1♡	1♠
	2♣	2♡

a) ♠ A Q 6 5
♡ Q 4
◇ 6 5
♣ A K Q 7 6

b) ♠ A 7 6 5
♡ J 6 5
◇ 6 5
♣ A K J 5

c) ♠ A K 6 5
♡ Q 7 6
◇ 7
♣ A Q J 7 6

d) ♠ A J 6 5
♡ K 7 6
◇ 6 5
♣ A K J 6

Hand (c) is correct; again, once West's 2♣ preference shows weakness, East needs a good hand to bid again and suggest game. Hand (a) would bid 3♣ over 2♣. Hand (b) would pass 2♣; hand (d) would open 1NT.

	WEST	EAST
		pass
16	1♡	2♠

a) ♠ K J 10 7 6 5
♡ 4
◇ 6 5 4
♣ 8 5 3

b) ♠ A K J 8 7
♡ A 6
◇ 7 6 4
♣ 10 6 5

c) ♠ K Q 10 8 7
♡ 8 7
◇ A 6 5
♣ Q 8 7

d) ♠ A Q 6 5 4
♡ K J 7 6
◇ 6 5
♣ 6 5

Hand (d) is correct: West's opening bid has improved East's hand. The jump shift by a passed hand promises a fit and is forcing (see Tip 9 in this section). Hand (a) would bid 2♠ only if using weak jump shifts; hand (b) would have opened the bidding; hand (c) would respond only 1♠ — it's a good hand, but no better than it was.

	WEST	EAST
		1NT
17	3♡	4◇

a) ♠ 7 6 5
♡ K 6 5
◇ A K Q 6 5
♣ K J

b) ♠ A 7 6
♡ 7 6
◇ A K Q 9 7
♣ K 7 6

c) ♠ A 5
♡ 7 6
◇ K Q J 7 6 5
♣ A Q 7

d) ♠ A 5
♡ A Q 7 6
◇ A K 6 5
♣ 8 7 5

Hand (d) is correct: the advance cuebid promises maximum strength, super heart support and diamond values. Hand (a) would just raise 3♡ to 4♡; hand (b) would bid 3NT over 3♡; hand (c) would open 1◇ (I hope).

	WEST	EAST
(18)	1♠	3♣
	3♠	4♡

a) ♠ K
  ♡ A K 6 5
  ◇ 7 6
  ♣ A K J 7 6 5

b) ♠ A 6
  ♡ A K 4
  ◇ 6 5
  ♣ A Q 8 6 5 4

c) ♠ K 6
  ♡ A 6 5
  ◇ K 5 4
  ♣ A K J 6 5

d) ♠ K Q 4
  ♡ A 5
  ◇ 6 5
  ♣ A K J 6 5 4

Experts avoid using a jump shift unless they know which suit will be trumps; otherwise, they need room to find a trump suit. Hands (a) and (b) would therefore start by responding 2♣; hand (c) would respond 3♣ but would rebid 3NT over 3♠. Hand (d) is correct; if West bids 4♠ next, East will raise to 5♠, asking him to bid a slam with a diamond control.

	WEST	EAST
(19)		1◇
	1♠	2♣
	3◇¹	3♠

1. Invitational.

a) ♠ Q J 5
  ♡ 4
  ◇ A 7 6 5 4
  ♣ A J 5 4

b) ♠ J 5 4
  ♡ 6
  ◇ A K 8 7 6
  ♣ A K 7 6

c) ♠ Q 4
  ♡ 6 5
  ◇ A K 5 4 3
  ♣ A Q 5 4

d) ♠ K Q 3
  ♡ 5
  ◇ A 6 5 4 3
  ♣ A Q 5 4

Hand (b) is correct. Hand (a) should raise 1♠ to 2♠; even though West has only three trumps, he should limit his minimum hand quickly. Hand (c) would bid 4◇ or even 5◇ over 3◇; hand (d) would jump to 4♠ over 3◇, suggesting three strong spades.

	WEST	EAST
(20)		1◇
	1♡	2♣
	2NT	3♠

a) ♠ A 9 6
  ♡ 5
  ◇ A Q J 6 3
  ♣ A 10 6 5

b) ♠ A 4
  ♡ 7
  ◇ K Q 6 5 4
  ♣ K J 10 7 6

c) ♠ A 6
  ♡ 7
  ◇ A K 6 5 4
  ♣ K Q 10 5 4

d) ♠ 10 7 6 3
  ♡ —
  ◇ A K 5 4 2
  ♣ A K 5 4

East cannot have 'real' spades, as in hand (d) — he would have rebid 1♠ over 1♡. Hand (c) is correct: East is showing a strong minor two-suiter and suggesting that slam is possible. With a less distributional hand, like (a), he would raise 2NT to 3NT; with a weaker hand, like (b), he would sign off in 3♣ over 2NT;

	WEST	EAST
		1◇
21	1♠	2♣
	2♡	2♠

a) ♠ K J 5
  ♡ 6
  ◇ A J 10 4 3
  ♣ K 5 4 3

b) ♠ Q 4
  ♡ K 4
  ◇ A Q 10 4 3
  ♣ A 10 5 4

c) ♠ Q 5
  ♡ 6 5
  ◇ A J 5 4 2
  ♣ A Q 5 4

d) ♠ K J 2
  ♡ 5
  ◇ A Q 7 6 5
  ♣ A Q 5 4

Hand (c) is correct. Hand (a) would raise 1♠ to 2♠; hand (b) would bid 2NT over 2♡; hand (d) would jump to 3♠ over 2♡.

	WEST	EAST
		1◇
22	1♠	3♠

a) ♠ K Q 4
  ♡ A Q 3
  ◇ A K 5 4 3
  ♣ 4 3

b) ♠ K J 5 4
  ♡ A 5
  ◇ A K J 6
  ♣ 6 5 4

c) ♠ K J 5 4
  ♡ A 5
  ◇ A K J 5 4
  ♣ 5 4

d) ♠ A Q 6 5
  ♡ 6
  ◇ A K J 5 4
  ♣ A 6 5

Hand (c) is correct: East's sequence denies balanced distribution. Hand (a) has only three spades so would improvise with a reverse to 2♡ over 1♠, intending to support spades next; hand (b) would open 1NT; hand (d) is too strong for 3♠ and would try 3♣ or 4♡ (splinter).

	WEST	EAST
		1◇
23	1♠	2NT
	3♡	4♠

a) ♠ K Q
  ♡ A Q
  ◇ A Q 9 7 6
  ♣ Q 9 6 2

b) ♠ 10 7 6 5
  ♡ A Q 3
  ◇ A K 5 4
  ♣ A Q

c) ♠ A K 5
  ♡ Q 5 4
  ◇ A Q 4 3
  ♣ A 7 6

d) ♠ J 7 6
  ♡ A K
  ◇ A Q 5 4 3
  ♣ K Q 5

Hand (a) would bid 3NT over 3♡ and might rebid 2♣ or 3♣ instead of 2NT. On (b) most experts would raise 1♠ directly to 4♠; some would try 2NT first given the poor trumps, but might then bid 3♠ over 3♡. Hand (d) would bid only 3♠ over 3♡. Hand (c) is correct because East's jump suggests strong spades. Principle: *a player who jumps when he doesn't need to has strength in the suit he jumps in.*

Players who adhere to the Principle of Fast Arrival believe that a 4♠ bid here shows no interest in any other contract. Since the auction will usually end at 4♠ anyway, bidding it directly suggests a less promising hand than does a slower approach. My book *The Bidder's*

Bible includes a discussion of Fast Arrival. It is a flawed concept in several ways, but to justify a jump to 4♠ on this auction, opener must be sure spades is the best strain (and not notrump, say). Also, if slam is in the picture, trump quality is a vital factor, and opener must reassure responder that trump quality is not a deterrent.

If this kind of jump is played, as it should be, to show strength in a suit, then on an auction such as

WEST	EAST
	1◇
1♡	1♠
2♣	2◇
3♠	

West has a singleton diamond and good spades. On this next auction he has shown good clubs:

WEST	EAST
	1◇
1♡	1♠
3♣	3◇
3♠	

	WEST	EAST
		1♡
24	1♠	2♠
	2NT	3♡

a) ♠ J 5 4	b) ♠ J 7 6 5	c) ♠ K J 5	d) ♠ K J 5
♡ A K 6 5 4	♡ A K 6 5 4	♡ A J 10 6 5 4	♡ A K 10 9 6 5
◇ 7 6	◇ 5 4	◇ 5 4	◇ K 5
♣ A J 6	♣ A 4	♣ A 4	♣ 6 5

Hand (c) is correct: East shows three spades, six hearts and minimum values. Hand (a) might raise to 2♠ but would just pass 2NT; hand (b) would bid 3♠ or 4♠ over 2NT; hand (d) would jump to 4♡ over 2NT.

	WEST	EAST
		1♣
25	1◇	1♡
	2♣	2NT

a) ♠ A Q 3	b) ♠ A 5 4	c) ♠ Q 4 3	d) ♠ A Q
♡ J 5 4 3	♡ K 5 4 3	♡ Q 5 4 3	♡ Q 10 6 5
◇ 5 4 3	◇ 6	◇ A 7	◇ A 10
♣ A K 2	♣ A K Q 5 4	♣ A K J 4	♣ A J 5 4 3

Hand (d) is correct. Hand (a) would pass 2♣. Hand (b) would

BECOMING A BRIDGE EXPERT

try for game despite West's weak preference but wouldn't be eager to bid notrump; East would try 3♣ or 2♠. Hand (c) would open 1NT, of course.

The record of major championships is full of disasters caused by a difference of opinion over whether or not a bid was forcing. The deal below, from a U.S. Trials, was reported in *The Bridge World*.

TIP 2

IS IT FORCING?

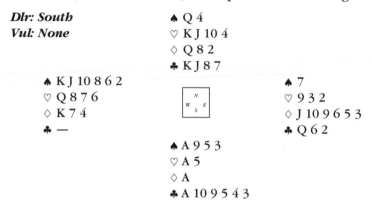

Dlr: South
Vul: None

```
                    ♠ Q 4
                    ♡ K J 10 4
                    ◇ Q 8 2
                    ♣ K J 8 7
♠ K J 10 8 6 2              ♠ 7
♡ Q 8 7 6         N         ♡ 9 3 2
◇ K 7 4        W     E      ◇ J 10 9 6 5 3
♣ —               S         ♣ Q 6 2
                    ♠ A 9 5 3
                    ♡ A 5
                    ◇ A
                    ♣ A 10 9 5 4 3
```

At one table North-South overreached to 7♣. After the ♠J opening lead, South could have succeeded but didn't. (A complex squeeze would make the grand slam on any lead.) In the replay:

WEST	NORTH	EAST	SOUTH
			1♣
2♠	3♠	pass	4♣
all pass			

North-South weren't using negative doubles, so North started with a cuebid, angling for notrump. When South rebid 4♣ — he was setting the trump suit before cuebidding — North passed with his junky hand.

It's unclear to what level North's 3♠ cuebid should be forcing (to game, or just to 4♣), but if practiced expert partnerships can have such misunderstandings, it's no wonder that casual partnerships have them. The more time a partnership devotes to defining auctions, the better its results will be. Here are twenty-five bidding sequences; decide whether or not the last bid is forcing. I'll tell you how I think it should be played, but the answer isn't always clear-cut. In the end, the only 'correct' answers are the ones on which you and your partner agree.

	WEST	EAST
(1)	1♣	1♡
	1♠	

	WEST	EAST
(2)	1◇	1♠
	2♣	2♠
	3◇	

	WEST	EAST
(3)	1◇	1♡
	1♠	3◇

	WEST	EAST
(4)	1◇	1♡
	1♠	2♣[1]
	2♡	3◇
	1. Fourth-suit forcing.	

	WEST	EAST
(5)	1◇	1♡
	1♠	2♣[1]
	2◇	3◇
	1. Fourth-suit forcing.	

	WEST	EAST
(6)	1◇	1♡
	1♠	3♡

	WEST	EAST
(7)	1◇	1♡
	1♠	2NT

	WEST	EAST
(8)	1◇	1♠
	2♠	3◇

	WEST	EAST
(9)	1♡	1♠
	2♣	3♡

	WEST	EAST
(10)	2♣	2◇
	2♡	3♣[1]
	3♡	
	1. Second negative.	

BECOMING A BRIDGE EXPERT

	WEST	EAST
(11)	1♡	2♡
	2♠	3♣

	WEST	EAST
(12)	1♣	1♠
	2♣	2♢
	2NT	3♣

	WEST	EAST
(13)	1♡	2♣
	3♣	

	WEST	EAST
(14)	1♠	2♣
	2♠	

	WEST	EAST
(15)	1♡	2♣
	2♡	2♠
	2NT	3♣

	WEST	EAST
(16)	pass	1♢
	2NT	3♢

	WEST	EAST
(17)	1♢	1♠
	2♡	3♢
	4♢	

	WEST	EAST
(18)	1♣	1♠
	3♣	4♣

	WEST	EAST
(19)	1♣	1♠
	2♣	2♡

	WEST	EAST
(20)	1♢	1♠
	2♢	2NT
	3♠	

	WEST	EAST
(21)	3♣	3♡

1 · CONSTRUCTIVE BIDDING

	WEST	EAST
(22)	1NT	2♡[1]
	2♠	3♣
	1. Transfer.	

	WEST	EAST
(23)	1♡	2♣
	2NT	

	WEST	EAST
(24)	1♡	2♣
	2NT	3♡

	WEST	EAST
(25)	1◊	2♣
	2♡	3♣

MY PREFERENCES

1. **Not forcing.** Some pairs play it as forcing, but that gives responder a problem with, for example,

   ♠ K 8 5   ♡ J 7 5 3 2   ◊ 7 5 4   ♣ Q 6

2. **Not forcing.** Neither 2♣ nor 2♠ was forcing, so 3◊ can't be.

3. **Forcing.** If this sequence isn't forcing, a missed 5-3 heart fit may result.

4. **Not forcing.** This, I think, should be the invitational sequence, but opinions vary about how far the auction should be forcing after a 'fourth-suit' bid by responder. Discuss this sequence and the previous one with your favorite partner.

5. **Not forcing.** Game may be in doubt even if responder has fair values.

6. **Not forcing.**

7. **Not forcing.** With enough strength for game, responder could bid 3NT or try 2♣.

8. **Forcing.** But if the partnership style is to raise to 2♠ often with three-card support, then not forcing makes sense.

9. Not forcing.

10. Not forcing if the 2♣ opening promises only nine playing tricks, but forcing if it guarantees ten or more.

11. Forcing — unless, perhaps, using four-card majors.

12. Forcing. If responder had real club support with invitational strength, he'd raise to 3♣ at his second turn. However, if responder's second bid had been 2♡, the inference would be weaker: some players might feel constrained to show the hearts, especially playing matchpoints, on a hand such as

♠ A 10 7 6 4   ♡ K J 7 4   ◇ 7   ♣ J 7 5

13. Not forcing. This is one of those 'not forcing but never passed' auctions, but if a bid isn't forcing, it isn't.

14. Forcing. This is no problem for pairs who play the 2♣ response as game-forcing. In Standard, responders have been known to pass 2♠ with minimum values and no spade fit; but since responder almost never passes, it makes sense to play the sequence as forcing.

15. Forcing. Responder's reverse is forcing to game.

16. Forcing, as most play. But since opener will sometimes have a minimum distributional hand, not forcing is playable.

17. Not forcing. Opener's reverse has shown strength and is considered game-forcing in some partnerships; but even 'game-forcing' auctions need not force to the five-level.

18. Not forcing. I'm in the minority here; most experts consider 4♣ forcing.

19. Forcing. A new suit by responder is forcing, but a case exists for playing 2♡ as not forcing here.

20. Forcing. Belated support is generally treated as forcing. Still, many players would raise to 2♠ with good three-card spade support and decent values. Therefore, a case exists for playing 3♠ as not forcing — implying distress (see Tip 10 in this section).

21. **Forcing.** Responder has no reason to bid a new suit with a weak hand.

22. **Not forcing.** Most pairs play a new suit after a transfer as forcing. I prefer the invitational treatment since it lets me bid good games with minimum high-card values when the hands fit well.

23. **Not forcing** in Standard, assuming opener can rebid 2NT with nothing extra.

24. **Not forcing,** although opener will seldom pass. Again, this is not a problem in a forcing Two-over-One style. In Standard, this sequence used to be forcing since four-card majors were common, and a pass risked landing the partnership in a 4-3 fit. With five-card majors, a pass by responder is possible.

25. **Forcing.** But if opener can 'reverse' to 2♡ with no extra strength after a two-over-one response, not forcing is possible.

No matter what methods you choose, you and partner must agree. If you aren't sure whether a bid is forcing, avoid making it — place the contract or make a bid partner can't misinterpret. Look at this deal:

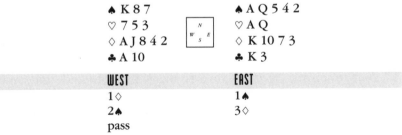

	♠ K 8 7		♠ A Q 5 4 2
	♡ 7 5 3		♡ A Q
	◇ A J 8 4 2		◇ K 10 7 3
	♣ A 10		♣ K 3

WEST	EAST
1◇	1♠
2♠	3◇
pass	

East thought 3◇ was forcing; West wasn't sure. Theory aside, East could have tried for slam by jumping to 4◇, a bid West couldn't misunderstand. For a related discussion, see Tip 13 in this section.

By 'sensible,' I mean a system that will produce the best results in practice, not in theory. Jeff Meckstroth-Eric Rodwell ('Meckwell', as they are known) use a complex system that constantly changes. Meckwell are professionals, and their long hours of work have paid off in world titles. Longtime partnerships who have spent hundreds of hours discussing their methods can benefit from a complicated style; but when two players strike up a casual partnership, simpler is better. If you play an unfamiliar system or convention, the chance of a misunderstanding outweighs the chance of any gain.

I often watch two players form an impromptu partnership on OKbridge, the Internet bridge server. The exchange is usually abbreviated, and might go something like this:

"NF Stayman Capp 1430 Bergen, pard?"

"No Bergen but supp dbls."

"OK."

Well, it's fine to agree on a few conventions — the fewer the better if you don't have time to discuss them. But style is as important as system; if I had just two minutes to discuss methods with a new partner, I'd ask whether his approach is sound or aggressive. Does he overcall on solid values or on a whim? Are his preempts 'textbook'? Does he like to open light, shapely hands? These *treatments* — different ways of playing natural bids (such as the range for a 1NT opening) — are as important to agree on as conventions. Look at this example:

TIP 3

CHOOSE A SENSIBLE SYSTEM

Dlr: East
Vul: E-W

	♠ A 10 6 4	
	♡ 3	
	◇ A 10 6 5 4	
	♣ J 5 3	

♠ Q J 9 7 5		♠ 8 3
♡ 10 9 5		♡ K 8 7 6 2
◇ K J	N W E S	◇ 3 2
♣ K 10 2		♣ A 9 8 4

	♠ K 2	
	♡ A Q J 4	
	◇ Q 9 8 7	
	♣ Q 7 6	

WEST	NORTH	EAST	SOUTH
		pass	1◇
pass	1♠	pass	1NT
pass	3◇	pass	3NT
all pass			

When this deal came up on OKbridge, North thought his jump

preference to 3♢ was invitational. South thought it might be forcing, and as a result North-South landed in 3NT with 23 points.

In an experienced partnership, North might bid 2♣, new minor forcing, over 1NT. South would try 2♡, and now North's conversion to 3♢ would invite. Or perhaps a direct jump to 3♢ by North over 1NT would, by agreement, be invitational. But this is a common sequence even a casual partnership ought to discuss. If I could ask one 'treatment' question of a new partner, it would be, "Are responder's secondary jump rebids and preferences forcing or invitational?"

What happened to 3NT on this deal? West led the ♠7, and South missed a chance when he played low from dummy and won with the king. He continued with the ♢A and another diamond, and West won and led the ♠Q. South took the ace and led a heart: deuce, queen, five. He might have cashed some diamonds next but instead led a club to the deuce, jack and ace. A club return by East at this point would have given the defense five tricks, but East returned a heart. When South's jack won, he was home with four diamonds, three hearts and two spades.

On the first heart, West might have played the ten, denying the jack, instead of signaling count; but East had enough information to make the winning play. East was playing South for a hand such as

♠ K 2   ♡ A Q 9 4   ♢ Q 9 8 7   ♣ Q 10 6

but then South would have started on clubs earlier to set up his ninth trick. By taking an early heart finesse, South might give the defense time to establish a heart for the setting trick.

Many casual partnerships go into battle with the popular Two-over-One Game-forcing style, in which an unpassed responder's bid of a new suit at the two-level usually forces to game. Two-over-One reminds me of the upgrades to word-processors that appear regularly. They have lots of extra bells and whistles and let you delete a word in six new and different ways. They may be better in theory, but my experience is that the best word processor is the one the user is most comfortable with — and in my case that's my old dinosaur, Wordstar.

Marshall Miles boldly wrote that nobody could become a world-class player using Two-over-One. I think Marshall was saying it's hard to develop good judgment when you use a system with so many constraints. I'll go further: *my experience suggests that Two-over-One is less effective than old-fashioned methods, especially in casual partnerships.*

One of the many flaws in Two-over-One is that responder can't show his side strength with an invitational hand. Suppose you hold

♠ A K Q 9 7   ♡ A 6 4 2   ◇ 6   ♣ Q 6 5

You open 1♠, and partner responds 1NT, forcing. You rebid 2♡, and he jumps to 3♠, inviting game. Do you bid 4♠ now? Sorry, partner has

♠ J 10 4   ♡ Q 7 3   ◇ A K 8 4   ♣ 7 4 2

The opening lead is a club, and they take three clubs and exit with a trump. The ♡K is wrong, and you lose two hearts as well. Down two.

Did you say you'd pass 3♠? Sorry, you missed a good game. Partner has

♠ J 10 4   ♡ Q 7 3   ◇ 7 4 2   ♣ A K 8 4

You ruff the second diamond, draw trumps and try the clubs. They split 4-2, but the ♡K is onside. Making four. Using old-fashioned methods, the bidding on the second pair of hands would go

♠ A K Q 9 7	♠ J 10 4
♡ A 6 4 2	♡ Q 7 3
◇ 6	◇ 7 4 2
♣ Q 6 5	♣ A K 8 4

OPENER	RESPONDER
1♠	2♣
2♡	2♠
4♠	

but on the first pair of hands, after

♠ A K Q 9 7	♠ J 10 4
♡ A 6 4 2	♡ Q 7 3
◇ 6	◇ A K 8 4
♣ Q 6 5	♣ 7 4 2

OPENER	RESPONDER
1♠	2◇
2♡	2♠

opener might pass, disliking the misfit.

The advent of lighter opening bids hasn't made Two-over-One more accurate. I watched a good pair bid these hands as follows:

♠ 8 4 2	♠ Q 5
♡ Q 10 5	♡ A K J 8 7 6
◇ A Q 7	◇ J 6 3
♣ A J 5 2	♣ 7 3

WEST	EAST
	1♡
2♣	2♡
4♡	

Down one. If East is going to open hands like that, West mustn't force to game — but how can he not?

Sometimes responder will want to force to game — for a while.

♠ 9 4 2		♠ J 6
♡ 6		♡ A K Q 8 7
◊ A J 5 4 2		◊ Q 6 3
♣ A K 9 4		♣ 7 3 2

WEST	EAST
	1♡
2◊	2♡
3♣	3◊
Groan.	

West would love to pass but cannot. The 2◊ response created a game force, and East might bid the same way with a much better hand. Even a slam could be cold.

A fundamental problem with Two-over-One is illustrated by this deal from an IMP game on OKbridge.

♠ 3		♠ A K Q J 10 7 4
♡ 7 5 3		♡ A 10
◊ A K 10		◊ 7
♣ A Q 9 8 5 2		♣ 10 6 3

WEST	NORTH	EAST	SOUTH
		1♠	pass
2♣	pass	2♠(!)	pass
3◊	pass	3♡	dbl
pass	pass	4♠	all pass

Since West's 2♣ was forcing to game, East saw no need to jump despite his massive trick-taking power, club fit and red-suit controls; he could rebid 2♠ 'to save space'. This bid told West nothing. Neither did East's 3♡; and whatever his 4♠ was supposed to show, West didn't get the message. Using old-fashioned methods, I would expect:

WEST	EAST
	1♠
2♣	3♠
4♣	4♡[1]
5◊	6♠

1. Cuebid. With hearts, East would bid 2♡ over 2♣.

The actual auction was a typical Two-over-One debacle: murky 'minimum bidding', with much suggested-implied-inferred. Nobody ever made a good descriptive bid, and neither player had any idea what his partner held. I consistently see Two-over-One players produce equally unsuccessful auctions.

When I cited this deal in my column in the Spectator, the monthly online publication for OKbridge subscribers, several readers wrote in rebuttal, citing chapter and verse from books on Two-over-One. Their contention was that East, not the system, was at fault: East should have jumped to 3♠ over 2♣ to show a solid suit. One Spectator reader suggested that my deal was a poor example of Two-over-One's shortcomings; he contended that in fairness I should have shown how proponents of Two-over-One would bid it. Well, the actual East-West were experts, but I couldn't call them Two-over-One 'proponents' if that implies authority. I can't say they were a regular partnership, but I believe they had played together before. In any case, they must have felt at ease with Two-over-One, else they wouldn't have been using it. Yet they produced an auction I found incomprehensible.

But let's say I did pick a poor example. How about these hands, which a Two-over-One pair bid in *The Bridge World*?

	♠ K 9 5 3 2			♠ Q 4
	♡ A Q J 4	N		♡ K
	◇ A K	W　E		◇ Q 10 7 5 4 2
	♣ 8 4	S		♣ A K 7 3

WEST	EAST
1♠	2◇
2♡	2NT
3◇	3♠
3NT	pass

No doubt 'proponents of Two-over-One' would bid these hands to the excellent slam; but East-West weren't 'proponents' — only multiple national champions. The Two-over-One advocates may again insist that the system wasn't at fault: West should have bid more or East should have bid more. I know what I consistently see when even experienced players use Two-over-One: failure to make a descriptive, value bid, leaving the partnership groping.

We could argue the theoretical merits of Two-over-One forever; we all have prejudices about what systems work best. But the fact is that deals are bid at the table, and most players are interested in actual gains, not theoretical ones. Moreover, no system is more effective than the players using it. Most of us were brought up on simple methods. We all know what a jump rebid of 3♠ means in Standard; but in Two-over-One, its meaning depends on your partner's biases or on whose book he has read.   In fact, if you play Two-over-One, you'll meet dozens of ambiguous sequences. I can illustrate that with one of my own disasters: I was trying to play Two-over-One in an unpracticed partnership, and we had this simple auction:

OPENER	RESPONDER
1♠	2♦
3NT	

Opener thought 3NT showed extra strength; responder did not. It cost a missed slam that mama-papa bidders would have reached in ten seconds — and it cost a Vanderbilt match. The practical test of a system is the results it achieves — not only for partnerships who have discussed their methods at length, but for casual partnerships who are concerned with ease of use and avoiding catastrophic misunderstandings. Playing any system without thorough discussion is foolhardy; that is the real lesson. But if your system is Two-over-One, you magnify the problem. If that's the system you choose, fine; but get ready to do your homework — lots of it.

One final observation: two good players using simple methods will beat two poor players using a system that is theoretically superior. Systems and conventions don't make winners.

The late Dr. Carl Sagan spent much time trying to discredit the misconceptions and superstitions that permeate society. But Sagan was a scientist. He refused to dismiss such things because of his own biases; he insisted that they be examined to see whether they contained any truth. Some modern ideas in bidding strike me the same way. They may excite us and tweak our imagination; they may achieve an occasional triumph. But do they gain points in the long run? We must study their results and see.

I was watching an IMP game recently on OKbridge, where East-West clearly wanted to get their money's worth by bidding as much as possible. Among other weapons, they brandished an opening bid of two of a major to promise a moderate hand with length both in that major and an unspecified minor. Gadgets such as this can make life miserable for opponents; and within thirty minutes, East-West got to use their toy twice.

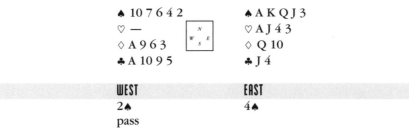

♠ 10 7 6 4 2
♡ —
◇ A 9 6 3
♣ A 10 9 5

♠ A K Q J 3
♡ A J 4 3
◇ Q 10
♣ J 4

WEST	EAST
2♠	4♠
pass	

East was safe enough in raising to 4♠, but couldn't imagine that West had three first-round controls and that 6♠ was almost cold. (A minor-suit lead lets declarer establish a pitch for his loser in the other minor suit. With a trump lead, West still has good chances; he might try the double finesse in clubs.) I expect if West restrains himself and passes as dealer, East will open 1♠, West will jump to 4♡, promising a big spade fit and heart shortness, and East has an easy 6♠ bid: since West has no points in the major suits, he must have the minors sewed up. That time, East-West's gadget interfered with their own constructive bidding. Well, one loss proves nothing, but three deals later, this happened:

♠ 8 7 3
♡ A Q
◇ A 5
♣ A K Q 8 5 2

♠ —
♡ J 7 6 3 2
◇ K Q 10 4
♣ 10 7 6 3

WEST	NORTH	EAST	SOUTH
		2♡	2♠
3♣	4♠	pass	pass
dbl	all pass		

Four spades doubled went down one. I believe it could have been down two, but East-West got poor compensation for their missed grand slam. Maybe this result was partly attributable to bad judgment: East might have pulled West's double to 5♣, or West might have risked 5♣ himself; if East was short in spades, as the auction indicated, he probably had a few clubs. Still, East-West were led down the garden path by their methods.

Poorly defined bids such as East's 2♡ strike me as 'Futile Willie' actions (read S.J. Simon's classic *Why You Lose at Bridge* if you're not familiar with this character). Players who use them are saying they don't think they can win with discipline and good judgment in the auction and solid card play. They must resort to 'bidding' methods that turn deals into a lottery. Later, I watched another pair using a similar toy:

Dlr: West
Vul: Both

```
                  ♠ A 8 7 4 3 2
                  ♡ 3
                  ◇ Q J 6 3
                  ♣ K 4
 ♠ Q 10 6                           ♠ K 9 5
 ♡ K 8 5            N               ♡ A J 7 2
 ◇ A 10 4        W     E            ◇ 9 8 7 2
 ♣ 9 7 3 2          S               ♣ 8 6
                  ♠ J
                  ♡ Q 10 9 6 4
                  ◇ K 5
                  ♣ A Q J 10 5
```

WEST	NORTH	EAST	SOUTH
pass	pass	pass	2♡[1]
pass	2♠	pass	3♣
all pass			

1.   Hearts and a minor, allegedly 9-11 points.

West had a marked trump lead, and South took five trumps, two diamonds and a spade. Down one. Meanwhile, 2NT or 2♠ would make. It's a free country; but for my money, North-South were playing losing bridge.

Misunderstandings are always more likely with complex conventions. This was a celebrated deal from the 1989 Venice Cup semifinal between West Germany and the Netherlands.

Dlr: West
Vul: N-S

```
              ♠ —
              ♡ Q 10 8 7 5 4 2
              ◇ A 10 7 6
              ♣ 10 3
♠ K 9 8 5 2                    ♠ A Q 10 7
♡ 6              N             ♡ J
◇ 9 8 3       W   E           ◇ K J
♣ A 8 6 2         S           ♣ K Q 9 7 5 4
              ♠ J 6 4 3
              ♡ A K 9 3
              ◇ Q 5 4 2
              ♣ J
```

WEST	NORTH	EAST	SOUTH
pass	3♡[1]	dbl	4♣[2]
dbl	pass[3]	pass	pass[4]

1. Hearts or solid clubs
2. "She must have clubs."
3. "Partner would have passed the double, unless she really has clubs."
4. "She must have clubs."

The Dutch defense slipped and beat four clubs doubled only 1700.

Before you adopt any convention, ask yourself these questions:

1. *Is the convention effective? Does it do what it's supposed to?*
2. *How often will I get to use it?* Don't bother with a convention to solve a problem that occurs once every ten years.
3. *What is the loss? Does the convention replace a useful natural bid?* Most players use Gerber in only one or two sequences because 4♣ is often the first cuebid in a slam auction.
4. *Is the convention easy to remember?* Recalling the details of a complex convention leaves you with less mental energy for more important matters.

Some players, I fear, use a convention or treatment just because everybody else does, not because it has a proven record of gaining points. Consider 'inverted raises', in which the old-style meanings of double and single raises in a minor suit are flip-flopped: a double raise is weak; a single raise is strong and forcing. The idea is that you can preempt with weaker hands but save room for investigation with better ones. One problem is that it's easy to 'play' inverted raises, but few partnerships have a disciplined bidding structure after the strong single raise. What usually ensues is some ill-defined groping toward 3NT — which works well only if 3NT happens to be the right contract. Another flaw is that responder often has a weak hand with trump support, but not the type of hand suitable for the double raise. I watched an expert pair on OKbridge bid these hands.

```
    ♠ 7 6 4              ♠ J
    ♡ A Q 7      N       ♡ K 8
    ◊ Q 10 7 6  W   E    ◊ A K 9 5 2
    ♣ 10 5 2      S      ♣ A K J 6 4
```

WEST	EAST
	1◊
1NT	3♣
3◊	3♡
4♡	5♣
5◊	pass

The diamond slam is worth bidding. A spade will usually be led, but not always; and even if the defenders cash their spade trick, East succeeds if the club finesse wins or if South has the bare ♣Q. The auction got off on the wrong foot when West couldn't raise 1◊ to 2◊ and had to respond 1NT. East's pass of 5◊ clearly reflected the fear of a trump loser, so their inability to ascertain trump quality interfered with East-West's own constructive bidding. If the East hand were

♠ A ♡ K 8 ◊ A 9 8 5 2 ♣ A K Q 6 4

then 6◊ would be odds-on, but the auction might be similar — except that East would be even more reluctant to bid it since West's diamonds could be J-x-x or Q-x-x.

Auctions are always more comfortable when the trump suit is set early. If West can start with a raise, I'd expect an easy jaunt to slam:

WEST	EAST
	1◊
2◊	4♣
4♡	6◊

I saw the next deal in another expert game on OKbridge.

BECOMING A BRIDGE EXPERT

Dlr: South
Vul: N-S
IMPs

```
                    ♠ 4
                    ♡ A 6 2
                    ◇ J 10 8 5 2
                    ♣ K Q J 6
   ♠ Q 9 8 6                        ♠ K 10 7 5 3
   ♡ K 10 8 5          N            ♡ 9 7 3
   ◇ K              W     E         ◇ 9 7 3
   ♣ 8 7 4 2           S            ♣ 9 5
                    ♠ A J 2
                    ♡ Q J 4
                    ◇ A Q 6 4
                    ♣ A 10 3
```

WEST	NORTH	EAST	SOUTH
			1◇
pass	2◇¹	pass	3NT
all pass			

1.   Inverted.

West led a heart, and South was presumably so distressed at missing the excellent slam that she ducked in dummy, jeopardizing the game if East won and switched to a spade. As it was, South made five, but 6◇ would have made also. What went wrong?

Perhaps the players were at fault, not the system. Maybe North should show his clubs before raising diamonds (as he'd likely do in a curmudgeonly style) or respond 3♠, a splinter raise. Maybe South's 3NT was presumptuous, but 2NT would not have been forcing; if 3NT was meant to suggest a balanced hand too strong for a 1NT opening, North perhaps should bid again.

Maybe South should test the water with 2♠ over 2◇, but would it do him any good? If North believed that bid was a probe for notrump, he'd have no thoughts of slam. If North tried 3♣ next, what bid could South make as a gentle slam suggestion? If South bid 3◇, would it be forcing? Do you know whether your regular partner would treat it as forcing? I see no clear answers, only lots of maybes. Maybe 'inverted minors' are too esoteric for mortal men.

Any method can betray you if you haven't discussed all its ramifications. In a U.S. Team Trials, two experts bid these hands to a less-than-optimum contract:

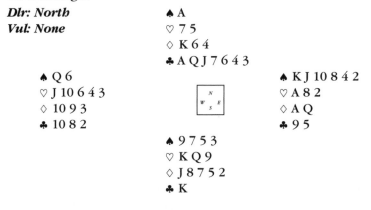

♠ Q J 6 2　　　　　　　　♠ A 8 5
♡ A K 8 7 3　　　　　　♡ Q J 10
◇ 9　　　　　　　　　　◇ A Q
♣ Q 9 2　　　　　　　　♣ A 7 4 3

WEST	EAST
2◇[1]	2NT[2]
3♣[3]	3♠[4]
pass[5]	

1.　　　　Flannery; minimum opening, four spades, five hearts.
2.　　　　Asks for distribution.
3.　　　　4-5-1-3.
4.　　　　Forcing, he thought.
5.　　　　Rejecting the 'invitation'.

One recent trend is to doubles that are 'cooperative' or 'action'. The original proponent of this method was Humpty Dumpty in *Alice Through the Looking Glass* ("When I double, it means exactly what I want it to mean..."). I watched this deal during a teaching session on OKbridge.

Dlr: North　　　　　　♠ A
Vul: None　　　　　　♡ 7 5
　　　　　　　　　　　　◇ K 6 4
　　　　　　　　　　　　♣ A Q J 7 6 4 3

♠ Q 6　　　　　　　　　　　　　　　♠ K J 10 8 4 2
♡ J 10 6 4 3　　　　　　　　　　♡ A 8 2
◇ 10 9 3　　　　　　　　　　　　◇ A Q
♣ 10 8 2　　　　　　　　　　　　♣ 9 5

　　　　　　　　　　　　♠ 9 7 5 3
　　　　　　　　　　　　♡ K Q 9
　　　　　　　　　　　　◇ J 8 7 5 2
　　　　　　　　　　　　♣ K

WEST	NORTH	EAST	SOUTH
	1♣	1♠	pass
pass	2♣	2♠	?

South thought for several seconds and doubled. West passed, and North huddled... and took out to 3♣. The commentator lauded North's action. South's double was for penalty, she said, but North had a minimum and an undisclosed seventh club. With only 50 points to gain, to pass the double was too close. North made an overtrick, and I reached for an aspirin. I suspect North may have thought South's double was 'showing cards', whatever that means. It was not. South says he can beat 2♠, and at IMPs, he isn't doubling for a one-trick set; he may have East nailed. North has a normal hand. His seventh club should be no surprise. Even if you ignore the ethical implications of South's pause before doubling — and ethical problems are common when partnerships indulge in ambiguous doubles — North should pass the double and expect a plus.

Of course, if South is going to make a you-figure-it-out double on that type of hand — with no trump tricks and limited defense — North should pull. But suppose South leads the ♣K against 2♠ doubled. East might make the contract with inspired guessing, but the defense will usually get six tricks. Wonder what the result might be if South had a real penalty double? What should South actually do over 2♠? It's not clear (to me), but I'd rather pass or even compete with 3♣ than double 2♠.

Here's another example of the kind of problem that these 'ambiguous' doubles create:

IMPs, neither side vulnerable

WEST	NORTH	EAST	SOUTH
		1◇	1♡
pass	1♠	2♣	?

♠ A6   ♡ A J 7 5 3 2   ◇ K 6   ♣ A 9 4

In theory, South's best call may be a double (maximum values for his overcall, no great support for spades, defensive values in East's suits), giving North the option of defending. But unless North can be trusted implicitly to play South for this type of hand, South should prefer a different action. An innocent North might expect South to hold

♠ 6   ♡ A K 7 5 3   ◇ A 6 3   ♣ K J 9 4.

In another OKbridge teaching session, I saw this auction:

WEST	NORTH	EAST	SOUTH
	1♠	2◇	dbl[1]
pass	2♠	3◇	dbl

1.   Negative.

Again, the commentator announced that South's second double was 'card-showing'. This time I couldn't stand it. "What should South do if his hand is

♠ x   ♡ A J x x   ◇ K 9 x x   ♣ K 10 x x

I typed. "Should he pass?"

WHEN YOU SUSPECT HOW THE CARDS LIE, BE BOLD

IMPs, both vulnerable

♠ Q 3 ♡ J 9 5 3 ◇ K J 3 ♣ A 9 5 4

WEST	NORTH	EAST	SOUTH
	1♠	2◇	?

What do you say?

Your diamond honors are equivalent to the A-Q, and you should bid 3NT despite the possible deficiency in points. The full deal:

```
                 ♠ A J 10 8 4
                 ♡ A K 6
                 ◇ 8 6
                 ♣ J 7 3
 ♠ 7 6 5 2                        ♠ K 9
 ♡ Q 10 8 7 2        N            ♡ 4
 ◇ 9 4            W     E         ◇ A Q 10 7 5 2
 ♣ Q 8              S             ♣ K 10 6 2
                 ♠ Q 3
                 ♡ J 9 5 3
                 ◇ K J 3
                 ♣ A 9 5 4
```

West led the ◇9, and East let South's jack win. South lost the spade finesse, and East shifted to a low club. South ducked, won the club return, took the ♡AK and ran the spades. East's last three cards were the ◇A and the ♣106, so South bared his ◇K and kept the ♣95. He then led a club, and East had to yield the ninth trick.

At the other table, North-South found trouble.

WEST	NORTH	EAST	SOUTH
	1♠	2◇	dbl
pass	2♡	pass	3♡
all pass			

South's negative double would have been fine with a hand such as

♠ Q 2 ♡ Q 7 5 3 ◇ A 4 3 ♣ K 10 5 4

With a primary diamond card, South could look for a heart contract or try to steer the play of notrump to North. North masterminded when he tried 2♡ instead of rebidding 2♠. Three hearts went down 200 for a 13-IMP swing.

Most declarers are apt to add a point for their masterful dummy play, and sometimes add more than one point when they can foresee an edge.

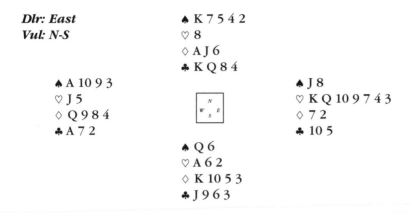

Dlr: East
Vul: N-S

♠ K 7 5 4 2
♡ 8
◇ A J 6
♣ K Q 8 4

♠ A 10 9 3
♡ J 5
◇ Q 9 8 4
♣ A 7 2

♠ J 8
♡ K Q 10 9 7 4 3
◇ 7 2
♣ 10 5

♠ Q 6
♡ A 6 2
◇ K 10 5 3
♣ J 9 6 3

WEST	NORTH	EAST	SOUTH
		3♡	pass
pass	dbl	pass	3NT
all pass			

South risked 3NT because he expected to isolate East's hearts by holding up the ace, and West rated to have the missing honors in the other three suits. When West led the ♡J, South won the second heart, led to the ♣K and returned a club to the jack. West won and exited with a club. South won with the queen and led a spade to his queen; West won and led another spade to dummy's king. South then cashed the ♣9. When West threw a spade, South finessed the ◇J, cashed the ◇A and exited with a spade from dummy, forcing West to lead into the ◇K10.

Another skinny game was reached on this deal after an opposing opening bid:

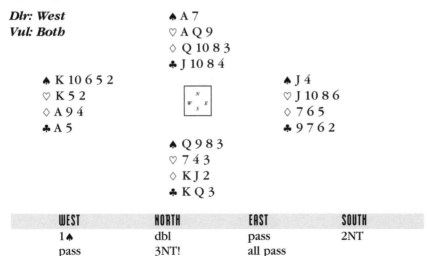

Dlr: West
Vul: Both

♠ A 7
♡ A Q 9
◇ Q 10 8 3
♣ J 10 8 4

♠ K 10 6 5 2
♡ K 5 2
◇ A 9 4
♣ A 5

♠ J 4
♡ J 10 8 6
◇ 7 6 5
♣ 9 7 6 2

♠ Q 9 8 3
♡ 7 4 3
◇ K J 2
♣ K Q 3

WEST	NORTH	EAST	SOUTH
1♠	dbl	pass	2NT
pass	3NT!	all pass	

North liked his good intermediates, and his ♡Q figured to be a winner. When West led the ♠5, South guessed well to put up dummy's ace, playing East for the jack or ten. (If South plays low from dummy, he goes down.) South next forced out the ♣A, and when West led another low spade to East's jack, South ducked. East exited with a club; but South won, forced out the ◇A and finessed successfully in hearts, winning three clubs, three diamonds, two hearts and a spade.

When an opponent steps in with a conventional bid to show a two-suiter, he may give you a hard time in the auction. Often, however, you can pay him back in the play.

Dlr: North
Vul: Both

```
                    ♠ K 10 4
                    ♡ 7 5
                    ◇ A Q 6 5 4
                    ♣ A 10 4
   ♠ Q 6 2                              ♠ A J 9 7 5
   ♡ 10 6              N                ♡ K J 9 8 2
   ◇ K 10 9 2        W   E              ◇ J 8
   ♣ J 9 8 2            S               ♣ 5
                    ♠ 8 3
                    ♡ A Q 4 3
                    ◇ 7 3
                    ♣ K Q 7 6 3
```

WEST	NORTH	EAST	SOUTH
	1◇	2◇¹	dbl
2♠	pass	pass	3♣
pass	3♠	pass	3NT
all pass			

1. Michaels: both majors.

West led the ♠2, and East won with the nine and switched to a heart. South took the queen, finessed the ◇Q and cashed the ◇A. When East followed, South had a blueprint of the deal. He returned a club to his king, finessed the ♣10, unblocked the ace, and got back to his hand with the ♡A to run the clubs for nine tricks. Without East's intervention, North-South probably wouldn't have bid game — nor would South have made it if they had.

As South, vulnerable at IMPs, you hold

♠ K 9   ♡ 9 3   ◊ A K 10 2   ♣ Q 8 7 6 5

WEST	NORTH	EAST	SOUTH
1♣	dbl	pass	?

What do you say?

Bid 3NT. The deal arose in a U.S. Team Trials.

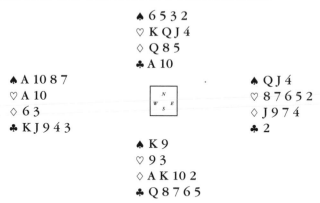

```
                    ♠ 6 5 3 2
                    ♡ K Q J 4
                    ◊ Q 8 5
                    ♣ A 10
♠ A 10 8 7                          ♠ Q J 4
♡ A 10                              ♡ 8 7 6 5 2
◊ 6 3                               ◊ J 9 7 4
♣ K J 9 4 3                         ♣ 2
                    ♠ K 9
                    ♡ 9 3
                    ◊ A K 10 2
                    ♣ Q 8 7 6 5
```

At many tables, North-South stalled out in this auction:

WEST	NORTH	EAST	SOUTH
1♣	dbl	pass	2NT
all pass			

South was afraid North might have a lightish double, but since the missing high cards were marked with West, South could have taken a bolder view. Despite North's minimum, the play for nine tricks was adequate, and four of the five pairs who reached 3NT made it.

TIP 6

BEFORE YOU BID, VISUALIZE THE PLAY

You're South at IMPs, both sides vulnerable, with

♠ K Q J 8   ♡ K Q J 9   ◇ A 7   ♣ 9 3 2

WEST	NORTH	EAST	SOUTH
1♣	dbl	pass	2♣
3♣	3♡	4♣	?

What is your plan?

At the ACBL 1999 Summer Championships, Brad Moss was sure that North had a singleton club and five hearts. If North's pattern was 4-5-3-1 or 3-5-4-1, a spade contract would produce an extra trick: South could ruff clubs in dummy and pitch his low diamond on the hearts. So Moss checked for aces and bid six spades.

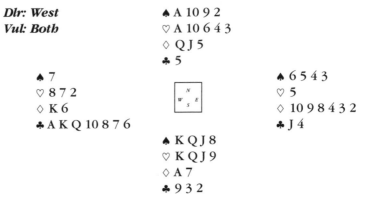

Dlr: West
Vul: Both

```
                    ♠ A 10 9 2
                    ♡ A 10 6 4 3
                    ◇ Q J 5
                    ♣ 5
  ♠ 7                              ♠ 6 5 4 3
  ♡ 8 7 2              N           ♡ 5
  ◇ K 6            W     E         ◇ 10 9 8 4 3 2
  ♣ A K Q 10 8 7 6     S          ♣ J 4
                    ♠ K Q J 8
                    ♡ K Q J 9
                    ◇ A 7
                    ♣ 9 3 2
```

A heart lead would sink the slam (declarer must let West in with the ♣A before drawing trumps, and he can give his partner a heart ruff), but West naturally led a high club and shifted to a trump. Moss won, ruffed a club, returned with the ◇A and ruffed a club with the ♠A. He could then draw trumps and run the hearts for twelve tricks. At the other table of the match, North-South got to six hearts, down one when the diamond finesse lost.

Novices and experts both count points; but before an expert places the contract, he imagines how the play will go. Think about this next hand. Playing IMPs, both sides vulnerable, South holds:

♠ 8 5 4 2 ♡ K 9 7 4 ◊ A Q J 6 ♣ 6

WEST	NORTH	EAST	SOUTH
		1♠	pass
2♠	3♡	3♠	?

South should consider bidding slam! North has a sound hand to climb in vulnerable at IMPs. The bidding marks him with spade shortness, perhaps a void, and if he doesn't have the ◊K, East probably does. Give North a reasonable minimum such as

♠ — ♡ A J 10 5 3 2 ◊ 10 9 3 ♣ A 7 4 2

and imagine how many tricks he'll win. Sometimes, by contrast, the auction will suggest pessimism.

Playing IMPs, both sides vulnerable, South holds

♠ A 7 5 ♡ J 4 ◊ K 10 8 4 ♣ K Q J 9

WEST	NORTH	EAST	SOUTH
			1♣
1♠	dbl[1]	pass	1NT
pass	2NT	pass	?

1. Negative.

Despite your maximum, you should pass. Your spade stopper is primary and easy to dislodge — a bad sign — and since three aces are missing, West may have an entry. He may get in to cash his spades before you can muster nine tricks. The full deal could be:

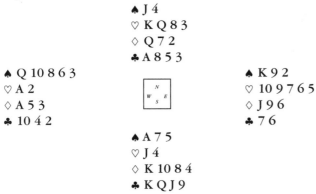

```
                    ♠ J 4
                    ♡ K Q 8 3
                    ◊ Q 7 2
                    ♣ A 8 5 3
♠ Q 10 8 6 3                        ♠ K 9 2
♡ A 2                               ♡ 10 9 7 6 5
◊ A 5 3                             ◊ J 9 6
♣ 10 4 2                            ♣ 7 6
                    ♠ A 7 5
                    ♡ J 4
                    ◊ K 10 8 4
                    ♣ K Q J 9
```

North has twelve points — a maximum for an invitation — but even 2NT will fail.

Similarly, as South, not vulnerable at IMPs, you hold:

♠ J 5 4 ♡ 4 ◇ J 8 6 4 ♣ A 7 5 4 3

WEST	NORTH	EAST	SOUTH
1◇	2◇[1]	dbl	2♠
pass	3♠	pass	?

1. Length in both majors.

Pass. Your hand isn't bad, but East-West have the balance of power; East's double promised strength. If you bid 4♠, a trump lead is as sure as snowflakes in January.

In a Vanderbilt match, an expert failed to foresee problems in the play on this deal:

Dlr: West
Vul: N-S

```
              ♠ 9 3
              ♡ K
              ◇ A K Q J 9 7 3
              ♣ K 8 2
♠ 5                            ♠ A Q J 10 7 6 2
♡ J 9 8 6 3      N             ♡ 10 4
◇ 6 4          W   E           ◇ 8 5 2
♣ Q 10 5 4 3     S             ♣ 9
              ♠ K 8 4
              ♡ A Q 7 5 2
              ◇ 10
              ♣ A J 7 6
```

WEST	NORTH	EAST	SOUTH
pass	1♣[1]	4♠	dbl[2]
pass	5◇	pass	5♡
pass	6◇	all pass	

1. 16+ points.
2. Values.

East led the ♠A and another spade, and West ruffed. South might have tried 6NT; if North has solid diamonds and no points in spades, twelve tricks are likely in notrump, but 6◇ is at risk.

Try this one. At IMPs, North-South vulnerable, South holds

♠ A 4 ♡ A 7 ◇ K 8 6 ♣ K Q J 9 8 3

WEST	NORTH	EAST	SOUTH
3♡	pass	pass	?

Bid 3NT, counting on North to provide a few values. The full deal might be

BECOMING A BRIDGE EXPERT

```
                ♠ K 8 6 3 2
                ♡ 6 4
                ◇ A 7 4 2
                ♣ 7 5
♠ 7                                      ♠ Q J 10 9 5
♡ K Q J 9 5 3 2      ┌─────┐           ♡ 10 8
◇ Q 10 5             │  N  │           ◇ J 9 3
♣ 6 4               │W   E│           ♣ A 10 2
                     │  S  │
                     └─────┘
                ♠ A 4
                ♡ A 7
                ◇ K 8 6
                ♣ K Q J 9 8 3
```

When West leads the ♡K, South can duck, win the next heart and force out the ♣A for ten tricks. But if South's heart holding were K-7, leaving West with a suit headed by the A-Q-J, a stab at 3NT would be less attractive; West would lead the ♡Q, and South couldn't hold up.

You are playing IMPs, neither side vulnerable, and you hold as South:

♠ 7 4   ♡ A 8 5 2   ◇ A J 7 2   ♣ J 7 2

WEST	NORTH	EAST	SOUTH
	1♣	pass	1♡
pass	2♡	pass	?

What do you say now?

Consider some hands with which North would accept a game try:

♠ A K 3   ♡ K 9 4 3   ◇ 10 5   ♣ A 9 6 3

At least four losers are all but certain.

♠ A 9   ♡ K 9 7 3   ◇ 10 5   ♣ A Q 8 6 3

Now 4♡ needs a 3-2 trump break plus a lucky club position.

♠ Q 8 6   ♡ K Q 4 3   ◇ 6 3   ♣ A K 10 6

Even if trumps break 3-2 and the club finesse wins, 4♡ isn't laydown.

If North has a normal minimum such as

♠ K 8 3   ♡ Q 7 4 3   ◇ 9 4   ♣ A K 6 3

he'll reject a try for game, but South may fail even in 3♡.

TIP 7

DON'T PLAY YOUR PARTNER FOR PERFECT CARDS

Clearly, then, you should pass. (Note that I gave North four trumps in all these examples, although he might raise with three.) What if North's hand is

♠ 8 5 3   ♡ K Q 10 4   ◇ Q 4   ♣ A K 10 9

True, now 4♡ is better than 50%. But it's wrong to try for game when you need specific cards from your partner. He'll accept on many hands when game chances are poor.

Barry Crane was the ACBL's leading masterpoint holder from 1968 until 1991, six years after his death. He used to tell his partners, "Don't play me for specific cards; I won't have them." The South play-

Dlr: South
Vul: N-S
Matchpoints

```
                    ♠ Q 6 5
                    ♡ 8 6 5
                    ◇ A J 6 5
                    ♣ Q 6 4
♠ K 2                                 ♠ 9 8 7
♡ J 10 9 7          N                 ♡ Q 3 2
◇ 10 8 7 2       W     E              ◇ 9
♣ A 10 8            S                 ♣ K J 9 7 3 2
                    ♠ A J 10 4 3
                    ♡ A K 4
                    ◇ K Q 4 3
                    ♣ 5
```

WEST	NORTH	EAST	SOUTH
			1♠
pass	2♠	pass	3◇
pass	4◇	pass	4♡
pass	4♠	all pass	

er on our next deal wasn't listening.

If South had jumped to 4♠ over 2♠, West would have led the ♡J. The actual daisy-picking auction induced him to lead a diamond. When South won in dummy and lost the trump finesse, West gave East a diamond ruff and got back in with the ♣A to give him another ruff for down two.

"Sorry," South told his partner. "If you had

♠ K Q 7   ♡ 8 6 5   ◇ A 8 6 5   ♣ 7 6 4

we could make 6◇." Perfect cards!

In a slam auction, you may have room to search out a perfect fit — but not when you're looking for game.

BECOMING A BRIDGE EXPERT

Dlr: South
Vul: None

	♠ Q 4 2		
	♡ A 8 3		
	◇ J 6 4 2		
	♣ Q 8 3		

♠ 9 7 5		♠ K 10 8
♡ Q 10 7 5 2		♡ K J 9 6 4
◇ A 8	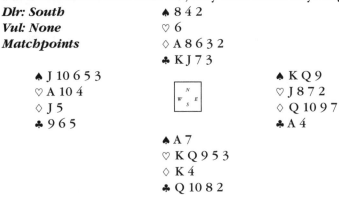	◇ Q 10 9
♣ 10 7 5		♣ J 9

	♠ A J 6 3		
	♡ —		
	◇ K 7 5 3		
	♣ A K 6 4 2		

WEST	NORTH	EAST	SOUTH
			1♣
pass	1NT	pass	2♠
pass	3♣	pass	3◇
pass	3NT	all pass	

Clubs broke 3-2 and the spade finesse worked, but 3NT still failed. A minor-suit game would have been against the odds. South thought 6◇ might make if North held

♠ K 5 2   ♡ J 9 4   ◇ A 6 4 2   ♣ Q 8 3

but he was giving North a perfect maximum. North will seldom have such a hand, and if South tries hard to reach game by bidding out his pattern, he may get too high. South should settle for a 2♣ rebid. If North bids 2◇ or 2♠ next to mark his values, South can reconsider; but if North can't act over 2♣, they won't miss anything.

Dlr: South
Vul: None
Matchpoints

	♠ 8 4 2		
	♡ 6		
	◇ A 8 6 3 2		
	♣ K J 7 3		

♠ J 10 6 5 3		♠ K Q 9
♡ A 10 4		♡ J 8 7 2
◇ J 5		◇ Q 10 9 7
♣ 9 6 5		♣ A 4

	♠ A 7		
	♡ K Q 9 5 3		
	◇ K 4		
	♣ Q 10 8 2		

WEST	NORTH	EAST	SOUTH
			1♡
pass	1NT	all pass	

East led the ♠K, and North lost four spades, the ♡A and the ♣A. A score of +90 was a bottom, since most North-Souths played in clubs for +110 or +130. South thought North might have strength in spades and diamonds and might do well in notrump. But instead of placing cards, South should simply have shown his second suit.

Players sometimes give partner perfect cards despite all the evidence that he cannot have them. In a Spingold match, another South player had a fit of optimism on this deal.

Dlr: West
Vul: Both

	♠ A J 5 3	
	♡ A 8 7 4	
	◇ J 7 6 3	
	♣ 8	
♠ K Q 9 7 4		♠ 8 2
♡ 6		♡ J 10 9 2
◇ 9 4		◇ 2
♣ A K 9 7 4		♣ Q 10 6 5 3 2
	♠ 10 6	
	♡ K Q 5 3	
	◇ A K Q 10 8 5	
	♣ J	

WEST	NORTH	EAST	SOUTH
1♣	dbl	2NT[1]	3♣
5♣	pass	pass	6◇
all pass			

1. Weak club raise.

North produced two aces, but 6◇ went down anyway. South imagined a dummy such as

♠ A K 7 5   ♡ A 8 7 4   ◇ J 7 6   ♣ 8 5

(although slam wouldn't be cold even then); but West had opened the bidding, after all. Dummy might have had

♠ K Q 7 5   ♡ A 8 7 4   ◇ J 7 6   ♣ K 5

When you have a good hand, it is tempting to hope that partner has precisely the cards that you need. Playing IMPs, neither side vulnerable, South holds

♠ A K 10 8 3 2   ♡ 4   ◇ A Q   ♣ A K Q 5

WEST	NORTH	EAST	SOUTH
			2♣
pass	2◇	pass	2♠
pass	2NT	pass	3♣
pass	4♠	pass	?

South can try for slam with a 5◊ cuebid but shouldn't bid slam himself. North has some spade support and one useful card. Will slam be a good bet? Some possible North hands for the auction:

♠ 9 6 4   ♡ Q 6 3   ◊ K 9 5 2   ♣ 9 6 4

This is as much as South can rightfully expect; slam is about 50%.

♠ 9 6 5 4   ♡ A 6 3   ◊ 8 6 4   ♣ 9 6 4

Now 6♠ is a heavy favorite, but this is a favorable dummy. South can't count on North for either four trumps or an ace.

♠ J 5 4   ♡ K 7 5   ◊ 9 6 4 2   ♣ J 6 3

Opposite this hand, even 5♠ may go down though that result would be unlucky.

A final example. Playing IMPs, both sides vulnerable, you hold as South

♠ 5   ♡ A Q 10 7 5 3   ◊ Q 7 6 4 3   ♣ 4

WEST	NORTH	EAST	SOUTH
	1◊	pass	1♡
pass	1NT	pass	?

What do you say?

If North has a perfect maximum hand such as

♠ A 8 2   ♡ J 4   ◊ A J 10 5 2   ♣ A 8 3

then 6◊ will be a good contract. But since partners never have perfect minimums, much less maximums, just bid 4♡.

Playing matchpoints, both sides vulnerable, you hold as South:

WEST	NORTH	EAST	SOUTH
	1♣	4◊	4NT
pass	5♡[1]	pass	?

1. Two aces.

♠ A 6   ♡ K 10 8 7 6 4 3 2   ◊ A   ♣ K Q

What do you say?

Bid 6♡, not 7♡. You can't tell how many hearts North has, but a timid view is best. Even if partner has the ♡A doubleton, the chance of a 3-0 break is greatly increased by East's preempt. If North has the singleton ace, the odds of a 2-2 break must be 4-1 against.

My wife's grandfather, an Alabama cotton farmer who was still a man of his own mind when he passed on at the age of 98, had a simple solution when his daughters henpecked him: he quietly turned

TIP 8

DON'T IGNORE THE THREAT OF BAD BREAKS

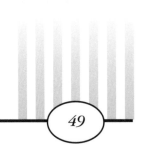

off his hearing aid and sat in his chair in peace. The old saying is that blind opening leads don't exist, but deaf opening leaders do. A bidding fault I've noticed in myself and in others is a predisposition to deafness in the bidding.

Playing matchpoints, both sides vulnerable, you hold as North.

♠ Q 7 4   ♡ 6 5 3   ◊ J 7 5 3   ♣ A 6 5

WEST	NORTH	EAST	SOUTH
			1♠
2NT	pass	3◊	3♡
pass	?		

It's tempting to jump to 4♠. After all, your hand could have been hopeless, and instead you have three good trumps plus an ace. Nevertheless, South may have stuck out his neck to compete; and since it's matchpoints, you have less to gain by bidding a close game. Furthermore, the bidding has substantially increased the chance of bad breaks in your key suits. The full deal may be

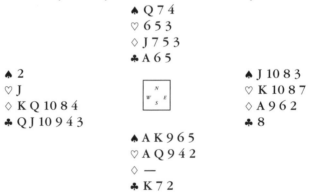

```
                      ♠ Q 7 4
                      ♡ 6 5 3
                      ◊ J 7 5 3
                      ♣ A 6 5
   ♠ 2                                  ♠ J 10 8 3
   ♡ J                                  ♡ K 10 8 7
   ◊ K Q 10 8 4        N                ◊ A 9 6 2
   ♣ Q J 10 9 4 3    W   E              ♣ 8
                        S
                      ♠ A K 9 6 5
                      ♡ A Q 9 4 2
                      ◊ —
                      ♣ K 7 2
```

West leads the ◊K against a spade contract, South ruffs and might weave his way to ten tricks. He cashes the ♠A and continues with a low heart to West's jack. South ruffs the next diamond, goes to the ♣A, returns a heart to his nine, gets back with the ♠Q and leads a heart to the queen. Dummy discards diamonds on the ♡A and the fifth heart. East ruffs, but whether he returns a diamond, giving up a ruff-sluff, or his last trump, South gets two more tricks. If South is good enough to produce that series of plays, I suspect you'll get a good result on this deal whether or not you're in game.

I often see a player face a bidding decision after his opponents have climbed all over the auction with a preempt or a conventional two-suited takeout such as a Michaels Cuebid. His fear of missing a laydown game overshadows the clear threat of bad breaks, and on he goes — to defeat. (True, some hands are easier to play when the opponents have blueprinted their distribution in the auction; but 5-0 trump breaks are hard to cope with.) I was watching an all-expert game on OKbridge when this deal appeared.

Dlr: South
Vul: None

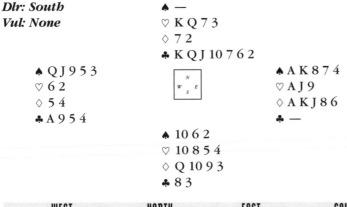

```
                    ♠ —
                    ♡ K Q 7 3
                    ◇ 7 2
                    ♣ K Q J 10 7 6 2
♠ Q J 9 5 3                              ♠ A K 8 7 4
♡ 6 2                                    ♡ A J 9
◇ 5 4                                    ◇ A K J 8 6
♣ A 9 5 4                                ♣ —
                    ♠ 10 6 2
                    ♡ 10 8 5 4
                    ◇ Q 10 9 3
                    ♣ 8 3
```

WEST	NORTH	EAST	SOUTH
			pass
pass	5♣	6♣	pass
6♠	all pass		

Sometimes when they preempt, you just have to shoot it out with them — and East did, with his full-blooded 6♣ cuebid. West's hand looked mammoth: his fifth spade was a winner, he had an ace and he could surely ruff vast numbers of clubs in dummy. Plenty of reasonable hands for East would make a grand slam laydown. But West wisely settled for 6♠; he knew foul splits were likely.

North led the ♡K, and when dummy hit, 7♠ looked like a good bet. West took the ♡A and the ♠Q, cashed the ◇AK, ruffed a diamond, crossed to the ♠K and ruffed a diamond. He drew South's last trump, threw a heart from dummy on the ♣A and claimed twelve tricks, losing a heart. With trumps 3-0 and diamonds 4-2, the thirteenth trick wasn't there: West had to draw three rounds of trumps before he could enjoy a heart discard from his hand on dummy's fifth diamond; but then he couldn't ruff a heart. Nor could West ruff three clubs in dummy and draw trumps to cash the good diamond.

Who do you think was at fault on this next deal?

Dlr: East
Vul: N-S

		♠ A Q J 10 8 5	
		♡ —	
		◇ 9 3	
		♣ J 10 8 5 2	

♠ 7			♠ K 6
♡ K 7 6 4 2			♡ A 9 8 3
◇ K 7 5			◇ A Q 6 4 2
♣ A K 6 3			♣ Q 4

		♠ 9 4 3 2	
		♡ Q J 10 5	
		◇ J 10 8	
		♣ 9 7	

WEST	NORTH	EAST	SOUTH
		1◇	pass
1♡	2♠	3♡	pass
4♣	pass	4◇	pass
5♣	pass	6♡	all pass

Down two. Apportion the blame between West and East.

I'd give West more of the blame, even though East made the final error when he jumped to 6♡. East thought he was obliged to bid slam since he had a spade control; but if that had been all West needed for slam, he'd have bid 5♡ over 3♡. So East should have used his judgment and signed off at 5♡. But West also pushed too hard. Six hearts would have been a gamble if North hadn't bid; as it was, the preempt at unfavorable vulnerability made bad splits likely. Once West had made his slam try with 4♣, he should have signed off at 4♡ over 4◇, and left any further moves to his partner.

When the opponents are in the auction, don't turn off your hearing aid; turn it up.

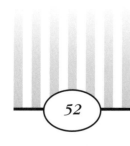

TIP 9

DESCRIBE
YOUR HAND

This may seem an unlikely tip. Isn't describing a hand what bidding amounts to? The problem is that players (1) fail to make their most descriptive bid; (2) place the contract too quickly. Here's an example of the first of these errors:

Playing IMPs, both sides vulnerable, you hold as South

♠ A 8 5   ♡ A 10 3   ◇ A K J 3   ♣ 9 6 2

WEST	NORTH	EAST	SOUTH
			1NT
pass	2♣	pass	2◇
pass	2♡	pass	?

Your 1NT showed 16 to 18 points. North's sequence is invitational: he has a five-card suit with about eight points. What do you say?

Your hand isn't bad: prime values, a working jack and heart support. Many players would bid 3♡ to try for game, but the right bid is 3◇, locating your side strength (without heart support you would return to notrump). Partner will bid 4♡ on

♠ 9 7 4 2   ♡ K Q 8 5 2   ◇ Q 9 4   ♣ 3

but with

♠ 9 7 4 2   ♡ K Q 8 5 2   ◇ 4   ♣ Q 7 3

he'll return to 3♡.

Here's a common situation where the same principle applies. Playing IMPs, both sides vulnerable, you hold as South

♠ 10 8 4   ♡ K J 7 3   ◇ 8 7 4   ♣ K 10 3

WEST	NORTH	EAST	SOUTH
	1♠	pass	2♠
pass	3♣	pass	?

Bid 3♡. Since you have weak trumps and a minimum, you can't bid 4♠ over partner's game try, but you can let partner know where your values are. If he needs help in hearts — a hand such as

♠ A Q J 9 3   ♡ A Q 2   ◇ 2   ♣ Q J 8 2

he'll jump to an odds-on game.

Players often 'bid out their pattern' to try for slam, letting partner judge whether he has fitting cards:

	WEST	EAST	
♠ A K 8 2			♠ Q 10 7 4 3
♡ 3			♡ A 7 4
◇ A Q J 7 2			◇ 9 3
♣ A J 3			♣ K 8 2

WEST	EAST
1◇	1♠
3♣	3NT
4♠	5♡
6♠	

After West's sequence, East knows his ♡A and ♣K are working cards. But if West raised 1♠ to 4♠, he'd suggest balanced distribution, and East would pass.

Playing IMPs, neither side vulnerable, you hold as South:

♠ J 7 6 3　♡ 5　◇ A K J 3　♣ 9 7 4 2

WEST	NORTH	EAST	SOUTH
			pass
pass	1♠	pass	?

Bid 3◇. A passed-hand jump shift promises a fit and is forcing. North might hold

♠ A K 8 5 2　♡ A J 6　◇ 8 6 2　♣ J 5

South can't afford to temporize with a 2◇ response, since he'd risk being dropped there; and North might pass a jump to 3♠. But over 3◇, North can try 3♡, suggesting a reasonable opening bid with heart values, and South can bid 4♠.

A 'limit raise' shows good trumps, prime values and a shapely hand. However, if you have side-suit values, help your partner judge by bidding your side suit first — even with good support. At IMPs, neither side vulnerable, you hold as South

♠ K J 4 3　♡ 6 3　◇ A Q 10 2　♣ 5 4 3

WEST	NORTH	EAST	SOUTH
			1♠
pass	?		

Bid 2◇. If North rebids 2♡, return to 2♠. He'll bid again with

♠ A Q 7 6 5　♡ A J 9 4　◇ J 4 3　♣ 2

but will pass with

♠ A Q 7 6 5　♡ A J 9 4　◇ 3　♣ J 7 6

Of course, in a game-forcing Two-over-One system, with invitational values you can't both raise and show your side suit (not the least of that style's drawbacks).

The second error I mentioned was hurrying to place the contract. On the next deal, two players erred by making the final decision before they had to.

Dlr: South
Vul: Both

```
                    ♠ 7 4
                    ♡ Q 3
                    ◇ K Q J 9 2
                    ♣ A J 6 2
     ♠ K Q 8                         ♠ J 9 5 3 2
     ♡ J 9 8 5          N            ♡ A 6
     ◇ 10 6          W     E         ◇ 8 5 3
     ♣ 9 7 5 4          S            ♣ Q 10 8
                    ♠ A 10 6
                    ♡ K 10 7 4 2
                    ◇ A 7 4
                    ♣ K 3
```

BECOMING A BRIDGE EXPERT

WEST	NORTH	EAST	SOUTH
			1♡
pass	2♢	pass	2NT
pass	3♣	pass	3♢
pass	3♡	pass	3NT
all pass			

This was the auction at one table of a team game. West led the ♠K, ducked, and continued with the queen. South won the third spade and finessed the ♣J for his ninth trick. Down two. At Table 2, the first six bids were the same, but South then tried 4♡. West led the ♠K again, and South lost a spade and three trumps.

Both Souths placed the contract too soon; they should have hedged by bidding 3♠ over 3♡. This bid would have suggested spade strength (but not so much that South wanted to insist on notrump) and weakish hearts. Perhaps North-South would then have reached 5♢.

This final example includes a common auction where more options are available than you might think. Playing IMPs, both sides vulnerable, you hold as South,

♠ K 8 2   ♡ A 7   ♢ A K J 4   ♣ J 8 6 3

WEST	NORTH	EAST	SOUTH
			1NT¹
pass	4NT	pass	?

1.   15-17.

What do you say?

South has a close decision. The actual South tried 6NT and found dummy with

♠ A 9 4   ♡ K 9 5   ♢ Q 10 6 3   ♣ A K 2

The clubs produced three tricks, but South still had only eleven tricks in all. Since South has prime values but no extra high-card strength, a minor-suit slam may be best. Over 4NT, South can probe with 5♣. North will try 5♢ and South can raise to 6♢ for +920.

You are playing matchpoints, both sides vulnerable, and you hold as South:

♠ A K 3　♡ 10 6 4　◇ A 10 3　♣ K 10 5 3

WEST	NORTH	EAST	SOUTH
	1♡	pass	2NT
pass	3◇	pass	?

TIP 10

SUPPORT YOUR PARTNER

What do you say?

I hate to report that South bid 3NT, and everyone passed. The full deal:

```
                ♠ Q 7 4
                ♡ A Q J 5 2
                ◇ K Q 7 2
                ♣ 6
  ♠ 10 6                         ♠ J 9 8 5 2
  ♡ 8 3          N               ♡ K 9 7
  ◇ J 9 8 4   W     E            ◇ 6 5
  ♣ A J 9 4 2      S             ♣ Q 8 7
                ♠ A K 3
                ♡ 10 6 4
                ◇ A 10 3
                ♣ K 10 5 3
```

West led a club, and 3NT went down one with 4♡ icy. To reach a winning contract, all South had to do was bid 3♡ over 3◇, showing his support for North's first suit.

Supporting partner's suit is so fundamental that it hardly seems to require a tip; but players persist in withholding support for no good reason. Suppose you open 1NT, and your partner responds 3♡. You hold

♠ A 10 4　♡ Q 7 3　◇ Q J 7 2　♣ A K 3

A genius looks at his flat pattern and insists on 3NT. A sound player looks at his three-card heart support and prefers the disciplined raise, which is what his partner wants to hear. Responder's hand may be

♠ 8 3　♡ K J 10 5 2　◇ A K 4　♣ 9 6 2

The 1961 Bermuda Bowl saw this depressing display.

```
  ♠ A 4                   ♠ Q J 7 2
  ♡ A 6 4       N         ♡ 10
  ◇ A Q 9 7 3  W     E    ◇ K J 6
  ♣ 10 8 2       S        ♣ A K Q 7 6
```

BECOMING A BRIDGE EXPERT

WEST	EAST
1◊	2♣
2NT	3♠
3NT	

West, with three aces, a good side suit and a ruffing value, should have taken a 4♣ preference over 3♠; or instead East could have tried 4◊ over 3NT. Since nobody wanted to support anybody, East-West played their grand slam at game.

Eight years later, in a U.S. Team Trials, the story was the same.

♠ A 9 3   ♠ 2
♡ A   ♡ J 10 7 5
◊ K 10 4   ◊ A Q 7 5 3
♣ Q 10 9 8 7 5   ♣ A K 4

WEST	NORTH	EAST	SOUTH
1♣	1♠	2◊	pass
3◊	pass	3♡	pass
3♠	dbl	redbl	pass
3NT	all pass		

East started well when he bid 2◊. However, his 3♡ instead of 4♣ or a 3♠ cuebid was questionable, and his pass of 3NT was indefensible.

It seldom turns out badly to support your partner. In the 1974 Spingold final, two experts each held

♠ 7   ♡ A K 8 4   ◊ A 6 4   ♣ K J 10 7 6

The auction started the same way at both tables: partner opened 1◊, they responded 2♣, partner bid 2♠ (not guaranteeing great strength), and they tried 3♡. Partner then bid 3NT. One player passed; one showed his support with 4◊ and eventually reached 6◊. The hand opposite was

♠ A Q J 2   ♡ Q 5 2   ◊ K J 10 9 3 2   ♣ —

and the slam came home.

Suppose you open 1◊, and your partner responds 1♡. What do you say with

♠ 64   ♡ K Q 5   ◊ A J 8 5 3   ♣ A 6 4

Raise to 2♡. Even with only three trumps, this action is best. Resolve close decisions in favor of supporting partner. A raise often makes the auction easier, especially when opener has minimum values; if he doesn't raise directly, he may have lost his chance.

```
               ♠ K Q 5              ♠ J 9 6 4 2
               ♡ A Q 8 6 3   ┌─────┐  ♡ 4
               ◊ J 8 6 3     │  N  │  ◊ K Q 2
               ♣ 3           │W   E│  ♣ J 9 6 2
                             │  S  │
                             └─────┘
```

WEST	EAST
1♡	1♠
2◊	pass

East can't bid again, and the 5-3 spade fit is lost.

```
               ♠ K J 4                 ♠ Q 8 7 3
               ♡ A 4          ┌─────┐   ♡ Q 10 3
               ◊ K 10 6 5 3 2 │  N  │   ◊ A 4
               ♣ J 5          │W   E│   ♣ K 6 4 2
                              │  S  │
                              └─────┘
```

WEST	EAST
1◊	1♠
2◊	2NT
3♠	3NT
pass	

West should have raised 1♠ to 2♠. Then he could sign off in 3◊ over 2NT.

One final deal: at IMPs, both sides vulnerable, you hold as South,

    ♠ K 10 5 2   ♡ 8 4   ◊ 8 5 3   ♣ 9 8 6 3

WEST	NORTH	EAST	SOUTH
	2♣	pass	2♡[1]
pass	3♣	pass	?

1.   Less than 4 points.

What do you say now?

When I watched the deal on OKbridge, South tried 3♠. He was clearly angling for notrump, since when North bid 3NT next, South passed. It was a safe contract but not the best spot, which happened to be 6♣. North held

    ♠ A   ♡ A Q 5   ◊ A 4   ♣ A K 10 7 5 4 2

North probably hated bidding 3NT, but South could have had

    ♠ Q J 6 5 4   ♡ 8 6 4   ◊ J 9 5 3   ♣ 3

To reach the good slam, South needed to support his partner.

BECOMING A BRIDGE EXPERT

♠ J 7 4　♡ A J 4　♢ 9 6 4　♣ K 8 5 2

Your partner opens 1♠, you raise to 2♠ and he tries 3♢. As far as you know, he's trying for game; he wants you to bid it with even a mediocre raise that has diamond values. What do you say now?

Bid 3♠. Although you have a high-card maximum, your honors in hearts and clubs may be useless. Players are often seduced by the point-count into trying 3NT in these situations; but opener, who usually has a shapely hand, often returns to the agreed suit. If you arrive in 4♠, you may find:

DON'T BE A SLAVE TO THE POINT COUNT

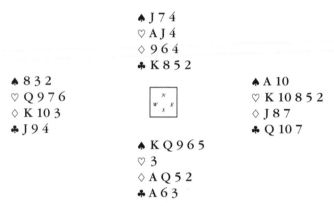

```
                ♠ J 7 4
                ♡ A J 4
                ♢ 9 6 4
                ♣ K 8 5 2
  ♠ 8 3 2                      ♠ A 10
  ♡ Q 9 7 6         N          ♡ K 10 8 5 2
  ♢ K 10 3      W     E        ♢ J 8 7
  ♣ J 9 4          S           ♣ Q 10 7
                ♠ K Q 9 6 5
                ♡ 3
                ♢ A Q 5 2
                ♣ A 6 3
```

Luck is average: the ♢K is wrong, but both spades and diamonds break evenly. South has a maximum for his try for game, and North's ♣K is a working card, but nine tricks are the limit. What went wrong?

The point-count is useful in evaluating the trick-taking potential of balanced hands. In assessing unbalanced hands, players must be careful; illusions are common. For example, aces and kings are undervalued on the 4-3-2-1 scale, but queens and jacks are overvalued.

As North, at IMPs, neither side vulnerable, you hold

♠ J 6 5 3　♡ Q 7 4　♢ J 7 5　♣ Q 9 3

South opens 1♡, West passes. What do you say?

If you raise to 2♡, South will jump to 4♡ with

♠ A K 2　♡ A K J 8 3　♢ Q 10 6 3　♣ 4

The defense takes two diamonds and a diamond ruff, a club and a spade. The North hand has too many secondary values, which may be useless in a suit contract, to make an encouraging raise. A 1NT response instead keeps game chances alive but may let North-South stop safely in 2♡.

The value of honors can change as the bidding evolves.

Dlr: South
Vul: Both

```
                ♠ A 10 6 2
                ♡ Q J 10 7 3
                ◇ Q 2
                ♣ 8 6
♠ 3                              ♠ J 9 8 4
♡ 9 8              N             ♡ A 2
◇ K 10 6 3      W     E          ◇ J 9 8 7
♣ A Q J 9 4 3      S             ♣ 10 7 2
                ♠ K Q 7 5
                ♡ K 6 5 4
                ◇ A 5 4
                ♣ K 5
```

WEST	NORTH	EAST	SOUTH
			1◇
2♣	dbl	pass	2♡
pass	3♡	pass	4♡
all pass			

West led a spade, and South went down one in 4♡, off two clubs, the ♡A and a spade ruff. He should have passed 3♡; on this auction, the ♣K was worth nothing.

Players are taught to count extra points for a long suit, but the long cards in a poor suit may be worthless. Even if your partner has a fit, you may not have time to establish your suit.

```
        ♠ A 10 5 3              ♠ K J 4
        ♡ K 4        N          ♡ A 6
        ◇ A K 4 3   W   E       ◇ 7 6 2
        ♣ Q 10 4       S        ♣ J 9 8 3 2
```

WEST	NORTH	EAST	SOUTH
1NT	pass	3NT	all pass

The defense led hearts, and West had no play for 3NT. Since East's long suit was ragged, it was the wrong time to take an aggressive view; but if East had held

♠ J 4 2   ♡ A 6   ◇ 7 6 2   ♣ K J 9 3 2

instead, 3NT would have been cold.

Having strong trumps is nice — but this too can be illusory.

Dlr: South
Vul: N-S

♠ 10 7 5 3
♡ K 7 6 2
◇ A J 6
♣ A 4

♠ A K Q J 2
♡ A J 3
◇ 7 3
♣ K 10 2

WEST	NORTH	EAST	SOUTH
			1♠
pass	2NT[1]	pass	3♠
pass	4♣	pass	4♡
pass	5◇	dbl	pass
pass	5♡	pass	6♠
all pass			

1.   Forcing spade raise.

West led a diamond, and South was at the mercy of the heart finesse, which lost. South slightly overvalued his hand since the ♠J was a wasted point; he could expect to draw trumps without it. Trade South's ♠J and ♡J for the ♡Q, giving him

♠ A K Q 6 2   ♡ A Q 3   ◇ 7 3   ♣ K 10 2

and he has a chance for thirteen tricks.

Here's a final example of overvaluing minor honors (queens and jacks). Playing matchpoints, both sides vulnerable, you hold as West

♠ K Q J 4   ♡ A Q 5   ◇ Q 4   ♣ Q 6 4 3

WEST	EAST
	1NT
2♣[1]	2♠
3♠	4♣
4♡	4♠

1. Game-forcing Stayman.

What do you say?

The actual West counted his 16 points and raised to 5♠. East went on, but the combined hands were:

♠ K Q J 4   ♠ A 10 6 3
♡ A Q 5   ♡ J 4 2
◇ Q 4   ◇ A 10
♣ Q 6 4 3   ♣ A K 7 2

1 · CONSTRUCTIVE BIDDING

The cards lay badly, and the result was down two. West's bidding was too bold (especially 5♠, which East interpreted as a command to bid slam if he had a diamond control). With only one ace and one king, West should have passed 4♠.

TIP 12

IF IT'S A MISFIT, QUIT

Vulnerable at IMPs, as South you hold

♠ 6 ♡ A J 7 ◊ A K 8 5 2 ♣ K 7 5 2

WEST	NORTH	EAST	SOUTH
			1◊
pass	1♠	pass	2♣
pass	2♠	pass	?

What do you say now?

The actual South tried 2NT. The full deal:

```
              ♠ K J 8 7 5 3
              ♡ 9 2
              ◊ J 4
              ♣ A 9 4
♠ 10 4                          ♠ A Q 9 2
♡ Q 6 3          N              ♡ K 10 8 5 4
◊ Q 10 7 3    W     E           ◊ 9 6
♣ Q 10 8 6       S             ♣ J 3
              ♠ 6
              ♡ A J 7
              ◊ A K 8 5 2
              ♣ K 7 5 2
```

North, who had a maximum with a couple of fitting minor-suit honors, raised to 3NT. East doubled — he knew the spades wouldn't run — and everyone passed. West led the ♠10 to the jack and queen, and East shifted to the ♡10, trapping dummy's nine. South eventually managed six tricks and got out for -800. Since North's bidding had promised long spades but high-card weakness, South's 2NT was foolhardy: he had no source of tricks in notrump. South should have passed 2♠, where North's hand might produce a few tricks.

Principle: *when the deal is a misfit and your side has no compensating high-card values, stop bidding.* Don't keep groping for a good contract when there isn't one. Just quit and avoid a penalty double and a catastrophe. I remember playing in a Regional teams event with a player who had represented the U.S. in the Bermuda Bowl. I held:

♠ 4   ♡ A 6   ◇ A Q 7 5 3   ♣ A K 8 5 3

The bidding started 1◇ by me, 1♠ by partner, 2♣ by me — and everyone passed. Dummy hit with something like

♠ J 9 7 5 3 2   ♡ K 9 5 3 2   ◇ J   ♣ 6

I scrambled eight tricks for +90, and we gained a chunk of IMPs. At the other table, North couldn't resist bidding again and got his side way too high. My partner knew enough to get out while the getting was good; it didn't matter that 2♣ might not be an ideal contract. Incidentally, if your partner opens 1◇, it may pay to respond 1♡ instead of the textbook 1♠ on

♠ J 9 6 4 3   ♡ K J 8 5 3   ◇ 6   ♣ 10 7

if you plan to pass a 2♣ rebid from fright. You break even if opener has four spades, lose if he has a minimum with 3-1-5-4 distribution but gain if he has a minimum 1-3-5-4 or 1-4-4-4.

You're South, playing against Italy in the 1974 Bermuda Bowl final, and hold a fine hand:

♠ A Q J 4   ♡ A 2   ◇ K 5   ♣ K Q J 8 2

WEST	NORTH	EAST	SOUTH
1NT[1]	pass	pass	dbl
pass	2♡	pass	2NT
pass	3◇	pass	?

1.   13-15.

Both sides vulnerable. What do you say now?

```
                      ♠ 6 2
                      ♡ 9 8 6 4 3
                      ◇ J 10 7 3 2
                      ♣ 6
  ♠ K 10 5                              ♠ 9 8 7 3
  ♡ Q J 7         ┌─────┐               ♡ K 10 5
  ◇ A 4           │  N  │               ◇ Q 9 8 6
  ♣ A 9 5 4 3     │W   E│               ♣ 10 7
                  │  S  │
                  └─────┘
                      ♠ A Q J 4
                      ♡ A 2
                      ◇ K 5
                      ♣ K Q J 8 2
```

WEST	NORTH	EAST	SOUTH
1NT	pass	pass	dbl
pass	2♡	pass	2NT
pass	3◇	pass	3NT
pass	pass	dbl	pass
pass	4◇	pass	pass
dbl	all pass		

Down four, +1100 to Italy. Three notrump is usually the worst place to play a misfit; South would have avoided disaster by taking a disciplined 3♡ preference over 3◇.

A pair of deals from a Grand National Teams final show how experts cope (or fail to cope) with misfits.

Dlr: South
Vul: E-W

```
                    ♠ J 10 5 4 3
                    ♡ A 10 8 6 5
                    ◇ 9 3
                    ♣ 6
♠ Q 9 8 6 2                            ♠ 7
♡ 3                N                   ♡ K Q J 9 7 4
◇ A Q 7 6      W       E               ◇ 10 2
♣ K 9 7            S                   ♣ Q J 5 4
                    ♠ A K
                    ♡ 2
                    ◇ K J 8 5 4
                    ♣ A 10 8 3 2
```

WEST	NORTH	EAST	SOUTH
			1◇
pass	1♠	3♡	4♣
all pass			

North passed 4♣ in terror and was rewarded when his side had to pay only a 50-points-per-trick penalty. Down five, -250. At the other table the bidding went 1◇ by South, 1♠ overcall by West, 2♡ by East, 4♣ by South (North-South were playing a strong, artificial 1♣). When North took a preference to 4◇, West got out the hammer and collected 500.

BECOMING A BRIDGE EXPERT

Dlr: West
Vul: E-W

```
                    ♠ A 10 7 5 4
                    ♡ K 10 5 3
                    ◇ 5 3
                    ♣ K 5
  ♠ Q J 9 8                          ♠ 3 2
  ♡ A J 9 8 2          N             ♡ 7 6 4
  ◇ A 6            W       E         ◇ Q 10 9 8
  ♣ 7 6                S             ♣ Q J 9 3
                    ♠ K 6
                    ♡ Q
                    ◇ K J 7 4 2
                    ♣ A 10 8 4 2
```

WEST	NORTH	EAST	SOUTH
pass	pass	pass	1◇
1♡	1♠	pass	2♣
pass	2NT	pass	3♣
pass	3NT(?)	all pass	

Down three. If North had been disciplined at his third turn and taken a 3◇ preference, South might have been down one.

One final example. Playing IMPs, neither side vulnerable, you hold as South:

WEST	NORTH	EAST	SOUTH
			1♣
1♠	pass	2♡	?

♠ K Q J 4   ♡ A 4   ◇ A   ♣ K J 8 7 6 3

What do you say?

Pass. The storm warning has been posted: you have length in West's suit and losers in your own long suit; East-West are not certain to have a fit, and North may have nothing. In a Bermuda Bowl, South tried 3♣ and was hit for -300. The full deal:

```
                    ♠ 9 6
                    ♡ J 8 5 2
                    ◇ Q 10 8 7 5 3
                    ♣ 2
  ♠ A 10 8 5 3                       ♠ 7 2
  ♡ 3                  N             ♡ K Q 10 9 7 6
  ◇ K 6 4          W       E         ◇ J 9 2
  ♣ A 10 9 5           S             ♣ Q 4
                    ♠ K Q J 4
                    ♡ A 4
                    ◇ A
                    ♣ K J 8 7 6 3
```

TIP 13

DON'T MAKE AMBIGUOUS BIDS

You are playing IMPs, both sides vulnerable, and you hold as West:

♠ A 10 3   ♡ 7   ◇ A J 8 7 2   ♣ A Q J 3

WEST	NORTH	EAST	SOUTH
1◇	pass	1♡	pass
2♣	pass	3♡[1]	pass
?			

1. Invitational.

What do you say?

Bid 3NT. This bid may look simple and obvious to you and me; but the actual West chose the murky bid of 3♠.

♠ A 10 3		♠ J 4
♡ 7	N W E S	♡ K J 9 8 6 4
◇ A J 8 7 2		◇ Q 5 3
♣ A Q J 3		♣ K 8

WEST	EAST
1◇	1♡
2♣	3♡
3♠	4◇
4♡	5♣
6♣	6♡
pass	

West succeeded in confusing East, who was afraid to bid 3NT with nothing in spades; and when East heard West bid 4♡ next, he assumed 3♠ had suggested a tolerance for hearts with slam interest. The result: disaster.

You're always careful to help your partner on defense with clear and accurate signals. By the same token, be careful not to offer him bids that lack clarity.

♠ A Q 7 6 2		♠ K 10 8 3
♡ K 3	N W E S	♡ A 7 4 2
◇ K 9		◇ A Q 10
♣ A J 4 2		♣ 8 5

WEST	EAST
	1◇
1♠	2♠
3♣	3♡
4◇	4♠
5♡	5♠
pass	

A U.S. pair missed this slam in a Bermuda Bowl, and the trouble began when East bid 3♡ instead of an honest 4♠. This bid planted doubt in West's mind about East's trump quality.

♠ A K J 3 2	♠ 9
♡ Q J 8 7 6 3	♡ K 9
◇ —	◇ Q 9 8 6
♣ Q J	♣ A 10 7 5 4 2

WEST	EAST
1♠	1NT
4♡	4♠

On this deal in the same event, East wasn't sure what West had and ran from 4♡. Four spades went down a lot, while in the other room East-West bid

WEST	EAST
1♠	2♣
2♡	2NT
4♡	

making four.

This next example shows a common situation in which many players go astray. At matchpoints, neither side vulnerable, you hold as South:

♠ 6 4   ♡ 9 5 3   ◇ K Q 8 3   ♣ A 10 8 3

North opens 1♣. A raise to 2♣ is unambiguous and descriptive (and shuts out a major-suit overcall by the next player). A 1◇ response won't put partner in the picture.

Here's another example of unnecessary confusion:

♠ A 6	♠ 9 4
♡ A K 6 4 3	♡ Q 8 5
◇ A Q 8 6 4	◇ K 9 7 3
♣ 7	♣ J 6 4 2

WEST	EAST
1♡	2♡
3◇	3♡
3♠	4♡

West's bidding was imprecise: although East might have done better to bid 4◇ over 3♠, he was never sure of his partner's intentions and kept signing off. West should jump to 4◇ over 2♡, unambiguously showing slam interest. East would raise to 5◇, and West could bid 6◇.

Experts seldom respond 3NT to an opening one-bid (and only with 4-3-3-3 distribution) because it uses up bidding space and makes slam investigation harder. Still, I'd rather bid a straightforward

3NT than subject partner to an ambiguous auction such as this one:

♠ 7 4 2	♠ A K 3
♡ A 6	♡ K J 8 2
◇ Q 6	◇ K 10 4
♣ A K J 8 7 3	♣ Q 9 5

WEST	EAST
1♣	1♡
2♣	2◇
2♡	2♠
2NT	3NT

East tried to cut his way through the jungle, inventing forcing bids, but couldn't squeeze any useful information from West. It was impossible to bid slam with any confidence, and East gave up. At the other table, East-West reached a good spot in fewer bids.

WEST	EAST
1♣	3NT
4♣	4♠
6♣	

If you aren't sure how your partner will interpret a bid, don't make it.

♠ A K 6 4 3	♠ 8
♡ 7 5	♡ A 8 4 3
◇ A Q 6 5	◇ K J 9 4 2
♣ A Q	♣ 8 6 4

WEST	EAST
1♠	1NT[1]
3◇	4♡
pass	

1. Forcing.

After 4♡ went down, East explained that West should have treated 4♡ as a cuebid in support of diamonds. Perhaps East was right in theory, but West wasn't up to the task.

Here's another example of expecting more from partner than you should:

♠ K Q 8 5 2	♠ A J 9 6 3
♡ 6	♡ K 10 8 2
◇ K Q 7	◇ 6 3
♣ Q 10 7 3	♣ A 6

WEST	NORTH	EAST	SOUTH
		1♠	dbl
redbl	2♡	dbl	pass
4♡	all pass		

Since East was an inexperienced player, West — it was me — got what he deserved with the fancy 4♡ splinter bid.

One last example: at matchpoints, both sides vulnerable, you hold as South:

♠ J 10 5   ♡ A K 4 3   ◊ A K J 2   ♣ K 5

WEST	NORTH	EAST	SOUTH
			1◊
pass	1♠	pass	2NT
pass	3◊	pass	?

What do you say?

Bid 3♠. The actual South got cute and tried 3♡ to show where his values were. North had to return to 3NT, which was passed out, and the full deal was

```
                ♠ Q 9 6 4 3
                ♡ 7 5
                ◊ Q 10 6 4
                ♣ A 7
♠ A 2                           ♠ K 8 7
♡ J 9 8 2          N            ♡ Q 10 6
◊ 8 5           W     E         ◊ 9 7 3
♣ Q 10 8 4 2       S            ♣ J 9 6 3
                ♠ J 10 5
                ♡ A K 4 3
                ◊ A K J 2
                ♣ K 5
```

West led a club to beat 3NT, while 4♠ would have made an overtrick.

Playing IMPs, both sides vulnerable you hold as South:

♠ K J 8 3   ♡ Q J 8 2   ◊ A J 6   ♣ 6 2

WEST	NORTH	EAST	SOUTH
	1♡	pass	3♡
pass	4♣	pass	?

Your 3♡ was forcing. What do you say now?

Sign off in 4♡. Your values are not slammish. The actual South cuebid his ◊A instead, and North then jumped to 5♡ on

♠ 10 5   ♡ A K 10 6 5   ◊ 7 4   ♣ A K Q 8

TIP 14

**A CUEBID
SHOWS
SLAM
INTEREST**

Everyone passed. The opening lead against 5♡ was a diamond, and North eventually misguessed spades to go down one. Perhaps North's 5♡, which demanded that South bid a slam if he had a spade control, was too aggressive; but North was surely worth a second slam try, and a 5♣ cuebid might have led to the same result. A cuebid shows slam interest. I consider this to be true, but many experts wouldn't: they would feel South had to cuebid 4◊.

Cuebidding is a superior slam-bidding method. After a trump suit is agreed, a bid of another suit at the game level or higher shows slam interest and promises a control: usually the ace, sometimes the king, rarely shortness. Partner can sign off, bid slam or cuebid himself. After a while, the partnership decides how high to play. Here are some typical cuebidding auctions:

```
♠ 7 2              ♠ J 5 3
♡ A K J 6 4        ♡ Q 9 5 2
◊ K 3              ◊ A Q 5
♣ A Q J 4          ♣ K 7 6
```

WEST	EAST
1♡	3♡
4♣[1]	4◊[2]
4♡[3]	5♣[4]
5◊[5]	5♡[6]

1. "I have the ♣A."
2. "I have the ◊A."
3. "My slam interest is only mild."
4. "I'm still interested, and I have the ♣K."
5. "I have the ◊K, but no spade control."
6. "I don't have one either."

With the lack of a spade control evident, the partnership stops safely in 5♡.

```
♠ K 3              ♠ Q J 4 2
♡ A K J 6 4        ♡ Q 9 5 2
◊ 7 2              ◊ A 6 3
♣ A Q 10 4         ♣ K 6
```

WEST	EAST
1♡	3♡
4♣	4◊
4♡	5♣[1]
6♡	

1. "I have the ♣K, and I'm still interested."

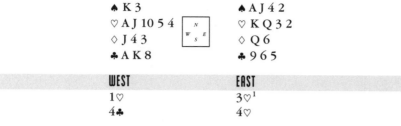

WEST	EAST
1♡	3♡[1]
4♣	4♡

1. Forcing.

Since East has a minimum, he refuses to go past game to cuebid. But suppose the East hand were

♠ J 6 5   ♡ K Q 3 2   ◇ A 10 5 2   ♣ Q 6

Many experts would cuebid 4◇ despite their minimum because they feel it's 'free' on the way to 4♡ and does not especially encourage slam. But this approach compromises the biggest advantage of cuebidding: to let both partners use their judgment. My tip: cuebids are constructive; a cuebid shows slam interest.

My files are full of deals in which a 'free' cuebid led to a poor result. This one comes from an Olympiad Teams final:

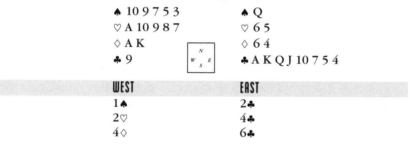

WEST	EAST
1♠	2♣
2♡	4♣
4◇	6♣

Eleven tricks were the limit. If the East-West bidding style required West to cuebid the ◇A, East's 6♣ was unjustified.

WEST	EAST
1♠	3♠[1]
4◇	4♡
4NT	5◇
6♠	

1. Forcing.

A heart lead beat the slam, but since South had the ♣AQ, any lead would have beaten it. A better auction would have stopped earlier:

WEST	EAST
1♠	3♠
4◇	4♠
5◇[1]	5♡[2]
5♠[3]	

1. "I'll try again."
2. "I do have the ♡A."
3. "We're off the ♣A, plus a possible heart and a possible diamond."

Notice that the players in these examples were top internationals. Here's another deal from a Bermuda Bowl:

♠ 10 3	♠ A K J 8 7 5 2
♡ K 9 7 2	♡ A 8 6 3
◇ A J	◇ 8
♣ A J 7 4 3	♣ 2

WEST	EAST
1♡[1]	2♠
3♣	3♡
4◇	4♡
pass	

1. 1♣ would have been forcing.

I'm not sure what went wrong here, since 6♡ requires little more than a 3-2 trump break. If East had thought West's 4◇ cuebid showed a willingness to bid slam, surely he would have done more than bid 4♡. I suspect, though, that East thought West was obliged to cuebid on any old hand with the ◇A. In that case, East couldn't afford another forward-going move.

Earlier in this Section, in Tip 3, I discussed some of the problems of the 'Two-over-One game-force' style. Here's another: players are often obliged to try for slam when they'd rather not.

Dlr: West
Vul: Both

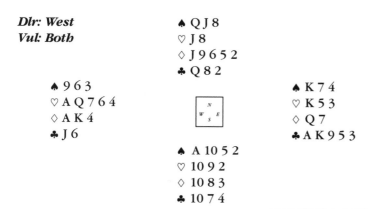

```
                    ♠ Q J 8
                    ♡ J 8
                    ◊ J 9 6 5 2
                    ♣ Q 8 2
    ♠ 9 6 3                          ♠ K 7 4
    ♡ A Q 7 6 4                      ♡ K 5 3
    ◊ A K 4                          ◊ Q 7
    ♣ J 6                            ♣ A K 9 5 3
                    ♠ A 10 5 2
                    ♡ 10 9 2
                    ◊ 10 8 3
                    ♣ 10 7 4
```

WEST	NORTH	EAST	SOUTH
1♡	pass	2♣[1]	pass
2♡	pass	3♡	pass
4◊	pass	4♠	pass
5◊	pass	5♡	all pass

1. Forcing to game.

Since East's 3♡ was forcing, West felt obliged to show the ◊A. Since West's hand was unlimited, East felt obliged to show his spade control. They wound up at the five-level, down two after the defense took three spades and then arranged an uppercut. The other East-West pair bid 1♡-2♣, 2♡-3NT, making five. When players use system as a substitute for judgment, problems are bound to occur.

Again, in a Bermuda Bowl:

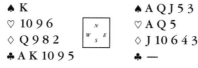

```
♠ K                          ♠ A Q J 5 3
♡ 10 9 6                      ♡ A Q 5
◊ Q 9 8 2                     ◊ J 10 6 4 3
♣ A K 10 9 5                  ♣ —
```

WEST	EAST
pass	1◊[1]
3◊	3♠[2]
4♣	4♡
5♣	5◊
6◊ (dbl)	pass

1. Canapé.
2. Extra values, but at most, 16 points.

East had bad trumps, and West's 4♣ cuebid signaled duplication of values. East should have bid a discreet 4◊ instead of suggesting slam with the 4♡ cuebid. If East's 4♡ cuebid was mandatory, something is wrong with the 'cooperative' style.

Here's an example of how cooperation should work. As West, vulnerable at IMPs, you hold:

♠ K Q J 4 ♡ 6 4 ◊ A Q J 8 3 ♣ Q 2

You open 1◊, your partner responds 1♠, you raise to 3♠ and he tries 4♣. What do you say now?

Bid 4♠. Since your three queens and two jacks give you a questionable 3♠ bid, it would be indiscreet to cooperate with partner's slam try. The actual auction was

	♠ K Q J 4		♠ A 10 8 3
	♡ 6 4	N W E S	♡ Q 7 3
	◊ A Q J 8 3		◊ 9 2
	♣ Q 2		♣ A K 7 4

WEST	EAST
1◊	1♠
3♠	4♣
4◊	5♣
5♠	pass

It's easy to say that 4◊ promised nothing extra, but it was human nature for East to be encouraged enough to cuebid again. The diamond finesse lost, and 5♠ failed. West should have saved his 4◊ cuebid for a more slammish hand such as

♠ K J 6 4 ♡ A 5 ◊ A K 8 4 3 ♣ 8 5

This section includes some secret bits of gambitry I've seen experts employ.

Gambit 1. *Top players know that if a slam is possible, it's best to tell partner early, then go easy; experts jump-shift on many hands that lack the old-fashioned requirement of 19 points.*

You are South, playing IMPs, both sides vulnerable, and you hold:

♠ A K J 4 3 ♡ 5 4 ◊ K J 5 4 ♣ A 2

North opens 1◊ and East passes. What do you say?

Bid 2♠, intending to support the diamonds next. Jump shifts work best when they suggest slam and get opener involved in the decision. If responder knows where the hand should play, he should jump if a suitable minimum hand for opener will produce slam. If you respond 1♠ instead, the auction may continue

NORTH	SOUTH
1◇	1♠
1NT	3◇[1]
3NT	?

1. Forcing, luckily.

Would you be comfortable passing now? You still won't feel you've done your hand justice. North could hold

♠ Q 2   ♡ K 8 2   ◇ A Q 7 2   ♣ K 9 7 3

However, if he signs off after 1◇-2♠, 2NT-3◇, you have an easy pass.

Your partner opens 1♠, and you hold

♠ K Q 5 4 3   ♡ 7   ◇ A K J 4 3   ♣ 3

Jump to 3◇, intending to support spades next. A spade slam is icy if opener has

♠ A 10 7 6 2   ♡ A J 6   ◇ Q 2   ♣ J 5 4

so an immediate slam signal is mandatory. Likewise, if your partner opens 1♡, jump to 3◇ on

♠ 8 6 2   ♡ A K 7   ◇ A K J 10 3   ♣ 9 3

A jump shift will get you to slam when he has the right minimum, such as

♠ K J 4   ♡ Q J 8 5 3   ◇ Q 4   ♣ A 7 6;

and let you stay low opposite

♠ Q 7 5   ♡ Q J 8 5 3   ◇ Q 4   ♣ A K 6

Failure to jump on a hand like these was costly in a Bermuda Bowl final:

```
          ♠ 5 3                    ♠ A K
          ♡ A K 4 3 2    ┌─────┐   ♡ 9 5
          ◇ A K 5 2      │  N  │   ◇ 10 6 4 3
                         │W   E│
          ♣ 10 3         │  S  │   ♣ A K Q J 5
                         └─────┘
```

WEST	EAST
1♡	2♣
2◇	2♠
3♣	3♠
3NT	

Slam was never in the picture. East could have started with a jump to 3♣, and perhaps East-West would have reached 6♣.

Gambit 2. *When your partner preempts, many tactical responses are possible (a gentle lift to the four-level, for example, may be effective). However, a psychic 3NT bid may be a credible-sounding action.*

Playing IMPs, with East-West vulnerable, you hold as North:

♠ A J 8 3   ♡ 8 3 2   ◇ A 7 3   ♣ 10 8 5

South opens 3◇ and West passes. East-West are probably cold for 4♡. How can you stop them from bidding it? A psychic 3♡ response won't work against good players. You probably have a paying sacrifice in 5◇, but if you leap there right away, the opponents will surely double. A raise to 4◇ is possible, but North actually tried 3NT. The full deal:

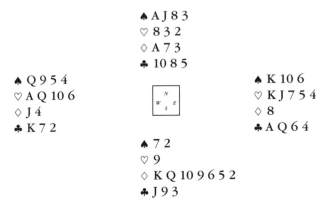

```
              ♠ A J 8 3
              ♡ 8 3 2
              ◇ A 7 3
              ♣ 10 8 5
♠ Q 9 5 4                    ♠ K 10 6
♡ A Q 10 6          N        ♡ K J 7 5 4
◇ J 4           W     E      ◇ 8
♣ K 7 2             S        ♣ A Q 6 4
              ♠ 7 2
              ♡ 9
              ◇ K Q 10 9 6 5 2
              ♣ J 9 3
```

If North had passed, East would have doubled and reached 4♡. If North had bid 4◇, East might still have doubled, and West might have doubled even if East passed. But the 3NT bid had an air of legitimacy that kept both East and West quiet. If someone had doubled 3NT, North would have run to 4◇, of course; but everyone passed. South went down five, -250, but North's bid gained nine IMPs since his teammates were +650 in 4♡.

Gambit 3. *If you're in the mood to gamble against good opponents, you might try passing your partner's opening bid with a fair hand.*

At matchpoints, both sides vulnerable, you hold as South

♠ 6   ♡ K 10 9 6   ◇ K 9 5 2   ♣ Q 10 6 4

If North opens 1♠, and East passes, consider passing. If West balances, you can double anything and hope for +200 or more.

Gambit 4. *Few casual players use 'fourth-suit' bids, but expert part-nerships can't do without them.*

In an auction such as

WEST	EAST
1♢	1♡
1♠	2♣

East may have clubs but doesn't promise them. His 2♣ signifies nothing except a desire to hear West bid again. East might hold

♠ 7 6		♠ Q 6
♡ A K 5 4	*or*	♡ A K 6 4
♢ K J 8 7		♢ A 10 5
♣ A 6 5		♣ 8 6 4

On the first hand, he wants to force in diamonds, but a jump preference to 3♢ may be invitational in his methods; on the second hand, he wants to hear South bid notrump or support hearts.

The rise in popularity of 'fourth-suit' bids is partly attributable to matchpoint duplicate, in which accurate partscores are as valuable as good games and slams. In the old Goren style, which was oriented to rubber bridge, most jump rebids and raises were forcing, allowing for ease in game and slam bidding; but duplicate players need more invitational sequences.

At matchpoints, neither side vulnerable, you hold as South:

♠ A 5 4   ♡ 7 6   ♢ K J 9 4 3   ♣ A Q 4

WEST	NORTH	EAST	SOUTH
	1♣	pass	1♢
pass	1♡	pass	?

Bid 1♠. You've no idea of the best contract, and even if 3NT is your spot, North should be declarer if he has a hand such as

♠ Q 6   ♡ A K 4 3   ♢ 8 2   ♣ K J 9 5 3

If he bids 1NT next, you'll raise to 3NT; if he rebids the clubs or takes a diamond preference, you'll steer clear of notrump.

Gambit 5. *I've seen top players get a good result with a bluff 1NT response (forcing, usually) when they have a poor hand but support for partner. The idea is make the opponents misjudge the fit.*

Dlr: South
Vul: Both

```
                    ♠ A 8 4 3
                    ♡ 3 2
                    ◇ 9 5 2
                    ♣ 9 7 6 2
   ♠ K 5                              ♠ 9 2
   ♡ Q 8 6 5 4         N              ♡ K 10 9 7
   ◇ Q 3          W         E         ◇ A K 10 6 4
   ♣ K Q 4 3          S              ♣ 8 5
                    ♠ Q J 10 7 6
                    ♡ A J
                    ◇ J 8 7
                    ♣ A J 10
```

WEST	NORTH	EAST	SOUTH
			1♠
pass	2♠	pass	pass
dbl	pass	3♡	all pass

North scraped up a raise to 2♠, but after two passes, West was willing to balance. East took nine tricks in 3♡, losing two spades, a trump and a club. But at the other table:

WEST	NORTH	EAST	SOUTH
			1♠
pass	1NT[1]	pass	2♣
pass	2♠	all pass	

1. Forcing.

Now neither East nor West was willing to act. It sounded as if North had only a tolerance for spades, and East-West weren't sure they had a spot to play in. When West led the ♣K, South wound up with nine tricks.

Gambit 6. *Experts occasionally operate by responding in a three-card major.*

Dlr: North
Vul: None

```
                    ♠ Q 6
                    ♡ Q J 7 6
                    ◇ A K J 5 4
                    ♣ A 3
   ♠ A J 7 4 3                        ♠ K 10 8
   ♡ 10 3           ┌─────┐           ♡ 9 8 5 4
   ◇ 9 6 2          │  N  │           ◇ 10 7
   ♣ Q 9 7          │W   E│           ♣ K J 10 4
                    │  S  │
                    └─────┘
                    ♠ 9 5 2
                    ♡ A K 2
                    ◇ Q 8 3
                    ♣ 8 6 5 2
```

WEST	NORTH	EAST	SOUTH
	1◇	pass	1NT
pass	2NT	pass	3NT

West led a spade for down one. But in the replay, South was reluctant to respond 1NT with prime heart values and nothing in spades.

WEST	NORTH	EAST	SOUTH
	1◇	pass	1♡(!)
pass	3♡	pass	4♡(!!)
all pass			

East-West found the best defense: West led the ♠A and continued, and East took the king and led a third spade. South discarded dummy's low club instead of ruffing and soon claimed his game.

Gambit 7. *Try for nine tricks rather than ten.*

Playing matchpoints, both sides vulnerable, you hold as North:

♠ A Q J 8 5 3   ♡ 7 6 5   ◇ 10 5   ♣ J 3

South opens 1NT (15-17), and West passes. What do you say?

I used to do well at matchpoints by raising 1NT to 3NT on hands with a six-card major suit but scattered values:

♠ Q 6   ♡ A Q 10 7 5 2   ◇ Q 7   ♣ J 5 4

That may have been a questionable action, but I'm certain if North is going to bid a game on the spade hand above, it should be 3NT. The hand is so threadbare that North should play for a nine-trick game. There may also be an advantage in having the opening lead come up to South's hand. The full deal may be

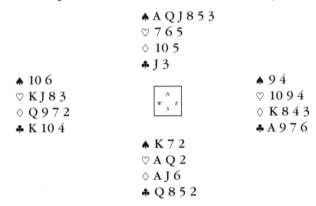

♠ A Q J 8 5 3
♡ 7 6 5
◇ 10 5
♣ J 3

♠ 10 6   ♠ 9 4
♡ K J 8 3   ♡ 10 9 4
◇ Q 9 7 2   ◇ K 8 4 3
♣ K 10 4   ♣ A 9 7 6

♠ K 7 2
♡ A Q 2
◇ A J 6
♣ Q 8 5 2

Any lead except a spade gives South an easy nine tricks; but 4♠ is in jeopardy.

DUMMY PLAY

2

Most players think dummy play is easier than defense, but I disagree. Although defenders often have difficult guesses, they can usually survive by applying basic principles and counting. I think to become a fine declarer takes longer since dummy play offers more scope for variety and creativity. The first step, though, is a mastery of elementary skills...

KNOW YOUR CARD COMBINATIONS

Dlr. South
Vul. None

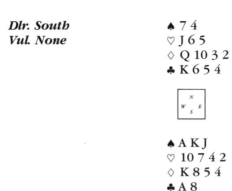

♠ 7 4
♡ J 6 5
◇ Q 10 3 2
♣ K 6 5 4

♠ A K J
♡ 10 7 4 2
◇ K 8 5 4
♣ A 8

WEST	NORTH	EAST	SOUTH
			1NT
pass	pass	all pass	

West leads a low spade, and you capture East's queen. How do you continue?

You have five top tricks and therefore need two in diamonds. A safety play is available: lead low to the queen. If it wins, return a diamond; you can win two diamond tricks even if East has no more. If East captures the ◇Q with the ace and returns a spade, go to dummy with the ♣K and return a diamond, planning to play the eight if East follows low. If instead he shows out, take the king and lead toward the ten.

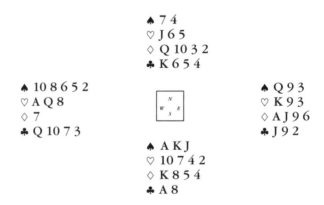

♠ 7 4
♡ J 6 5
◇ Q 10 3 2
♣ K 6 5 4

♠ 10 8 6 5 2   ♠ Q 9 3
♡ A Q 8   ♡ K 9 3
◇ 7   ◇ A J 9 6
♣ Q 10 7 3   ♣ J 9 2

♠ A K J
♡ 10 7 4 2
◇ K 8 5 4
♣ A 8

Declarer seldom attacks a suit without factoring in the bidding and the defenders' play so far. He may also have to consider problems such as avoidance and communication. Nevertheless, knowing the best way to handle combinations of cards 'in isolation' is a basic skill. How would you play each of these card combinations for the indicated number of tricks? Assume no clues from the bidding or play.

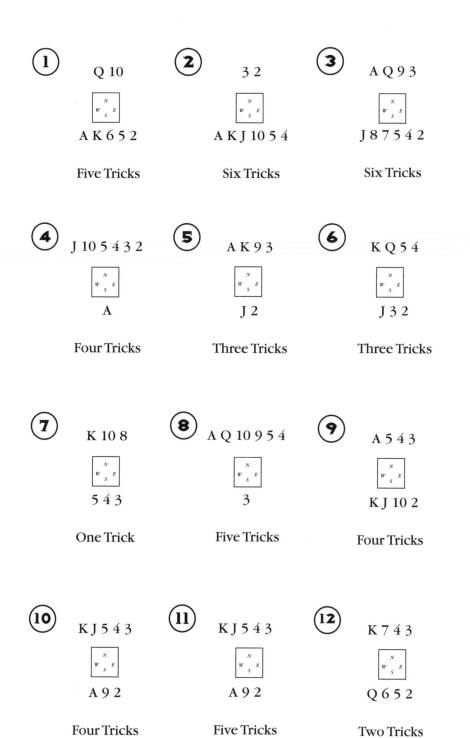

1
Q 10

	N	
W		E
	S	

A K 6 5 2

Five Tricks

2
3 2

	N	
W		E
	S	

A K J 10 5 4

Six Tricks

3
A Q 9 3

	N	
W		E
	S	

J 8 7 5 4 2

Six Tricks

4
J 10 5 4 3 2

	N	
W		E
	S	

A

Four Tricks

5
A K 9 3

	N	
W		E
	S	

J 2

Three Tricks

6
K Q 5 4

	N	
W		E
	S	

J 3 2

Three Tricks

7
K 10 8

	N	
W		E
	S	

5 4 3

One Trick

8
A Q 10 9 5 4

	N	
W		E
	S	

3

Five Tricks

9
A 5 4 3

	N	
W		E
	S	

K J 10 2

Four Tricks

10
K J 5 4 3

	N	
W		E
	S	

A 9 2

Four Tricks

11
K J 5 4 3

	N	
W		E
	S	

A 9 2

Five Tricks

12
K 7 4 3

	N	
W		E
	S	

Q 6 5 2

Two Tricks

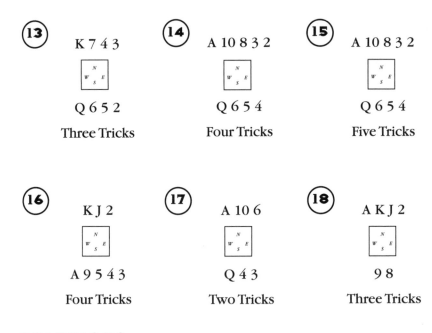

13 K 7 4 3

Q 6 5 2

Three Tricks

14 A 10 8 3 2

Q 6 5 4

Four Tricks

15 A 10 8 3 2

Q 6 5 4

Five Tricks

16 K J 2

A 9 5 4 3

Four Tricks

17 A 10 6

Q 4 3

Two Tricks

18 A K J 2

9 8

Three Tricks

SOLUTIONS

1. **Low to the ten.** You will take five tricks 42% of the time.

2. **Low to the ten** without cashing the ace or king (48%). Qxxx with East is more likely than a singleton queen with West.

3. **Let the jack ride** in case East is void (50%).

4. **After cashing the ace**, lead low from the J10543, catering to Kx or Qx (65%).

5. **Low toward the jack**, then low to the nine if necessary (74%).

6. **Low to the king**. If it wins, lead low toward the queen (45%). The idea is to lead twice toward the hand with two honors. A similar combination is Q32 opposite J1054.

7. **Low to the eight**. If it loses to the queen or jack, low to the ten next; otherwise, low to the king (about 70%). (Pay off if fourth hand is good enough to win with an honor holding QJ9.)

8. **Low to the queen**, then play the ace (40%).

9. **Play the ace**, then low to the ten (53%).

10 and 11. For five tricks, low to the jack without cashing the ace (37%). (Finesse the nine next if West plays the queen — pay off to a falsecard of the queen from Q-10 doubleton). **For four tricks**, play the king and then lead low toward the A-9, intending to play the nine if right-hand opponent follows low (96%).

12 and 13. For three tricks, lead toward an honor and duck on the way back — an 'obligatory finesse' (14%). **For two tricks**, play low from both hands on the first lead in case the ace is singleton, then lead up to one of the honors (73%).

14 and 15. For four tricks, play ace and then low to the queen (78%). **For five tricks, lead the queen**, hoping for a singleton jack on your right (6%).

16. Cash the king and lead toward the jack. If the ten falls under the king, you can simply concede a trick to the queen. Your total chance of taking four tricks is 96%.

17. Lead low to the queen; if it loses, finesse the ten (74%). But if you had the nine in place of the six, you should let the queen ride, and if it loses, lead to the ten next (76%).

18. Let the nine ride; if it loses to the ten, lead to the jack (76%).

The foregoing quiz looked at suit combinations in isolation; but we seldom get to play them in that context. A lack of entries can affect how you handle a suit.

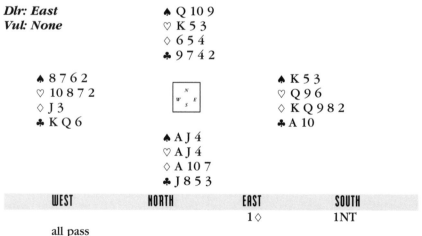

Dlr: East
Vul: None

```
                 ♠ Q 10 9
                 ♡ K 5 3
                 ◊ 6 5 4
                 ♣ 9 7 4 2
  ♠ 8 7 6 2                      ♠ K 5 3
  ♡ 10 8 7 2        N            ♡ Q 9 6
  ◊ J 3          W     E         ◊ K Q 9 8 2
  ♣ K Q 6           S            ♣ A 10
                 ♠ A J 4
                 ♡ A J 4
                 ◊ A 10 7
                 ♣ J 8 5 3
```

WEST	NORTH	EAST	SOUTH
		1◊	1NT

all pass

West led the ◊J, which South ducked, and continued with another diamond. South took the ace, led a heart to the king and let the

♠9 ride. The finesse worked, but when South led the ♠Q next, East covered. Since South couldn't return to dummy for a heart finesse, he took only six tricks. To get the extra entry he needs, South must lead the ♠Q first and underplay it with his jack if East ducks. South next lets the ♠10 ride and then leads a heart to the jack to fulfill the contract.

I watched the next deal on OKbridge.

Dlr: East
Vul: E-W

                ♠ K Q J 4
                ♡ J 4
                ◇ Q 6 4
                ♣ A K 6 2

                ♠ A 10 8 6 3
                ♡ K 7 2
                ◇ 5
                ♣ 9 7 5 4

WEST	NORTH	EAST	SOUTH
		1◇	1♠
pass	2◇	3◇	pass
pass	4♠	all pass	

South's 1♠ bid was lusty even at favorable vulnerability, but no harm was done this time. West led the ◇9, and East overtook with the ten and continued with the ace. South ruffed and drew trumps in two rounds. How should he continue?

South cashed the ♣AK and found this layout:

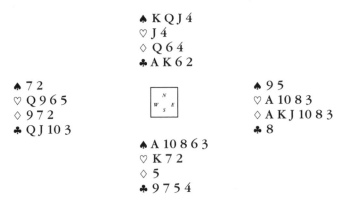

                ♠ K Q J 4
                ♡ J 4
                ◇ Q 6 4
                ♣ A K 6 2

♠ 7 2   ♠ 9 5
♡ Q 9 6 5   ♡ A 10 8 3
◇ 9 7 2   ◇ A K J 10 8 3
♣ Q J 10 3   ♣ 8

                ♠ A 10 8 6 3
                ♡ K 7 2
                ◇ 5
                ♣ 9 7 5 4

Although the ♡A was where it figured to be, South lost two clubs and went down. If clubs break 3-2, South is safe; if they break 4-1,

West is almost sure to have four since East has already shown up with two trumps and at least six diamonds. There are interesting endplay possibilities, but if South is going to attack the clubs himself, he must start by leading the ♣9, intending to let it ride if West plays the three. If East has a singleton club honor or the singleton three, South must lose two clubs; barring a defensive error, the only singleton he can handle is the eight. If in the actual deal West covers the ♣9 with the queen, South wins in dummy, returns the deuce to his seven and West's ten, and later finesses against West's jack.

Dlr: South
Vul: N-S

```
              ♠ A 4
              ♡ Q 5
              ◇ 6 5 4 3 2
              ♣ A 10 3 2
                  ┌─────┐
                  │  N  │
                  │W   E│
                  │  S  │
                  └─────┘
              ♠ K 10 8 7 5 3
              ♡ A K J
              ◇ A K
              ♣ K 7
```

WEST	NORTH	EAST	SOUTH
			1♠
pass	1NT	pass	3♡
pass	3♠	pass	4♠
pass	6♠	all pass	

West leads the ♡10. How do you play from here?

Lead the ♠10 at the second trick and let it ride if West plays low. The only singleton trump in the East hand you can handle is the nine; if East has any other singleton, two trump losers are all but certain. If West plays an honor on your ten (or if he plays the nine), take the ace and return a trump, covering East's card in case East has four trumps.

TIP 2

PLAN BEFORE YOU PLAY

Dlr: North
Vul: Both

♠ A 8
♡ A 10 8 4 2
◇ A 10 2
♣ K 4 3

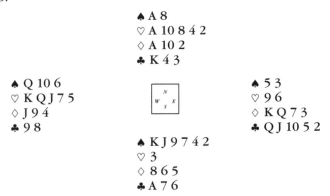

♠ K J 9 7 4 2
♡ 3
◇ 8 6 5
♣ A 7 6

WEST	NORTH	EAST	SOUTH
	1♡	pass	1♠
pass	1NT	pass	3♠
pass	4♠	all pass	

West leads the ♡K. How do you play the hand?

It looked like a routine deal — so the actual declarer took the ♡A, cashed the ♠A and finessed the ♠J. West took the queen and exited with his last trump, and South also lost two diamonds and a club.

♠ A 8
♡ A 10 8 4 2
◇ A 10 2
♣ K 4 3

♠ Q 10 6   ♠ 5 3
♡ K Q J 7 5   ♡ 9 6
◇ J 9 4   ◇ K Q 7 3
♣ 9 8   ♣ Q J 10 5 2

♠ K J 9 7 4 2
♡ 3
◇ 8 6 5
♣ A 7 6

South has a chance even if the trumps don't come in and the hearts don't break well — but only if he ruffs a heart at the second trick. He then takes the K-A of trumps. When both defenders play low, South ruffs another heart, cashes the ♣AK and ruffs a third heart. If hearts have broken 4-3, his fifth heart is now good. If the cards lie as in the diagram, he can cross to the ◇A and ruff dummy's last heart for his tenth trick while West follows.

It's easy to spot a good declarer: he never boots an easy hand and never plunges ahead without deciding on a line of play.

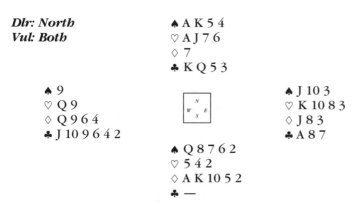

Dlr: North
Vul: Both

♠ A K 5 4
♡ A J 7 6
◇ 7
♣ K Q 5 3

♠ 9
♡ Q 9
◇ Q 9 6 4
♣ J 10 9 6 4 2

♠ J 10 3
♡ K 10 8 3
◇ J 8 3
♣ A 8 7

♠ Q 8 7 6 2
♡ 5 4 2
◇ A K 10 5 2
♣ —

WEST	NORTH	EAST	SOUTH
	1♣	pass	1♠
pass	4◇[1]	pass	5◇
pass	6♠	all pass	

1.   Spade support, diamond shortness.

West led the ♣J: king, ace, ruff. South then took the ◇A, ruffed a diamond and cashed the ace-king of trumps, hoping for a 2-2 break. When West showed out, South was in trouble. He threw a heart on the ♣Q, ruffed a club, cashed the ◇K and ruffed a diamond. East overruffed, and South also lost a heart.

South erred at the first trick and couldn't recover. Instead of ruffing the first club, he must pitch a heart, preserving an entry to his hand. He throws another heart on the next club, wins in dummy, takes the ◇A, ruffs a diamond, cashes the ace-king of trumps, ruffs a club and ruffs a second diamond. South can then ruff a club, draw East's last trump, and cash his winning diamonds and the ♡A.

A good declarer is skilled at controlling the tempo of the play. He pauses at the first trick and perhaps in the endgame, but he sets the pace for the other tricks — and inexperienced defenders may be caught up in his tempo and make a mistake. Moreover, declarer can create illusions like the one in the following deal.

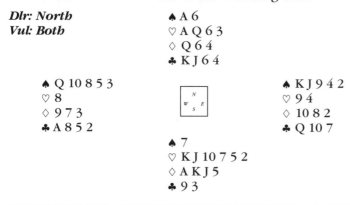

Dlr: North
Vul: Both

♠ A 6
♡ A Q 6 3
◇ Q 6 4
♣ K J 6 4

♠ Q 10 8 5 3
♡ 8
◇ 9 7 3
♣ A 8 5 2

♠ K J 9 4 2
♡ 9 4
◇ 10 8 2
♣ Q 10 7

♠ 7
♡ K J 10 7 5 2
◇ A K J 5
♣ 9 3

WEST	NORTH	EAST	SOUTH
	1NT	pass	3♡
pass	4♡	pass	5◇
pass	6♡	all pass	

West leads a spade to dummy's ace. Declarer has two possible approaches: one is to cross to his hand with a trump and lead a club immediately, forcing West to make a quick decision; the other is to draw trumps and run the diamonds to pitch dummy's last spade. Declarer takes his time, making sure West can count him for six trumps and four diamonds. South then leads a club, and if he has created the impression that he started with 2-6-4-1 distribution, West may rise with the ♣A (if he has it) to save the overtrick.

Even when your play seems obvious, stop and think the whole hand through before calling the first card from dummy.

Dlr: South
Vul: E-W

```
                        ♠ K 8 7
                        ♡ A 2
                        ◇ A J 3
                        ♣ A 9 8 4 2

   ♠ Q 9 5 2                              ♠ A J 10 3
   ♡ Q 9 5 3          N                   ♡ K J 10 8 6 4
   ◇ 7 4           W     E                ◇ 2
   ♣ Q 10 6           S                   ♣ 7 5

                        ♠ 6 4
                        ♡ 7
                        ◇ K Q 10 9 8 6 5
                        ♣ K J 3
```

WEST	NORTH	EAST	SOUTH
			4◇
pass	5◇	all pass	

When West led the ♡3, South took the ace, drew trumps and cashed the ♣AK. When both defenders played low, South led a third club, hoping East would win; but West took the queen and led a spade, and down South went. South does best to play low from dummy on the first heart! East wins and can do no better than to return a heart, and South throws a club. He can then draw trumps, cash the top clubs, ruff a club and return to dummy with a trump to run the clubs.

Here's a final deal on which the play to Trick 1 is critical:

Dlr: North
Vul: Both

♠ A 10 7 5
♡ Q 6
◇ A 7 3 2
♣ A 7 4

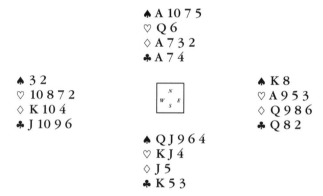

♠ Q J 9 6 4
♡ K J 4
◇ J 5
♣ K 5 3

WEST	NORTH	EAST	SOUTH
	1◇	pass	1♠
pass	2♠	pass	2NT
pass	4♠	all pass	

West leads the ♣J. Plan the play.

♠ A 10 7 5
♡ Q 6
◇ A 7 3 2
♣ A 7 4

♠ 3 2
♡ 10 8 7 2
◇ K 10 4
♣ J 10 9 6

♠ K 8
♡ A 9 5 3
◇ Q 9 8 6
♣ Q 8 2

♠ Q J 9 6 4
♡ K J 4
◇ J 5
♣ K 5 3

Count losers. You have one each in hearts and diamonds and a possible trump loser. You also have a club loser, but you can pitch a club from dummy on a winning heart and ruff a club.

Suppose you take the ♣K to try the trump finesse. East wins and returns a club — and you're too late to start the hearts; when East takes the ♡A, the defense will cash a club. Hence you must wait to draw trumps and first attack the hearts. However, it's not good enough to take the ♣K and lead a heart to the queen. East might duck, win the next heart and lead another club, stranding you in dummy with no quick entry to your hand for the good heart. Win the first club with the ace and lead the ♡Q. If the defense wins the second heart and continues clubs, you take the king and discard dummy's last club on the ♡K. Then it's safe to finesse in trumps.

TIP 3

ESTABLISH YOUR SIDE SUIT EARLY

Dlr: South
Vul: Both
Matchpoints

♠ 5 4 3
♡ K J
◇ 10 9 7 2
♣ A K 8 2

♠ K
♡ A Q 10 9 8 3
◇ J 6 5 3
♣ 7 4

WEST	NORTH	EAST	SOUTH
			2♡
pass	3♡	all pass	

West leads the ♠J to East's ace, and you ruff the spade return. How do you continue?

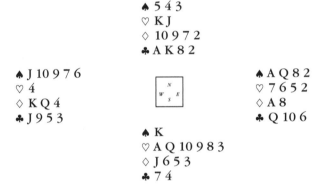

♠ 5 4 3
♡ K J
◇ 10 9 7 2
♣ A K 8 2

♠ J 10 9 7 6
♡ 4
◇ K Q 4
♣ J 9 5 3

♠ A Q 8 2
♡ 7 6 5 2
◇ A 8
♣ Q 10 6

♠ K
♡ A Q 10 9 8 3
◇ J 6 5 3
♣ 7 4

If you draw trumps, you will only have one left. You force out the ◇Q, ruff the next spade, take your ♣AK — and lose the rest: down one. You must lead a diamond at the third trick, ruff the spade return and concede a second diamond. Since dummy has no more spades, the defense can't gain by leading another spade. If they shift to a club, you win and concede the third diamond. You can win the next club, draw trumps and cash the good diamond.

Although East-West could make 3♠, they have no obvious way into the auction.

I've always felt good declarers are made and great declarers are born, but here's the single most important piece of dummy-play advice I know: *when a hand looks tough, and especially when trump control may be a problem, establish your side suit early.*

BECOMING A BRIDGE EXPERT

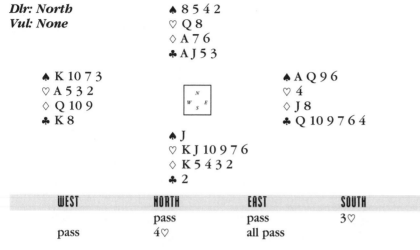

Dlr: North
Vul: None

♠ 8 5 4 2
♡ Q 8
◇ A 7 6
♣ A J 5 3

♠ K 10 7 3
♡ A 5 3 2
◇ Q 10 9
♣ K 8

♠ A Q 9 6
♡ 4
◇ J 8
♣ Q 10 9 7 6 4

♠ J
♡ K J 10 9 7 6
◇ K 5 4 3 2
♣ 2

WEST	NORTH	EAST	SOUTH
	pass	pass	3♡
pass	4♡	all pass	

West leads the ♠3; South ruffs the second spade and must immediately take the ace-king of diamonds and concede a diamond. He can then ruff the spade return and embark on a crossruff that is sure to produce ten tricks. If instead South starts on trumps at the third trick, West wins the second trump and forces South to ruff another spade. South must spend all his trumps to draw trumps, and when West wins a diamond trick, the defense cashes a spade for the setting trick.

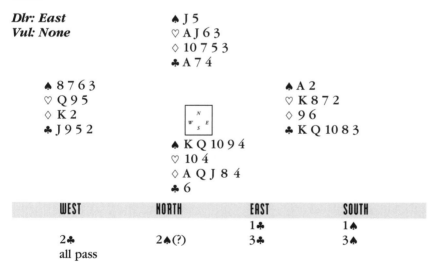

Dlr: East
Vul: None

♠ J 5
♡ A J 6 3
◇ 10 7 5 3
♣ A 7 4

♠ 8 7 6 3
♡ Q 9 5
◇ K 2
♣ J 9 5 2

♠ A 2
♡ K 8 7 2
◇ 9 6
♣ K Q 10 8 3

♠ K Q 10 9 4
♡ 10 4
◇ A Q J 8 4
♣ 6

WEST	NORTH	EAST	SOUTH
		1♣	1♠
2♣	2♠(?)	3♣	3♠
all pass			

I don't like the 2♠ bid, since South might misjudge — North's best action is a responsive double — and South might have tried 3◇ at his last turn; but against 3♠ West leads a club. Suppose South takes the ace and leads the ♠J, which wins, and then another spade losing to the ace. He ruffs East's club return, draws trumps, leads to the ♡A and lets the ◇10 ride. West wins, and the defenders cash a few hearts and clubs.

South may do better to try a diamond to his queen at the second trick. He ruffs the club return and leads a trump to the jack. East-West can still prevail if East ducks, wins the next trump and forces declarer with a club (then if West refuses to ruff until South leads a fourth round of diamonds, the defense can cut South off from his fifth diamond); but if East wins the first spade, South is safe.

Is it dangerous for South to take an early diamond finesse? Well, if East had a low singleton, he could get a ruff; but if West has the ◇K, East surely has the ♠A. The defense will still win only four tricks: a diamond, a heart, a ruff and the ♠A.

Dlr: East
Vul: Both

        ♠ A 10 9 5 4
        ♡ 10 8 6 5
        ◇ J
        ♣ A 10 5

                N
             W   E
                S

        ♠ J 8
        ♡ K Q 9 3
        ◇ A K 10 7 6 4 2
        ♣ —

WEST	NORTH	EAST	SOUTH
		1♣	1◇
pass	1♠	pass	2♡
pass	4♡	all pass	

West leads the ♣4. Plan the play.

        ♠ A 10 9 5 4
        ♡ 10 8 6 5
        ◇ J
        ♣ A 10 5

♠ Q 7 2   ♠ K 6 3
♡ 7 2   N   ♡ A J 4
◇ Q 8 5 3   W   E   ◇ 9
♣ J 9 8 4   S   ♣ K Q 7 6 3 2

        ♠ J 8
        ♡ K Q 9 3
        ◇ A K 10 7 6 4 2
        ♣ —

BECOMING A BRIDGE EXPERT

South threw a spade on the ♣A and led a trump to his king. He next took the ◇A and ruffed a diamond. East, U.S. expert John Solodar, discarded(!), refusing an easy overruff with the jack. South then ruffed a club and ruffed another diamond. Solodar discarded again (actually, he could have afforded to overruff this time) and South couldn't keep control to use the diamonds and wound up down two.

Credit East with good defense. If he overruffs when South ruffs the first diamond in dummy, South ruffs the club return and takes another diamond ruff. Whatever East does, his ace of trumps wins the defenders' last trick. But South is always safe if he starts the diamonds at the second trick: he cashes the ace and ruffs a diamond. If East discards (overruffing won't help), South leads a trump to his king and ruffs a diamond. East can get only his jack and ace of trumps.

TIP 4

ASSUME YOUR CONTRACT IS MAKABLE

Dlr: East	♠ K 7		
Vul: N-S	♡ A K 4 2		
	◇ 10 9 6 5		
	♣ J 10 8		

	N
W	E
	S

♠ J 4
♡ 8 5 3
◇ A Q J 4
♣ A Q 9 7

WEST	NORTH	EAST	SOUTH
		pass	1◇
pass	1♡	pass	1NT
pass	2NT	pass	3NT
all pass			

West leads the ♠2, and the contract is in the balance. Do you put up the king from dummy or play low?

You have no chance unless East has both minor-suit kings. But if East also had five spades to the ace, he'd doubtless have overcalled 1♠. You should put up the ♠K.

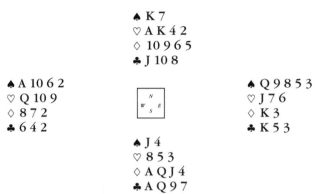

$$\spadesuit \; K\,7$$
$$\heartsuit \; A\,K\,4\,2$$
$$\diamond \; 10\,9\,6\,5$$
$$\clubsuit \; J\,10\,8$$

♠ A 10 6 2   ♠ Q 9 8 5 3
♡ Q 10 9   ♡ J 7 6
◊ 8 7 2   ◊ K 3
♣ 6 4 2   ♣ K 5 3

♠ J 4
♡ 8 5 3
◊ A Q J 4
♣ A Q 9 7

World Champion Bobby Goldman played correctly to make this game.

Declarers often make assumptions about the location of missing honors; the idea is to give themselves a chance for the contract. When you make an assumption, take note of where it leads.

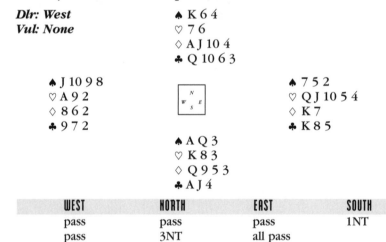

Dlr: West
Vul: None

♠ K 6 4
♡ 7 6
◊ A J 10 4
♣ Q 10 6 3

♠ J 10 9 8   ♠ 7 5 2
♡ A 9 2   ♡ Q J 10 5 4
◊ 8 6 2   ◊ K 7
♣ 9 7 2   ♣ K 8 5

♠ A Q 3
♡ K 8 3
◊ Q 9 5 3
♣ A J 4

WEST	NORTH	EAST	SOUTH
pass	pass	pass	1NT
pass	3NT	all pass	

West leads the ♠J, and South takes the queen and passes the ◊9, losing to the king. East shifts to the ♡Q, which wins, and continues with the ♡10. South must assume East has the ♣K. But if East had the ♡AQJ, ◊K and ♣K, he'd have opened the bidding; so South must duck the second heart also. He loses only three hearts and a diamond.

I was playing with a friend on OKbridge, and with North-South vulnerable, I was South holding:

♠ 8 6 4 2   ♡ A Q 7 5 3 2   ◊ Q 6   ♣ 7

WEST	NORTH	EAST	SOUTH
	1NT	dbl[1]	redbl
pass	pass	2♣	3♣
pass	3◇	pass	4♡
all pass			

1. Single-suited hand.

I wasn't too pleased with my bidding; but against 4♡ West led the
♣9, and I saw

♠ K J 9
♡ 10 4
◇ A K 10 5 3
♣ A J 5

```
    N
  W   E
    S
```

♠ 8 6 4 2
♡ A Q 7 5 3 2
◇ Q 6
♣ 7

I took the ♣A, and East played the deuce. A low trump from
dummy went to East's six, my queen and West's king. West led another club, and I ruffed East's ten and cashed the ♡A: West played the
eight and East the jack. Suppose I take the top diamonds next. If the
jack falls, I continue diamonds, pitching two spades. The worst that
can happen is that West ruffs and leads a spade, forcing me to guess.
If instead West turns up with ◇Jxxx, I can ruff a fourth diamond, lead
a spade myself and hope to guess right. I was certain, though, that
play would fail. West surely had the missing ♡9, and East's ♣2 at the
first trick troubled me. East was begging for a shift — obviously to
spades — and wouldn't want one if he had only the ace. My only
chance was to pitch three spades before West could ruff; if West had
to hold four diamonds, the odds were he'd have the jack.

So I took the ◇Q and led a diamond to the ten. The full deal was

♠ K J 9
♡ 10 4
◇ A K 10 5 3
♣ A J 5

♠ 10 7 3
♡ K 9 8
◇ J 9 8 2
♣ 9 8 3

```
    N
  W   E
    S
```

♠ A Q 5
♡ J 6
◇ 7 4
♣ K Q 10 6 4 2

♠ 8 6 4 2
♡ A Q 7 5 3 2
◇ Q 6
♣ 7

The defense got one spade and two trumps. "You sure are lucky," my partner typed. He was right, but I was also following the consequences of an assumption. As for the defense, West should have trusted East's signal. Since East had many clubs from which to choose, the deuce sent a clear message: "If you get in, shift!"

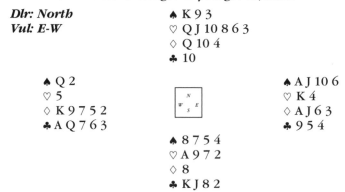

Dlr: North
Vul: E-W

```
                        ♠ K 9 3
                        ♡ Q J 10 8 6 3
                        ◇ Q 10 4
                        ♣ 10

  ♠ Q 2                                    ♠ A J 10 6
  ♡ 5                                      ♡ K 4
  ◇ K 9 7 5 2                              ◇ A J 6 3
  ♣ A Q 7 6 3                              ♣ 9 5 4

                        ♠ 8 7 5 4
                        ♡ A 9 7 2
                        ◇ 8
                        ♣ K J 8 2
```

East opened 1◇ in second seat, West temporized with 2♣ and North came in with 2♡. I'd have passed over that as East; but the actual East liked his ♡K and rebid 2♠ freely. South competed gently with 3♡, but West launched into 4NT, Blackwood: if East held as little as

♠ A K J ♡ x x x ◇ A Q x x x ♣ x

a diamond slam would be cold. East dutifully answered 5♡, and West bid 6◇, which was passed out. South cashed the ♡A and shifted to the ♣2. Declarer finessed with dummy's queen, winning, but cashed the ace-king of trumps next. When South showed out, declarer claimed down two, conceding a club.

After East wins the ♣Q at the second trick, he can see eleven tricks: five trumps (if he picks up the trump suit), three spades (if the ♠K is right), a heart and two clubs. The twelfth trick must come from a spade-club squeeze against South, but then South must hold length in spades as well as in clubs. North is likely to have six hearts on the bidding — he'd probably have opened 3♡ with a seven-card suit and South might have bid more with five-card support. North's ♣10 looks like a singleton; he probably had some distribution for his bid. If East assumes that North has no more than three spades so the squeeze will operate, he can also assume North has three diamonds.

East should take the ◇K at the third trick, finesse the jack and cash the ace. After taking the ♡K, he cashes two more trumps, leaving:

BECOMING A BRIDGE EXPERT

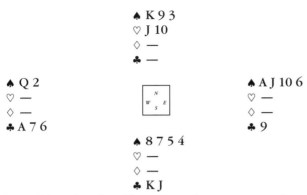

```
              ♠ K 9 3
              ♡ J 10
              ◇ —
              ♣ —
♠ Q 2                       ♠ A J 10 6
♡ —          ┌───┐         ♡ —
◇ —          │ N │         ◇ —
♣ A 7 6      │W E│         ♣ 9
             │ S │
             └───┘
              ♠ 8 7 5 4
              ♡ —
              ◇ —
              ♣ K J
```

In this position, South, still to discard, must surrender.

When you make an assumption, make the most of it:

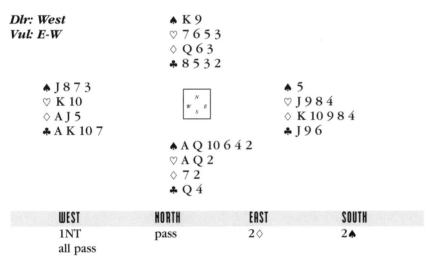

Dlr: West
Vul: E-W

```
                    ♠ K 9
                    ♡ 7 6 5 3
                    ◇ Q 6 3
                    ♣ 8 5 3 2
♠ J 8 7 3                          ♠ 5
♡ K 10          ┌───┐             ♡ J 9 8 4
◇ A J 5         │ N │             ◇ K 10 9 8 4
♣ A K 10 7      │W E│             ♣ J 9 6
                │ S │
                └───┘
                    ♠ A Q 10 6 4 2
                    ♡ A Q 2
                    ◇ 7 2
                    ♣ Q 4
```

WEST	NORTH	EAST	SOUTH
1NT	pass	2◇	2♠
all pass			

West cashes his top clubs and leads a third club, and South ruffs East's jack. South knows West started with four clubs and surely three diamonds. Since East probably has a diamond honor, West has the ♡K; and South must lose two hearts unless West has a doubleton. So South should assume West has 4-2-3-4 distribution. South leads a trump to dummy's nine and cashes the king. When East shows out, South leads a heart to his ace, draws trumps and leads a low heart.

Try the last example for yourself:

Dlr: West
Vul: Both

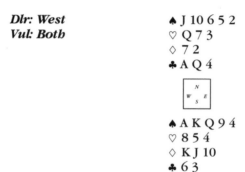

♠ J 10 6 5 2
♡ Q 7 3
◊ 7 2
♣ A Q 4

♠ A K Q 9 4
♡ 8 5 4
◊ K J 10
♣ 6 3

WEST	NORTH	EAST	SOUTH
1♡	pass	1NT	2♠
pass	3♠	all pass	

West cashes the ♡AK, East following with the jack and six. East ruffs the next heart and leads a low diamond. Your play.

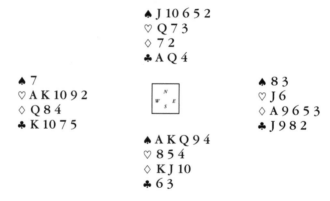

♠ J 10 6 5 2
♡ Q 7 3
◊ 7 2
♣ A Q 4

♠ 7
♡ A K 10 9 2
◊ Q 8 4
♣ K 10 7 5

♠ 8 3
♡ J 6
◊ A 9 6 5 3
♣ J 9 8 2

♠ A K Q 9 4
♡ 8 5 4
◊ K J 10
♣ 6 3

To have a chance, you must assume West has the ♣K; hence East needs the ◊A for his 1NT response. Play the ◊K.

♠ A K Q 9
♡ 7 5 3
◇ Q 6 4
♣ Q 6 2

```
  N
W   E
  S
```

♠ 8 7 6 4 2
♡ A K Q 2
◇ 7 5 3
♣ A

WEST	NORTH	EAST	SOUTH
			1♠
pass	3♠	pass	4♠
all pass			

West leads the ◇J. Dummy plays low, and East follows with the eight. When West continues diamonds, East takes the king and ace and shifts to the ♡J. Plan the play from here.

The only danger is a 4-0 trump break. Suppose you lead a trump to dummy, and East shows out. You can come back to the ♣A, return a trump to the ten and king, ruff a club, finesse the ♠9 and ruff dummy's last club. But then you have only hearts left; and when you lead one, West ruffs.

♠ A K Q 9
♡ 7 5 3
◇ Q 6 4
♣ Q 6 2

♠ J 10 5 3
♡ 4
◇ J 10 9 2
♣ K 10 7 3

```
  N
W   E
  S
```

♠ —
♡ J 10 9 8 6
◇ A K 8
♣ J 9 8 5 4

♠ 8 7 6 4 2
♡ A K Q 2
◇ 7 5 3
♣ A

It takes foresight to cater to a 5% chance, but South must cash the ♣A before leading the first trump. He can then ruff a club, lead a trump to the jack and king, ruff a club, finesse the ♠9, draw West's last trump and claim.

Good declarers are familiar with 'safety plays', which are like insurance. You pay a premium — you may lose the chance for the maximum number of tricks — but you're insured against a damaging loss.

TIP 5

CONSIDER WHAT CAN GO WRONG

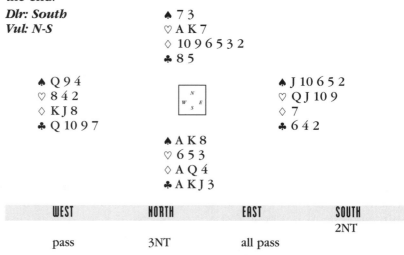

Dlr: South
Vul: Both

	♠ 10 5 3	
	♡ K 10	
	◇ K J 8 2	
	♣ J 7 5 2	

♠ A K J 8 6　　　　　　　　　　　♠ Q 9 7 2
♡ 4　　　　　　　　　　　　　　　♡ Q 9 7 5 3
◇ 9 6　　　　　　　　　　　　　　◇ 7 5
♣ Q 9 8 6 3　　　　　　　　　　　♣ K 10

	♠ 4	
	♡ A J 8 6 2	
	◇ A Q 10 4 3	
	♣ A 4	

WEST	NORTH	EAST	SOUTH
			1♡
1♠	dbl	2♠	4◇
pass	5◇	all pass	

South ruffed the second spade and expected at least eleven tricks. He drew trumps, crossed to the ♡K and returned the ♡10 to his ace. When West showed out, South was finished. He could ruff two hearts in dummy, but lost a heart and a club.

South assures the contract by letting the ♡10 ride. If West could win, South would discard three clubs from dummy on the ♡AJ8, losing one heart and one spade. As the cards lie, the ♡10 wins, and South takes the ♡A and ruffs two hearts in dummy, losing a club at the end.

Dlr: South
Vul: N-S

	♠ 7 3	
	♡ A K 7	
	◇ 10 9 6 5 3 2	
	♣ 8 5	

♠ Q 9 4　　　　　　　　　　　　♠ J 10 6 5 2
♡ 8 4 2　　　　　　　　　　　　♡ Q J 10 9
◇ K J 8　　　　　　　　　　　　◇ 7
♣ Q 10 9 7　　　　　　　　　　♣ 6 4 2

	♠ A K 8	
	♡ 6 5 3	
	◇ A Q 4	
	♣ A K J 3	

WEST	NORTH	EAST	SOUTH
			2NT
pass	3NT	all pass	

West leads the ♣10, and South wins with the jack. South may be tempted to go to dummy with a high heart and finesse the ◇Q; but

BECOMING A BRIDGE EXPERT

although that play offers a chance for thirteen tricks, it jeopardizes the contract. On the diagrammed deal, West would take the ◇K and return a heart, forcing out dummy's last entry to the diamonds. South should settle for eleven sure tricks by leading the ◇A and ◇Q.

This next deal combines my previous tip, regarding following up assumptions, with this one:

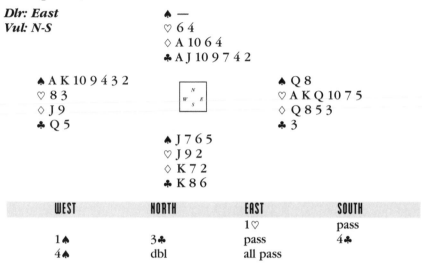

Dlr: East
Vul: N-S

```
                    ♠ —
                    ♡ 6 4
                    ◇ A 10 6 4
                    ♣ A J 10 9 7 4 2

♠ A K 10 9 4 3 2                        ♠ Q 8
♡ 8 3                N                   ♡ A K Q 10 7 5
◇ J 9              W   E                 ◇ Q 8 5 3
♣ Q 5                S                   ♣ 3

                    ♠ J 7 6 5
                    ♡ J 9 2
                    ◇ K 7 2
                    ♣ K 8 6
```

WEST	NORTH	EAST	SOUTH
		1♡	pass
1♠	3♣	pass	4♣
4♠	dbl	all pass	

North's double of 4♠ was conventional. It said to South, "I would like to bid 5♣; unless you think we can beat 4♠, you bid it." (It shows how far bidding has 'progressed' when a player must double to say he'd rather bid than defend.) But South sat for 4♠ doubled, and North led the ♣A and shifted to the ◇A and a diamond. South took the ◇K and led the ♣K, forcing dummy to ruff — the best defense. West then cashed the ♠Q. When North showed out, West conceded a trump, justifying South's decision to defend.

The bidding and the defense strongly suggest that South has all four missing trumps. Proceeding on that assumption, West should ruff a diamond at the fifth trick, lead a heart to dummy and ruff the ◇Q. He gets back to dummy with a heart and ruffs a good heart. West can then lead a trump to the queen at Trick 10. His last three cards are the ♠AK10, and the game is safe in harbor.

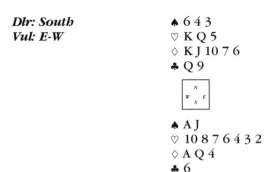

Dlr: South
Vul: E-W

♠ 6 4 3
♡ K Q 5
◇ K J 10 7 6
♣ Q 9

♠ A J
♡ 10 8 7 6 4 3 2
◇ A Q 4
♣ 6

WEST	NORTH	EAST	SOUTH
			1♡
1♠	2◇	pass	2♡
pass	3♡	pass	4♡
all pass			

West leads the ♠K. You take the ace and lead a trump to the king, and East discards the ♣8. How do you continue?

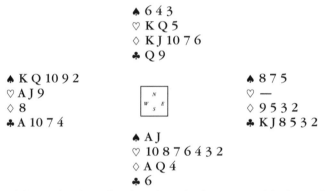

♠ 6 4 3
♡ K Q 5
◇ K J 10 7 6
♣ Q 9

♠ K Q 10 9 2
♡ A J 9
◇ 8
♣ A 10 7 4

♠ 8 7 5
♡ —
◇ 9 5 3 2
♣ K J 8 5 3 2

♠ A J
♡ 10 8 7 6 4 3 2
◇ A Q 4
♣ 6

South got back to his hand with the ◇A and led another trump; but West took the ace, cashed the ♠Q and underled his ♣A to East's jack. Back came a diamond, and West ruffed: down one. Since a diamond ruff was South's only danger, he should have led a club at the third trick, killing East's entry.

East-West seem to have let the vulnerability deter them in the auction; they might make game in either black suit.

Dlr: West
Vul: Both

♠ Q 9 7 5
♡ Q 4
◇ A 8 7 2
♣ 7 5 2

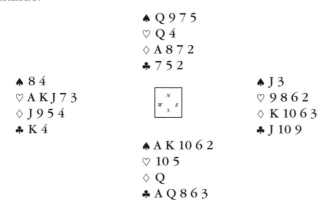

♠ A K 10 6 2
♡ 10 5
◇ Q
♣ A Q 8 6 3

WEST	NORTH	EAST	SOUTH
1♡	pass	2♡	2♠
pass	3♠	pass	4♠
all pass			

West cashes the ♡AK and shifts to a trump. How do you continue?

♠ Q 9 7 5
♡ Q 4
◇ A 8 7 2
♣ 7 5 2

♠ 8 4
♡ A K J 7 3
◇ J 9 5 4
♣ K 4

♠ J 3
♡ 9 8 6 2
◇ K 10 6 3
♣ J 10 9

♠ A K 10 6 2
♡ 10 5
◇ Q
♣ A Q 8 6 3

South drew trumps with the ace and queen and tried finessing the ♣Q. West produced the king, and East also got a club trick. Down one. What went wrong? East needed one king for his 2♡ raise and could have held the ♣K instead of the ◇K. South could find out, however, by leading the ◇Q after he drew trumps. When West failed to cover, South could place the ◇K with East — and the ♣K with West. South would then lead the ♣A and a low club, hoping that West's ♣K was doubleton .

Good declarers delay crucial decisions until they know as much about the deal as possible. When declarer actively goes digging for information, we call it a 'discovery play'.

Dlr: East
Vul: None
Matchpoints

	♠ Q 4 3 2	
	♡ A J 9 7	
	◊ 10 3	
	♣ A Q 3	

♠ A 9 5   ♠ J 10 8 7 6
♡ 3   N   ♡ Q 5 2
◊ Q 7 6 5 2   W E   ◊ K 9 4
♣ K J 10 7   S   ♣ 9 8

	♠ K	
	♡ K 10 8 6 4	
	◊ A J 8	
	♣ 6 5 4 2	

WEST	NORTH	EAST	SOUTH
		pass	pass
pass	1♣	pass	1♡
pass	2♡	pass	4♡
all pass			

West leads a diamond, and South takes East's king and returns a diamond to the queen. When West shifts to the ♣J, South finesses and the queen wins.

Since the contract is safe, South might cash the ace-king of trumps now and make four when West shows out. But a declarer who wants more information will lead a spade to the king next. When West turns up with the ♠A, South can be sure East has the ♡Q since West has shown ten points and didn't open the bidding in third position. So South can finesse in trumps against East for a valuable overtrick.

Dlr: West
Vul: N-S

	♠ K 6 2	
	♡ 5 2	
	◊ J 10 7 4	
	♣ A Q J 4	

♠ J 10 7   ♠ A 5
♡ K 6 3   N   ♡ 9 8 4
◊ A K 9 3   W E   ◊ 8 6 5 2
♣ 9 6 5   S   ♣ 8 7 3 2

	♠ Q 9 8 4 3	
	♡ A Q J 10 7	
	◊ Q	
	♣ K 10	

WEST	NORTH	EAST	SOUTH
pass	pass	pass	1♠
pass	2♣	pass	2♡
pass	2♠	pass	3♠
pass	4♠	all pass	

West cashes the ◇K and shifts to a club. South wants to lead a trump through the defender with the ace; if the ace is doubleton, South can duck on the next trump. To get information, South takes the ♣Q and tries the heart finesse. When West wins, South knows East has the ♠A since West has shown up with A-K-K but didn't open the bidding. So South wins the next club in dummy to lead a trump through East.

Sometimes declarer can postpone a critical play permanently:

Dlr: South
Vul: None

	♠ A Q 6 4	
	♡ J 6 5	
	◇ 10 9 5 4	
	♣ A Q	
♠ 10 7 5		♠ J 9 8
♡ A Q 9 4 2		♡ 10 3
◇ K 3		◇ 8 7 6
♣ J 9 3		♣ K 10 8 7 2
	♠ K 3 2	
	♡ K 8 7	
	◇ A Q J 2	
	♣ 6 5 4	

WEST	NORTH	EAST	SOUTH
			1◇
1♡	1♠	pass	1NT
pass	3NT	all pass	

West leads a low heart, and South correctly puts up the jack, winning the trick. Suppose he takes the diamond finesse next. West wins and shifts to a club, and South is in a pickle. He has three diamonds, three spades, a club and a heart, and either a 3-3 spade break or a winning club finesse will provide a ninth trick. But South must guess which play to try; if he loses the club finesse, East will return a heart, and West will run the hearts.

To preserve his options, South must test the spades before he finesses in diamonds. When spades split, South is sure of nine tricks even when the diamond finesse loses; but if spades break badly, South knows he has to risk the club finesse.

Dlr: North
Vul: None
Matchpoints

	♠ A 3	
	♡ 10 7 4	
	♦ 9 7 4 3	
	♣ K J 10 2	
♠ 9 7 6 5 2		♠ K 8 4
♡ Q 2	N W E S	♡ K J 5
♦ Q J 10 5		♦ A K 8 2
♣ Q 7		♣ 9 5 4
	♠ Q J 10	
	♡ A 9 8 6 3	
	♦ 6	
	♣ A 8 6 3	

WEST	NORTH	EAST	SOUTH
	pass	1♦	1♡
1♠	2♡	2♠	pass
pass	3♡	all pass	

North's 3♡ with weak trumps was bold, but South ruffed the second diamond and lost a spade finesse. He ruffed East's diamond return and ducked a trump. West won and led a fourth diamond, and South ruffed and cashed the ♡A.

South next crossed to the ♠A and returned dummy's last trump to East's king. He won the spade return and was ready — finally — to tackle the clubs. South knew East had balanced distribution and had seen him produce 14 HCP: ♠K, ♡KJ, ♦AK. If East had the ♣Q too, he'd have opened 1NT; so South played West for the ♣Q and made his contract.

Dlr: East
Vul: Both

	♠ K 10 9 5	
	♡ 7 4	
	♦ Q 10 4 2	
	♣ K Q 4	
	N W E S	
	♠ A J 8 7 2	
	♡ 10 5 3	
	♦ K 5	
	♣ A J 8	

WEST	NORTH	EAST	SOUTH
		1♡	1♠
pass	3♠	pass	4♠
all pass			

West leads the ♡2. East takes the king and ace and shifts to the ♣10. Plan the play.

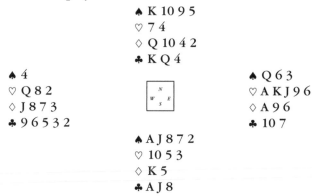

```
              ♠ K 10 9 5
              ♡ 7 4
              ◇ Q 10 4 2
              ♣ K Q 4
♠ 4                           ♠ Q 6 3
♡ Q 8 2         N             ♡ A K J 9 6
◇ J 8 7 3     W   E           ◇ A 9 6
♣ 9 6 5 3 2     S             ♣ 10 7
              ♠ A J 8 7 2
              ♡ 10 5 3
              ◇ K 5
              ♣ A J 8
```

You can attack the trumps immediately, trusting to good luck; or you can try to dig up a count of the defenders' distribution. Take the ♣K and lead a diamond to the king and a diamond back to the ten. East wins the ace and leads another club, and you win in dummy and discard the ♣A on the ◇Q. You then ruff a club, as East throws a heart, ruff your last heart in dummy and lead the last diamond. If East followed suit, you'd be back to guessing; but when he shows out, you know he started with five hearts, three diamonds, two clubs — and three spades. So you ruff the diamond, lead a trump to the king and finesse the jack with confidence.

You're declarer at 3NT; you opened 1NT, and your partner put you in game. West leads the ♠2, and you see

```
              ♠ 10 5
              ♡ A J 6 4
              ◇ K 10 5 3
              ♣ Q 9 4
                N
              W   E
                S
              ♠ A 9
              ♡ K Q 7 3
              ◇ A J 9 2
              ♣ K 5 3
```

East plays the jack, and you win immediately instead of betraying your weakness by holding up the ace. How do you continue? (The answer is not that you berate partner for not using Stayman.)

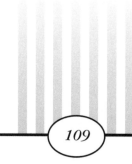

ASSUME A LOGICAL OPENING LEAD

Before taking a position in diamonds, cash the hearts. West follows once, then discards two spades and a club. The 'guess' for the ◇Q is now no guess. West's ♠2 suggested a four-card suit, and he had only one heart. If he had a five-card suit somewhere, he'd have had a more attractive lead, which suggests that his shape is 4-1-4-4; hence cash the ◇A and let the jack ride.

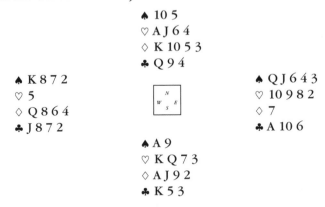

```
                    ♠ 10 5
                    ♡ A J 6 4
                    ◇ K 10 5 3
                    ♣ Q 9 4
  ♠ K 8 7 2                          ♠ Q J 6 4 3
  ♡ 5              ┌─────┐           ♡ 10 9 8 2
  ◇ Q 8 6 4        │  N  │           ◇ 7
  ♣ J 8 7 2        │W   E│           ♣ A 10 6
                   │  S  │
                   └─────┘
                    ♠ A 9
                    ♡ K Q 7 3
                    ◇ A J 9 2
                    ♣ K 5 3
```

As a defender, you try to conduct a logical defense. You usually lead and signal honestly and give your partner and the declarer credit for rational play. So declarers must assume the defenders know what they're doing — and treat the opening lead as a source of information.

Dlr: South
Vul: N-S

```
                    ♠ Q 7 5 2
                    ♡ J 9 2
                    ◇ A 5 3
                    ♣ Q 4 2
  ♠ 10 8 6 4                         ♠ A J 9 3
  ♡ A K 4          ┌─────┐           ♡ 7 3
  ◇ 10 8 4         │  N  │           ◇ Q J 9 7
  ♣ J 8 6          │W   E│           ♣ 9 7 3
                   │  S  │
                   └─────┘
                    ♠ K
                    ♡ Q 10 8 6 5
                    ◇ K 6 2
                    ♣ A K 10 5
```

WEST	NORTH	EAST	SOUTH
			1♡
pass	2♡	pass	3♡
pass	4♡	all pass	

West started with the ace and king of trumps, then led a third trump. South won in dummy and led a spade, but East rose with the ace and switched to the ◇Q. South won with the ace, threw a diamond on the ♠Q and started the clubs. Both defenders followed low to the ace and queen, and East played the nine on the next club. South then pondered — and finessed the ten to go down. Was this an unlucky misguess or a clear error?

It was an error. West was known to have a weak hand, and South played him for a low doubleton club as well as for A-K-x of trumps. But with two trump entries, West would surely have led his double-ton, hoping for a ruff.

Dlr: North
Vul: Both

```
                    ♠ 5 4
                    ♡ K J 4 2
                    ◇ 7 3
                    ♣ 7 6 4 3 2
    ♠ K J 6 2                        ♠ 10 9 8 7
    ♡ 10 9 8          N              ♡ —
    ◇ K 8 5 4      W     E           ◇ J 10 9 6 2
    ♣ 10 8            S              ♣ Q J 9 5
                    ♠ A Q 3
                    ♡ A Q 7 6 5 3
                    ◇ A Q
                    ♣ A K
```

WEST	NORTH	EAST	SOUTH
	pass	pass	2♣
pass	2◇	pass	2♡
pass	4♡	pass	6♡
all pass			

In a team event, South landed in 6♡ and got a trump lead. Declarer won in dummy and lost the spade finesse. He won West's trump return in his hand, took the ace-king of clubs, led a trump to dummy and ruffed a club. When West discarded, declarer took the ace of spades, ruffed a spade and tried the diamond finesse: down one.

North wasn't happy. He thought South should win the first trump in his hand and take the top clubs. South then leads a trump to dummy, ruffs a club high, returns a trump to dummy and ruffs a club. He gives up a spade and ruffs a spade in dummy to throw the queen of diamonds on the good club. Line 1 wins if one of two finesses works or if the clubs break 3-3: in all, about 84% plus the slight chance of a defensive error. Line 2 works when the clubs break 3-3 or 4-2 or otherwise when both finesses work. Total: about 88%. Percentage-wise, it's a tossup.

If I were declarer, I'd try the second play — but not because of percentages. When West leads a trump, clubs will probably break well; West won't have a singleton. Moreover, he's more likely to have the missing kings. *If your only excuse for a line of play is a complex calculation, look for something else.*

Dlr: East
Vul: E-W

	♠ Q 2	
	♡ A 8 2	
	◇ J 9 6 4 3 2	
	♣ 10 8	

♠ K 7 6 4		♠ 10 9 8
♡ 9 5 3	N W E S	♡ 6 4
◇ A Q		◇ 10 8 5
♣ Q 9 5 3		♣ K J 7 4 2

	♠ A J 5 3	
	♡ K Q J 10 7	
	◇ K 7	
	♣ A 6	

WEST	NORTH	EAST	SOUTH
		pass	1♡
pass	2♡	pass	4♡
all pass			

In a World Championship, both Wests led a trump against 4♡. One South won with dummy's eight and let the ♠Q ride. West won and led a second trump, and although South ruffed a spade in dummy, he lost two diamonds and a club. Down one. At the other table, South looked deeply into the deal and decided West's trump lead indicated side honors from which he was reluctant to lead. So South won the first trump in his hand and led a low spade.

West now had two losing options. If he took the king and led a another trump, South would cash the ♠Q, take the ♣A, pitch dummy's last club on the ♠A, ruff a club and lead a diamond. The defense would get two diamonds and a spade. If instead West withheld his ♠K, dummy's queen would win; then South would take the ace and ruff his other spades in dummy, losing two diamonds and a club.

A negative inference is clear from the opening lead on this last deal:

♠ K 6
♡ J 9 7 3
◇ Q 8 5
♣ K 10 7 3

♠ 10 4
♡ K Q 10 8 5
◇ A
♣ A J 9 6 2

WEST	NORTH	EAST	SOUTH
		1♠	2♡
pass	3♡	pass	4♡
all pass			

West leads the ♠2, and East takes the queen and ace and shifts to the ace and a low trump. You win, and West follows. Since you are confident of your guessing powers, you don't bother to lead the ◇Q from dummy next, hoping to smoke out the king so you can place the missing ♣Q. Instead you lead a club to the king and return a club. Both defenders follow low. Do you put up the ace or finesse the jack?

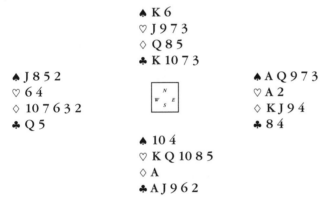

♠ K 6
♡ J 9 7 3
◇ Q 8 5
♣ K 10 7 3

♠ J 8 5 2
♡ 6 4
◇ 10 7 6 3 2
♣ Q 5

♠ A Q 9 7 3
♡ A 2
◇ K J 9 4
♣ 8 4

♠ 10 4
♡ K Q 10 8 5
◇ A
♣ A J 9 6 2

Put yourself in West's place and assume you'd defend logically. If you held a weak hand with a singleton club and two trumps and knew your partner had an opening bid (quite possibly with the ♣A or ♡A), what would your opening lead have been?

West leads the ♠J against your 3NT contract, and you see

Dlr: South
Vul: Both

```
              ♠ K 6 4
              ♡ J 6 4
              ◇ 8 3
              ♣ A J 10 7 4

                  N
               W     E
                  S

              ♠ Q 7
              ♡ K Q 7
              ◇ A K 9 6 4
              ♣ Q 9 3
```

WEST	NORTH	EAST	SOUTH
			1NT
pass	3NT	all pass	

When you play low from dummy, East contributes the three, and you win. The ♣9 loses to East's king, and East returns the ♡10. West takes the ace and leads the ♠10. What do you play from dummy?

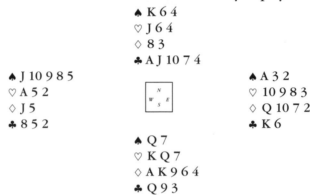

```
                    ♠ K 6 4
                    ♡ J 6 4
                    ◇ 8 3
                    ♣ A J 10 7 4
♠ J 10 9 8 5                            ♠ A 3 2
♡ A 5 2           N                     ♡ 10 9 8 3
◇ J 5          W     E                   ◇ Q 10 7 2
♣ 8 5 2           S                     ♣ K 6
                    ♠ Q 7
                    ♡ K Q 7
                    ◇ A K 9 6 4
                    ♣ Q 9 3
```

The actual South tried the king — and down he went. Really, South's play was an insult to the defense. If West had the ♠A, having led from A-J-10-x-x, East would have returned a spade when he took the ♣K, setting up the spades while West still had the ♡A for an entry. South should play low from dummy on the second spade, blocking the suit and salvaging the contract.

Just as declarer assumes a logical opening lead, he must assume the defenders will operate rationally in the middle game and the end game. If you rely on your opponents to apply sound defensive principles, inferences are available.

TIP 8

ASSUME THE DEFENDERS' PLAYS MAKE SENSE TO THEM

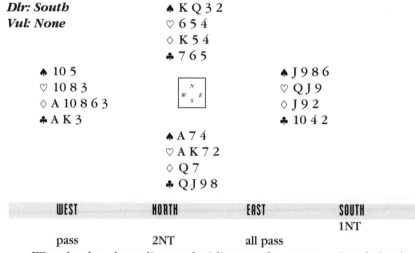

Dlr: South   ♠ K Q 3 2
Vul: None   ♡ 6 5 4
               ◇ K 5 4
               ♣ 7 6 5

♠ 10 5   ♠ J 9 8 6
♡ 10 8 3   ♡ Q J 9
◇ A 10 8 6 3   ◇ J 9 2
♣ A K 3   ♣ 10 4 2

               ♠ A 7 4
               ♡ A K 7 2
               ◇ Q 7
               ♣ Q J 9 8

WEST	NORTH	EAST	SOUTH
			1NT
pass	2NT	all pass	

West leads a low diamond, riding to the queen. South leads a spade to dummy and returns a club: deuce, jack, king. West then cashes the ◇A and leads another diamond to the king. On the next club, East plays the four. If South trusts West's defense, he'll play the eight. By clearing the diamonds instead of leading low a second time to maintain communication with East, West advertised a sure entry.

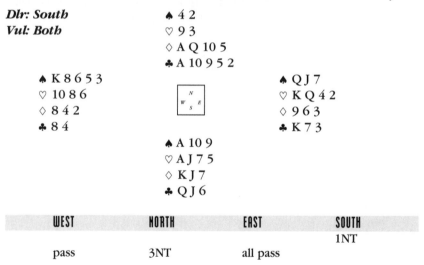

Dlr: South   ♠ 4 2
Vul: Both   ♡ 9 3
               ◇ A Q 10 5
               ♣ A 10 9 5 2

♠ K 8 6 5 3   ♠ Q J 7
♡ 10 8 6   ♡ K Q 4 2
◇ 8 4 2   ◇ 9 6 3
♣ 8 4   ♣ K 7 3

               ♠ A 10 9
               ♡ A J 7 5
               ◇ K J 7
               ♣ Q J 6

WEST	NORTH	EAST	SOUTH
			1NT
pass	3NT	all pass	

West led a spade, and South ducked East's jack and queen. Since East knew his partner couldn't have an entry to the long spades, he shifted to a low heart. South played low, and West took the ten and returned a heart to the queen and ace. When the club finesse lost, East cashed the ♡K for the setting trick. A capable East would shift to the ♡10 from a holding such as Q-10-4 or K-10-2, giving South no legitimate chance. If South trusted his opponent, he'd have played the jack on the first heart.

Declarer can often draw negative inferences from what defenders fail to do:

Dlr: North
Vul: N-S
Matchpoints

♠ A Q 2
♡ 10 9 2
◇ A Q 8 6 5
♣ J 3

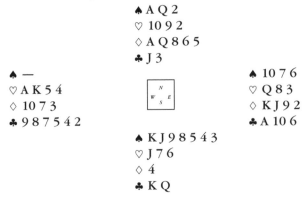

♠ K J 9 8 5 4 3
♡ J 7 6
◇ 4
♣ K Q

WEST	NORTH	EAST	SOUTH
	1◇	pass	1♠
pass	2♠	pass	4♠
all pass			

West cashes the ace and king of hearts and leads a heart to East's queen. East exits with a trump. If diamonds break 4-3 with the king onside, you can finesse the queen, set up two discards for your clubs and make the contract. But unless East looks catatonic, that play can't work: unless he held the ◇K, he'd cash the ♣A at Trick 4 and not give you a chance. Instead, take the ♠J and the ◇A, ruff a diamond, lead to the ♠Q and ruff a diamond. If the king doesn't fall (it won't), draw trumps and settle for down one.

♠ A Q 2
♡ 10 9 2
◇ A Q 8 6 5
♣ J 3

♠ —
♡ A K 5 4
◇ 10 7 3
♣ 9 8 7 5 4 2

♠ 10 7 6
♡ Q 8 3
◇ K J 9 2
♣ A 10 6

♠ K J 9 8 5 4 3
♡ J 7 6
◇ 4
♣ K Q

Dlr: West
Vul: N-S

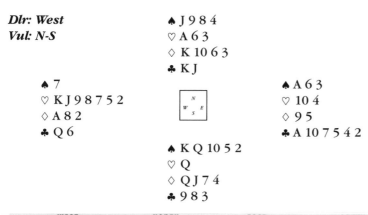

```
                    ♠ J 9 8 4
                    ♡ A 6 3
                    ◊ K 10 6 3
                    ♣ K J
  ♠ 7                              ♠ A 6 3
  ♡ K J 9 8 7 5 2                  ♡ 10 4
  ◊ A 8 2                          ◊ 9 5
  ♣ Q 6                            ♣ A 10 7 5 4 2
                    ♠ K Q 10 5 2
                    ♡ Q
                    ◊ Q J 7 4
                    ♣ 9 8 3
```

WEST	NORTH	EAST	SOUTH
1♡	dbl	pass	2♠
pass	3♠	pass	4♠
all pass			

North's raise to 3♠ was an error, but against 4♠, West led the ◊A. East signaled with the nine, and West led another diamond. South won and led a trump, and East took the ace and shifted to the ♡10: queen, king, ace. South then drew trumps, ran the diamonds and led a club. When West played low, South put up dummy's king — and went down.

If East did not hold the ♣A, he would have returned a club when he took the ♠A. Then a diamond ruff would always beat the contract. Hence South should have finessed the ♣J.

Dlr: South
Vul: N-S

```
                    ♠ 7 5
                    ♡ A J 10
                    ◊ A K 10 6 4
                    ♣ J 10 4

                    ♠ J 4
                    ♡ Q 7 2
                    ◊ J 3
                    ♣ A K Q 9 6 3
```

WEST	NORTH	EAST	SOUTH
			1♣
1♠	2◊	3♠[1]	pass
pass	4♣	pass	5♣
all pass			

1. Preemptive

West cashes the ace and king of spades and shifts to the ♡9. How will you play the hand?

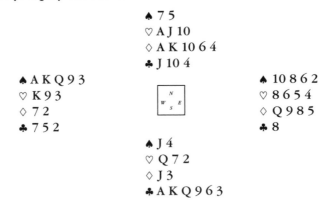

```
                    ♠ 7 5
                    ♡ A J 10
                    ◇ A K 10 6 4
                    ♣ J 10 4
  ♠ A K Q 9 3                        ♠ 10 8 6 2
  ♡ K 9 3                            ♡ 8 6 5 4
  ◇ 7 2                              ◇ Q 9 8 5
  ♣ 7 5 2                            ♣ 8
                    ♠ J 4
                    ♡ Q 7 2
                    ◇ J 3
                    ♣ A K Q 9 6 3
```

You should take the heart finesse. West's heart shift would be a needless risk if he had two or three low hearts. If your hand were

♠ J 4   ♡ K 2   ◇ 9 8 5   ♣ A K Q 9 6 3

he'd be presenting you with the contract .

EIGHT EVER, NINE NEVER? DON'T BELIEVE IT!

Dlr: West
Vul: N-S

```
                    ♠ K 9 6 4
                    ♡ A 4
                    ◇ J 4 2
                    ♣ A K 6 3

                    ♠ A J 10 5 3
                    ♡ 9 7
                    ◇ A 8 7 5
                    ♣ 8 4
```

WEST	NORTH	EAST	SOUTH
3♡	dbl	pass	4♠
all pass			

West leads the ♡Q, and you take the ace. How do you play the trumps?

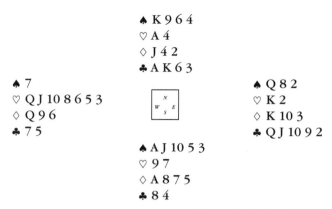

```
                    ♠ K 9 6 4
                    ♡ A 4
                    ◇ J 4 2
                    ♣ A K 6 3
♠ 7                                        ♠ Q 8 2
♡ Q J 10 8 6 5 3        N                  ♡ K 2
◇ Q 9 6              W       E              ◇ K 10 3
♣ 7 5                   S                  ♣ Q J 10 9 2
                    ♠ A J 10 5 3
                    ♡ 9 7
                    ◇ A 8 7 5
                    ♣ 8 4
```

The old maxim 'Eight ever, nine never' recommends cashing the ace and king. South did so — and lost two diamonds, a trump and a heart. On this deal, it was correct to finesse against East for the ♠Q. Since West's preempt had suggested seven hearts to East's two, the odds shifted away from a 2-2 trump break. Moreover, West was likely to have a singleton somewhere but would surely have led a side singleton. When he led a heart, the chance of finding him with a singleton trump soared.

It annoys me to hear reputable bridge teachers assault beginners with 'Eight ever, nine never'. Even if declarer has a guess, to try for the drop with nine trumps missing the queen is only a slightly better percentage play. Any indication from the bidding or defense should be enough to finesse instead.

Furthermore, declarer must consider the entire deal, not just one suit.

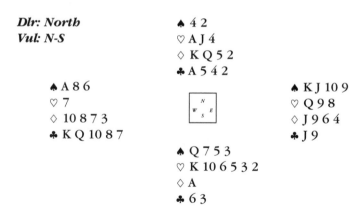

```
Dlr: North          ♠ 4 2
Vul: N-S            ♡ A J 4
                    ◇ K Q 5 2
                    ♣ A 5 4 2
♠ A 8 6                                    ♠ K J 10 9
♡ 7                     N                  ♡ Q 9 8
◇ 10 8 7 3          W       E              ◇ J 9 6 4
♣ K Q 10 8 7            S                  ♣ J 9
                    ♠ Q 7 5 3
                    ♡ K 10 6 5 3 2
                    ◇ A
                    ♣ 6 3
```

WEST	NORTH	EAST	SOUTH
	1♣	pass	1♡
pass	2♡	pass	4♡
all pass			

West leads the ♣K, and South takes the ace, comes to the ◇A, gets back with the ♡A and discards a club on the ◇K. South next leads a spade. East's jack wins, and he leads a trump. If South puts up the ♡K, he goes down two: East wins the next spade and cashes the ♡Q, and South can't ruff a spade in dummy. But if South plays low, the contract will be safe even if West wins; South could ruff one spade in dummy and pitch his last spade on the ◇Q.

On the next deal, declarer can gather information before making his decision:

Dlr: South
Vul: Both

```
                        ♠ J 3
                        ♡ 9 7 6
                        ◇ Q J
                        ♣ K J 10 9 6 3
   ♠ 10 7 6 2                              ♠ 9 8 5 4
   ♡ 10 3              ┌──────┐            ♡ J 8 5 2
   ◇ 10 6 5 3          │ N    │            ◇ A K 9 7
   ♣ Q 7 2             │W   E │            ♣ 5
                       │  S   │
                       └──────┘
                        ♠ A K Q
                        ♡ A K Q 4
                        ◇ 8 4 2
                        ♣ A 8 4
```

WEST	NORTH	EAST	SOUTH
			2NT
pass	3NT	all pass	

West leads the ♠2, suggesting a four-card suit, and South wins and cashes his three top hearts. When West discards a diamond, South knows West had seven cards in diamonds and clubs, and they must be divided 4-3; West would have led from a five-card suit if he had held one. So South cashes the ♣A and finesses the jack.

Dlr: South
Vul: Both

```
                    ♠ Q 5
                    ♡ Q 4
                    ◇ J 7 5 3
                    ♣ A J 8 6 2
  ♠ J 9 8 2                          ♠ K 10 7 3
  ♡ J 8 5 2          N               ♡ K 9 6 3
  ◇ 8 4           W     E            ◇ A 10 9 2
  ♣ Q 7 3            S               ♣ 4
                    ♠ A 6 4
                    ♡ A 10 7
                    ◇ K Q 6
                    ♣ K 10 9 5
```

WEST	NORTH	EAST	SOUTH
			1NT
pass	3NT	all pass	

West leads the ♠2. East covers dummy's queen, and South wins the third spade and leads the ◇K. (South shouldn't try the clubs immediately since he'll have only seven tricks even if the queen falls.) East takes the ◇A, and the defense cashes a spade and exits with a diamond. South takes the queen and jack, and West discards. South then knows West started with four spades and two diamonds. If West had five hearts, he'd have led a heart against 3NT; so South places West with at least three clubs, cashes the ♣K and lets the ten ride.

'Eight ever, nine never' is for when brains run out.

Dlr: North
Vul: N-S

```
                    ♠ K 10 5 3
                    ♡ K J 4
                    ◇ Q 7 3
                    ♣ A K 3

                       N
                    W     E
                       S

                    ♠ A J 4
                    ♡ A 10 9 7 5 2
                    ◇ 8 2
                    ♣ 8 5
```

WEST	NORTH	EAST	SOUTH
	1NT	pass	4♡
all pass			

West leads the ◇J and a diamond to East's king. When East tries to cash the ◇A, you ruff. How do you continue?

Cash the ♡A, take the ace and king of clubs and ruff a club. Then lead another trump. If West shows out, you'll have to guess the ♠Q; but if West follows, finesse the ♡J.

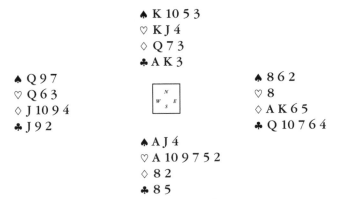

  ♠ K 10 5 3
  ♡ K J 4
  ◊ Q 7 3
  ♣ A K 3

♠ Q 9 7   ♠ 8 6 2
♡ Q 6 3   ♡ 8
◊ J 10 9 4   ◊ A K 6 5
♣ J 9 2   ♣ Q 10 7 6 4

  ♠ A J 4
  ♡ A 10 9 7 5 2
  ◊ 8 2
  ♣ 8 5

  As the cards lie here, the finesse wins. But if East could win this trick, he would be endplayed — forced to guess the ♠Q for you or lead a minor-suit card, giving you a ruff-sluff.

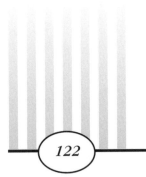

WITH EXTRA TRUMPS, LOOK FOR AN ENDPLAY

  ♠ K Q 10 9 7 5
  ♡ 9
  ◊ Q 10
  ♣ 8 7 3 2

  ♠ A J 8 6 2
  ♡ A J 2
  ◊ A 4
  ♣ A K 5

WEST	NORTH	EAST	SOUTH
			1♠
pass	4♠	pass	6♠
all pass			

West leads the ♣J and East plays the queen. Plan the play.

BECOMING A BRIDGE EXPERT

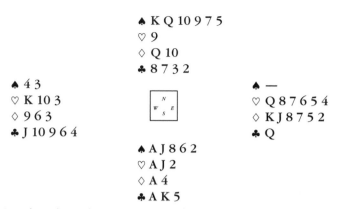

```
                          ♠ K Q 10 9 7 5
                          ♡ 9
                          ◇ Q 10
                          ♣ 8 7 3 2
    ♠ 4 3                                          ♠ —
    ♡ K 10 3                                       ♡ Q 8 7 6 5 4
    ◇ 9 6 3                                        ◇ K J 8 7 5 2
    ♣ J 10 9 6 4                                   ♣ Q
                          ♠ A J 8 6 2
                          ♡ A J 2
                          ◇ A 4
                          ♣ A K 5
```

South takes the ♣A and draws trumps. Since he has extra trumps, he can 'strip' the hearts, preparing an endplay. He cashes the ♡A, ruffs a heart, comes to the ♣K and ruffs his last heart. South then leads the ◇A and a diamond; and when East takes the king, he must lead a red card, letting South discard his last club as dummy ruffs.

When you have more trumps than you need — in both hands — always look for a throw-in; the conditions are ripe.

Dlr: South
Vul: N-S

```
                          ♠ 7 4 3
                          ♡ K J 9 8 3
                          ◇ A 7
                          ♣ A 6 3
    ♠ A Q J 8 5                                    ♠ 10 9
    ♡ 6 5 2                                        ♡ 4
    ◇ Q J 10                                       ◇ 9 8 4 3 2
    ♣ 10 7                                         ♣ Q J 9 8 4
                          ♠ K 6 2
                          ♡ A Q 10 7
                          ◇ K 6 5
                          ♣ K 5 2
```

WEST	NORTH	EAST	SOUTH
			1♡
1♠	3♡	pass	3NT
pass	4♡	all pass	

West led the ◇Q, and South won in dummy, drew trumps, took the ◇K and ruffed his last diamond. South then cashed the top clubs. When West followed, South knew West's distribution had been 5-3-3-2. So South next led the ♠K, snaring the defenders in an endplay. If West took three spades, he'd have to concede a ruff-sluff next; and if East won the second spade and cashed a club, he'd also have to yield a ruff-sluff and the contract.

One way to execute a throw-in is with a **loser-on-loser** play.

Dlr: West
Vul: N-S

```
              ♠ A Q 10 3
              ♡ 8 4 3
              ◇ Q 5 3
              ♣ K J 7
♠ 7 2                          ♠ 6
♡ K J 10 2      N              ♡ 9 7 5
◇ 10 6        W   E            ◇ J 9 8 2
♣ 10 9 8 5 2    S              ♣ A Q 6 4 3
              ♠ K J 9 8 5 4
              ♡ A Q 6
              ◇ A K 7 4
              ♣ —
```

WEST	NORTH	EAST	SOUTH
pass	pass	pass	1♠
pass	3♠	pass	6♠
all pass			

West led the ♣10: jack, queen, ruff. South drew trumps and cashed the top diamonds, hoping for a 3-3 break that would provide a heart discard. When instead West threw a club on the third diamond, South ruffed his last diamond in dummy and tried the heart finesse. West took the king and got another heart at the end.

If West has the ♣8 as well as the ♣9, the slam is on ice. After South draws trumps, he leads the ♣K from dummy, ruffs East's ace and takes the top diamonds. After South ruffs his last diamond, he leads the ♣7 and discards a heart, endplaying West.

Dlr: East
Vul: Both

```
              ♠ K 10
              ♡ 6 3
              ◇ A Q 8 2
              ♣ K J 10 7 2
                   N
                W     E
                   S

              ♠ J
              ♡ A K J 4
              ◇ K J 10 9 7 6
              ♣ 8 6
```

WEST	NORTH	EAST	SOUTH
		1♡	2◇
pass	5◇	all pass	

West leads the ♡7. Plan the play.

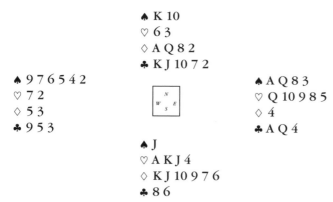

```
              ♠ K 10
              ♡ 6 3
              ◇ A Q 8 2
              ♣ K J 10 7 2
♠ 9 7 6 5 4 2                    ♠ A Q 8 3
♡ 7 2          N                ♡ Q 10 9 8 5
◇ 5 3        W   E              ◇ 4
♣ 9 5 3         S               ♣ A Q 4
              ♠ J
              ♡ A K J 4
              ◇ K J 10 9 7 6
              ♣ 8 6
```

North's leap to 5◇ was indelicate, but South can make the contract by playing East for both the missing aces. South wins the first heart with the jack, draws trumps, cashes the ace and king of hearts to discard the ♠10 from dummy and ruffs his last heart. South then leads the ♠K; and when East takes the ace, he must cash the ♣A or concede a ruff-sluff.

Dlr: West
Vul: Both

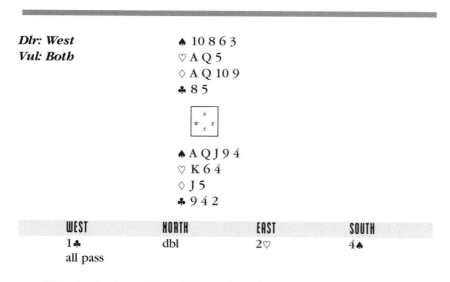

```
              ♠ 10 8 6 3
              ♡ A Q 5
              ◇ A Q 10 9
              ♣ 8 5
                 N
               W   E
                 S
              ♠ A Q J 9 4
              ♡ K 6 4
              ◇ J 5
              ♣ 9 4 2
```

WEST	NORTH	EAST	SOUTH
1♣	dbl	2♡	4♠
all pass			

TIP 11

LOOK FOR THE LOSER-ON-LOSER

West leads the ♣K, and East plays the queen. West shifts to the ♡10. Plan the play.

West probably has ♠Kxx; he intends to put East in with the ♣J to get a heart ruff. To counter that plan, take the ♡Q and lead a trump to your ace. Then finesse in diamonds. You'll throw one club on the ◇A and, even if the king is still out, your last club on the ◇Q. You lose a trump, a diamond and a club; but West can't put East in to get a ruff for the fourth defensive trick. This maneuver is a **Scissors Coup**.

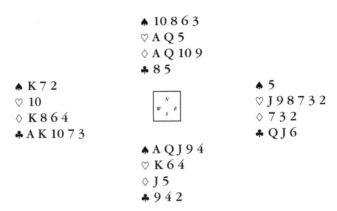

```
              ♠ 10 8 6 3
              ♡ A Q 5
              ◇ A Q 10 9
              ♣ 8 5
♠ K 7 2                          ♠ 5
♡ 10                             ♡ J 9 8 7 3 2
◇ K 8 6 4                        ◇ 7 3 2
♣ A K 10 7 3                     ♣ Q J 6
              ♠ A Q J 9 4
              ♡ K 6 4
              ◇ J 5
              ♣ 9 4 2
```

Easley Blackwood called the loser-on-loser play the 'faithful servant' because it's useful in so many situations. In the deal below, a loser-on-loser helps set up a suit.

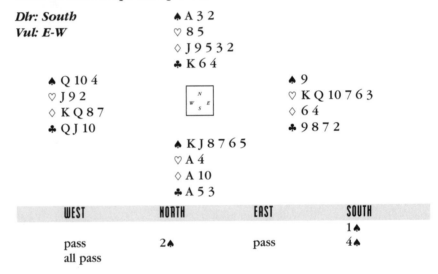

Dlr: South
Vul: E-W

```
              ♠ A 3 2
              ♡ 8 5
              ◇ J 9 5 3 2
              ♣ K 6 4
♠ Q 10 4                         ♠ 9
♡ J 9 2                          ♡ K Q 10 7 6 3
◇ K Q 8 7                        ◇ 6 4
♣ Q J 10                         ♣ 9 8 7 2
              ♠ K J 8 7 6 5
              ♡ A 4
              ◇ A 10
              ♣ A 5 3
```

WEST	NORTH	EAST	SOUTH
			1♠
pass	2♠	pass	4♠
all pass			

West leads the ♣Q. South takes the ace, cashes the ♠K and starts the diamonds by leading the ace and ten. West wins and leads another club, and South wins in dummy and leads the ◇J. When East discards, South throws his club loser. West takes the king; but South ruffs the next club, gets to dummy with the ♠A and discards his heart loser on the good ◇9. He loses a trump and two diamonds.

A loser-on-loser play may help declarer maintain trump control.

Dlr: West
Vul: E-W

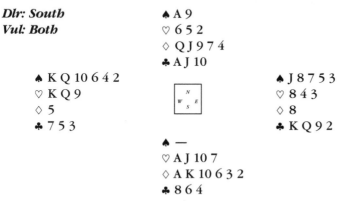

```
                    ♠ J 7 5
                    ♡ 10 6 5 3
                    ◇ K 8
                    ♣ K J 10 4
♠ Q 10 6 4                              ♠ K 9 3
♡ Q 7 2              ┌─────┐           ♡ A K J 9 8
◇ 10 9 5 2          │  N  │           ◇ 7 6
♣ A 6               │W   E│           ♣ 8 7 2
                    │  S  │
                    └─────┘
                    ♠ A 8 2
                    ♡ 4
                    ◇ A Q J 4 3
                    ♣ Q 9 5 3
```

WEST	NORTH	EAST	SOUTH
pass	pass	1♡	2◇
2♡	3◇	all pass	

After some questionable bidding, South must struggle at 3◇ with insufficient trumps. Suppose he ruffs the second heart and draws trumps, leaving him with none. When he forces out West's ♣A next, the defense can take three more hearts for down one. A loser-on-loser play lets South keep control: he discards a spade on the second heart, ruffs the third heart and draws trumps. Then when West takes the ♣A, he has no more hearts, and South can take five trumps, three clubs and a spade.

We saw in Tip 10 how declarer can use a loser-on-loser to execute an endplay. The next deal is similar, but 'avoidance' is a factor – declarer must not let East win a club trick and lead a heart through.

Dlr: South
Vul: Both

```
                    ♠ A 9
                    ♡ 6 5 2
                    ◇ Q J 9 7 4
                    ♣ A J 10
♠ K Q 10 6 4 2                         ♠ J 8 7 5 3
♡ K Q 9             ┌─────┐           ♡ 8 4 3
◇ 5                 │  N  │           ◇ 8
♣ 7 5 3             │W   E│           ♣ K Q 9 2
                    │  S  │
                    └─────┘
                    ♠ —
                    ♡ A J 10 7
                    ◇ A K 10 6 3 2
                    ♣ 8 6 4
```

WEST	NORTH	EAST	SOUTH
			1◇
1♠	3◇	4♠	5◇
all pass			

West led the ♠K, and South threw a club on the ace, drew trumps and tried a heart finesse. West won and shifted to a club, and South had to lose a club and another heart for down one. South should, instead, play low from dummy on the first spade and discard a losing club. If West shifts to a club, South takes the ace, throws his last club on the ♠A, ruffs a club, leads a trump to dummy and ruffs a club. He returns to dummy with a trump and leads a heart to the ten, end-playing West.

Dlr: South
Vul: Both

♠ 8 4
♡ 7 4 3
♢ 10 5
♣ A 8 7 5 3 2

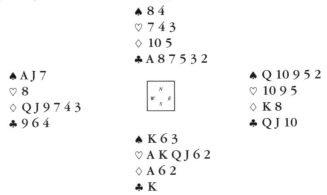

♠ K 6 3
♡ A K Q J 6 2
♢ A 6 2
♣ K

WEST	NORTH	EAST	SOUTH
			1♡
pass	1NT	pass	4♡
all pass			

In this final example, a loser-on-loser play helps avoid an overruff: West leads the ♢Q. You duck, and another diamond goes to East's king and your ace. Plan the play.

♠ 8 4
♡ 7 4 3
♢ 10 5
♣ A 8 7 5 3 2

♠ A J 7   ♠ Q 10 9 5 2
♡ 8   ♡ 10 9 5
♢ Q J 9 7 4 3   ♢ K 8
♣ 9 6 4   ♣ Q J 10

♠ K 6 3
♡ A K Q J 6 2
♢ A 6 2
♣ K

Unblock the ♣K and lead another diamond; but since East may have no more diamonds, discard a spade from dummy instead of ruffing. If West shifts to a trump, win and lead a spade. You'll be able to ruff one spade in dummy and pitch your last spade on the ♣A, losing only three tricks in all. If you ruff the diamond in dummy instead of discarding on it, East will overruff and return a trump, leaving you two tricks short.

Dlr: South
Vul: N-S

RUN YOUR LONG SUIT

```
               ♠ Q 10 5 4
               ♡ K 3
               ♢ A 7 5 3
               ♣ Q 7 5
                  ┌─────┐
                  │  N  │
                  │W   E│
                  │  S  │
                  └─────┘
               ♠ A K 9 7 3 2
               ♡ A 8 2
               ♢ Q 4
               ♣ K 2
```

WEST	NORTH	EAST	SOUTH
			1♠
dbl	redbl	2♡	pass
pass	2♠	pass	3♡
pass	4♢	pass	4♠
pass	5♡	pass	6♠
all pass			

West leads the ♡4. Plan the play.

Take the ♡K, draw trumps and lead the ♣2 through West, who must play low. Return a heart to your ace, ruff a heart and run all your trumps. After ten tricks, West must keep the ♣A and the guarded ♢K; hence no hearts. You can exit with a club, forcing him to lead from the ♢K and concede the slam.

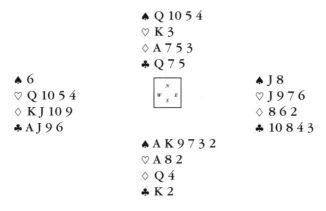

```
               ♠ Q 10 5 4
               ♡ K 3
               ♢ A 7 5 3
               ♣ Q 7 5
  ♠ 6                          ♠ J 8
  ♡ Q 10 5 4   ┌─────┐         ♡ J 9 7 6
  ♢ K J 10 9   │  N  │         ♢ 8 6 2
  ♣ A J 9 6    │W   E│         ♣ 10 8 4 3
               │  S  │
               └─────┘
               ♠ A K 9 7 3 2
               ♡ A 8 2
               ♢ Q 4
               ♣ K 2
```

Such *strip squeezes* are common. They require declarer to run every one of his trumps and (sometimes) judge in the end how the defender under pressure has discarded.

In one of Terence Reese's books, he devotes several pages to the merits of running a long suit and forcing discards from the defenders. A 'long' suit need not be so long to have its effect.

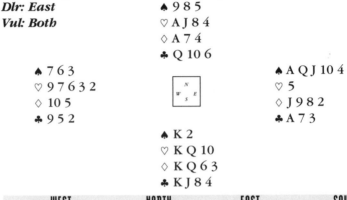

Dlr: East
Vul: Both

```
                    ♠ 9 8 5
                    ♡ A J 8 4
                    ◇ A 7 4
                    ♣ Q 10 6
    ♠ 7 6 3                          ♠ A Q J 10 4
    ♡ 9 7 6 3 2          N           ♡ 5
    ◇ 10 5          W       E        ◇ J 9 8 2
    ♣ 9 5 2              S           ♣ A 7 3
                    ♠ K 2
                    ♡ K Q 10
                    ◇ K Q 6 3
                    ♣ K J 8 4
```

WEST	NORTH	EAST	SOUTH
		1♠	1NT
pass	2♠	pass	2NT
pass	3NT	all pass	

South arrives at 3NT and is happy to see a couple of aces in dummy. Still, after West leads a spade, and East takes the ace and returns a spade, South's position looks hopeless. If South runs four hearts, though, it's East who is stuck. East can throw two clubs, but the last heart fixes him. He can't discard the ♣A; a diamond gives South an extra trick there; if East throws a spade, South can safely force out the ♣A.

Even if a defender isn't squeezed, he may err in discarding.

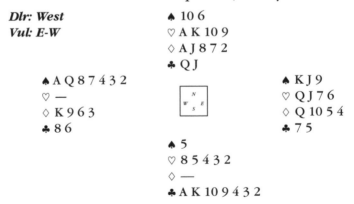

Dlr: West
Vul: E-W

```
                    ♠ 10 6
                    ♡ A K 10 9
                    ◇ A J 8 7 2
                    ♣ Q J
    ♠ A Q 8 7 4 3 2                  ♠ K J 9
    ♡ —                 N           ♡ Q J 7 6
    ◇ K 9 6 3       W       E        ◇ Q 10 5 4
    ♣ 8 6               S           ♣ 7 5
                    ♠ 5
                    ♡ 8 5 4 3 2
                    ◇ —
                    ♣ A K 10 9 4 3 2
```

At one table of a Vanderbilt semifinal match, North-South went down one in 5♡. In the replay:

BECOMING A BRIDGE EXPERT

WEST	NORTH	EAST	SOUTH
3♠	dbl	pass	6♣
all pass			

West led the ♠A and then the ♠Q. South ruffed and cashed five rounds of trumps, pitching two hearts from dummy. East, who thought he needed to keep his diamonds, also threw two hearts, and dummy's ♡AK picked up the suit. East, a world champion, might have interpreted West's ♠Q as a suit-preference signal (asking for a heart return if East ruffed), but that's easier to work out in retrospect. The fact is that discarding problems can tax the best players and partnerships.

Dlr: North
Vul: N-S
Matchpoints

♠ A 8
♡ J 8 4 2
◇ 6 4 3
♣ A K 6 5

```
      N
   W     E
      S
```

♠ K 7 6 3
♡ A Q 10 9 5
◇ K 8
♣ 9 2

WEST	NORTH	EAST	SOUTH
	1♣	1◇	1♡
pass	2♡	pass	4♡
all pass			

West leads the ◇5, and East takes the ace and returns the ◇Q to your king, as West follows with the seven. You'd like to make two overtricks; plan the play.

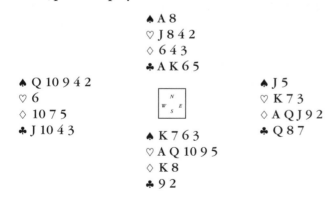

♠ A 8
♡ J 8 4 2
◇ 6 4 3
♣ A K 6 5

♠ Q 10 9 4 2
♡ 6
◇ 10 7 5
♣ J 10 4 3

♠ J 5
♡ K 7 3
◇ A Q J 9 2
♣ Q 8 7

♠ K 7 6 3
♡ A Q 10 9 5
◇ K 8
♣ 9 2

Most players would try for two spade ruffs in dummy and run into an overruff that held them to eleven tricks. The winning line, not obvious, is to go to the ♠A and draw trumps with the help of a finesse. West discards one spade and his last diamond safely. South can't cash another trump, since he needs a spade ruff in dummy; but he does just as well to lead a club to the king and ruff a diamond since West must discard again. If West throws a spade, South takes the ♠K and ruffs a spade, setting up his last spade; if West throws a club, South takes the ♣A and ruffs a club, setting up dummy's last club.

ATTACK YOUR WEAK SUIT!

Dlr: South
Vul: N-S

                    ♠ 8 6 4
                    ♡ Q 6 4
                    ◇ K 8 3
                    ♣ A J 5 2

                    ┌─────┐
                    │ N │
                    │W   E│
                    │ S │
                    └─────┘

                    ♠ K 10 5
                    ♡ A K 5 2
                    ◇ A Q 6 4
                    ♣ 10 3

WEST	NORTH	EAST	SOUTH
			1NT
pass	3NT	all pass	

West leads the ♠3, and East plays the queen. Plan the play.

Take the ♠K and return a spade. Since you have only eight sure tricks, and since West's lead marks him with no more than five spades, you have nothing to lose by letting West run the spades (if he will). Then East must make some uncomfortable discards.

                    ♠ 8 6 4
                    ♡ Q 6 4
                    ◇ K 8 3
                    ♣ A J 5 2

♠ A J 9 3 2   ♠ Q 7
♡ J 3   ┌─────┐   ♡ 10 9 8 7
◇ 10 2   │ N │   ◇ J 9 7 5
♣ Q 9 7 4   │W   E│   ♣ K 8 6
               │ S │
               └─────┘
                    ♠ K 10 5
                    ♡ A K 5 2
                    ◇ A Q 6 4
                    ♣ 10 3

If West runs all the spades, East will be hopelessly squeezed. If instead West shifts to a club, South can make two club tricks. Even if West wins the second spade and shifts to a red card (a play few Wests would find), South has a route to nine tricks.

The story goes that in an expert game a declarer found himself playing in notrump with three low clubs in dummy opposite the Q-10 doubleton. After winning the first trick in dummy in a different suit, he boldly led a club to his ten, which held. So he got back to dummy and led a club to his queen – and it held. After the deal, with the defenders in a tizzy, he told his partner that if he'd had the jack, he could have brought in the whole suit.

Declarers can obtain surprising results by doing what the defenders least expect. In the 1961 World Championship, Argentina's Eduardo Scanavino was South in a 'hopeless' contract.

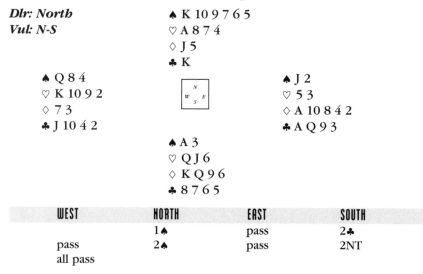

Dlr: North
Vul: N-S

♠ K 10 9 7 6 5
♡ A 8 7 4
◇ J 5
♣ K

♠ Q 8 4
♡ K 10 9 2
◇ 7 3
♣ J 10 4 2

♠ J 2
♡ 5 3
◇ A 10 8 4 2
♣ A Q 9 3

♠ A 3
♡ Q J 6
◇ K Q 9 6
♣ 8 7 6 5

WEST	NORTH	EAST	SOUTH
	1♠	pass	2♣
pass	2♠	pass	2NT
all pass			

West led the ♡10, and Scanavino won with the jack. If he set up the spades, the defense would shift to clubs and end up with at least six tricks; so Scanavino led a club himself, and East took dummy's king and returned a low diamond. South won with the jack, returned a diamond to his queen and led the ♣8 to West's ten. By now, West was convinced that South's weak spot was spades; so West switched to a spade, and dummy's ten held. Scanavino then took the ♠A and got back to dummy with the ♡A to run the spades.

Dlr: South   ♠ 10 6 4
Vul: N-S   ♡ A Q J
                  ◇ J 6 4 2
                  ♣ 7 5 4

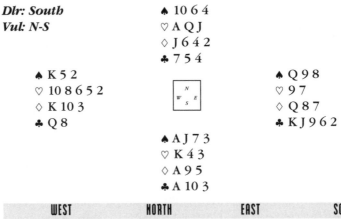

♠ K 5 2   ♠ Q 9 8
♡ 10 8 6 5 2   ♡ 9 7
◇ K 10 3   ◇ Q 8 7
♣ Q 8   ♣ K J 9 6 2

                  ♠ A J 7 3
                  ♡ K 4 3
                  ◇ A 9 5
                  ♣ A 10 3

WEST	NORTH	EAST	SOUTH
			1NT
pass	2NT	all pass	

In a team-of-four match, both Souths landed in 2NT and got a heart lead. At the first table, South won in dummy and tried a spade to his jack; West took the king and did well to find the shift to the ♣Q. South won the second club and tried the ♠A and another spade, but East won and ran the clubs for down one.

In the other room, South wasn't as eager to break the spades; he marked time by leading a club to his ten at the second trick. West won with the queen but was in darkness. He finally decided on a spade switch. This play would have been a winner if the full deal had been

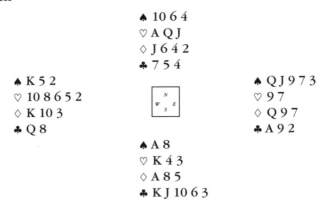

                  ♠ 10 6 4
                  ♡ A Q J
                  ◇ J 6 4 2
                  ♣ 7 5 4

♠ K 5 2   ♠ Q J 9 7 3
♡ 10 8 6 5 2   ♡ 9 7
◇ K 10 3   ◇ Q 9 7
♣ Q 8   ♣ A 9 2

                  ♠ A 8
                  ♡ K 4 3
                  ◇ A 8 5
                  ♣ K J 10 6 3

but as it was, South took East's ♠Q, returned a spade, and finished with three spades, three hearts, a diamond and a club.

Dlr: South
Vul: N-S

♠ A 6 4 2
♡ K Q 4
◇ A Q 3
♣ 5 4 3

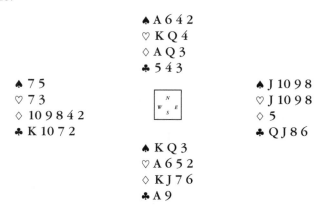

♠ K Q 3
♡ A 6 5 2
◇ K J 7 6
♣ A 9

WEST	NORTH	EAST	SOUTH
			1NT
pass	4NT	pass	6NT
all pass			

West leads the ◇10. Plan the play.

A possible reason for leading a weakish suit is to **rectify the count** for a squeeze. Here you have eleven top tricks and can get one more if either major suit breaks 3-3 or if one defender guards both majors. Since you must lose one trick before a 'simple' squeeze for twelve tricks can operate, take the ◇A and lead a club to your nine.

♠ A 6 4 2
♡ K Q 4
◇ A Q 3
♣ 5 4 3

♠ 7 5
♡ 7 3
◇ 10 9 8 4 2
♣ K 10 7 2

♠ J 10 9 8
♡ J 10 9 8
◇ 5
♣ Q J 8 6

♠ K Q 3
♡ A 6 5 2
◇ K J 7 6
♣ A 9

You win West's diamond return, cash the ♣A and finish the diamonds, discarding dummy's last club. East is squeezed. To run the diamonds first isn't good enough. East will pitch three clubs, and if you give up a club next, West will have a long diamond to cash.

TIP 14

LET YOUR OPPONENTS MAKE THE MISTAKES

Dlr: South
Vul: Both

♠ A 10 9 7
♡ K 7 6 3
◇ K 6 3
♣ A 6

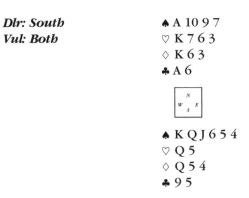

♠ K Q J 6 5 4
♡ Q 5
◇ Q 5 4
♣ 9 5

WEST	NORTH	EAST	SOUTH
			2♠
pass	4♠	all pass	

West leads the ♣K. Plan the play.

```
            ♠ A 10 9 7
            ♡ K 7 6 3
            ◇ K 6 3
            ♣ A 6
♠ 2                        ♠ 8 3
♡ J 9 2          N         ♡ A 10 8 4
◇ 10 9 8 2    W     E      ◇ A J 7
♣ K Q J 4 2      S         ♣ 10 8 7 3
            ♠ K Q J 6 5 4
            ♡ Q 5
            ◇ Q 5 4
            ♣ 9 5
```

You wouldn't think South could manage two heart tricks, but that assumes East-West are infallible. South won the first club and led a heart from dummy, winning with the queen when East ducked and West followed with the deuce. South then drew trumps and led another low heart from dummy. East stewed but put up the ace and led a club. West won; but since South could throw a diamond on the ♡K, he lost a heart, a club and one diamond.

East's defense was ill-judged but not a clear error: he would have been right if South's hand had been

♠ K Q J 6 5 4   ♡ Q J   ◇ 5 4   ♣ 9 5 4

West might have apologized for not playing the jack on the first heart, and could have complimented South for a good deceptive play.

Nobody ever became a winner by assuming his opponents were omniscient. Suppose you must play this suit:

J 6 5 3 2

A K 9 8 4

You have nothing to lose by leading the jack. If East plays low, you'll put up the ace; but you tempt East to cover with Q-10-7.

Suppose West leads the ♡J against your notrump contract in this position:

A K 6

J 10 9 2   7 5 4

Q 8 3

If you fear a shift, take the king and follow with the eight, concealing the three. West may think East has Q-4-3.

Another expert ruse is to give a defender in third position a headache by playing low from dummy.

Dlr: North
Vul: Both

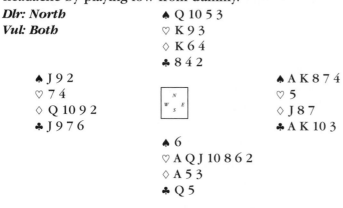

♠ Q 10 5 3
♡ K 9 3
◇ K 6 4
♣ 8 4 2

♠ J 9 2
♡ 7 4
◇ Q 10 9 2
♣ J 9 7 6

♠ A K 8 7 4
♡ 5
◇ J 8 7
♣ A K 10 3

♠ 6
♡ A Q J 10 8 6 2
◇ A 5 3
♣ Q 5

WEST	NORTH	EAST	SOUTH
	pass	1♠	2♡
pass	3♡	pass	4♡
all pass			

When West leads the ♠2, South follows with dummy's three. East can't know he could win with the seven and will play the king. He cashes the ♣K, West encourages and East continues with the ♣A and another club. South ruffs, leads a trump to dummy, ruffs a spade, returns to dummy with a trump and leads the ♠Q, pinning West's jack and settling up the ♠10 for a vital diamond discard.

Here's another example of the same ploy:

Dlr: North
Vul: Both

                ♠ K J 8 5
                ♡ Q 4
                ◇ K J 4 2
                ♣ A Q 7

♠ 10 9 6 4 2   ♠ A 7 3
♡ J 7   ♡ K 9 2
◇ 10 6 5 3   ◇ A Q 9 8 7
♣ 10 2   ♣ 8 4

                ♠ Q
                ♡ A 10 8 6 5 3
                ◇ —
                ♣ K J 9 6 5 3

WEST	NORTH	EAST	SOUTH
	1NT	pass	2◇
pass	2♡	pass	3♣
pass	3NT	pass	4♣
pass	5♣	pass	6♣
all pass			

This is a famous deal from a U.S. Team Trials. When West led the ◇5 (playing third- and fifth-best leads), South, Billy Eisenberg, casually called for dummy's deuce. Since East couldn't read the position, he followed with the queen; Eisenberg ruffed and later ruffed out the ◇A to get a discard for the ♠Q.

Some players have more talent than others, some are more successful; but no player can be a winner who thinks his opponents are infallible. How would you play 6♣ on this next deal when West leads the ◇J?

Dlr: North
Vul: None

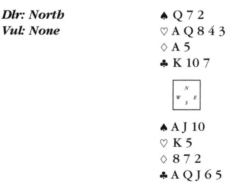

                ♠ Q 7 2
                ♡ A Q 8 4 3
                ◇ A 5
                ♣ K 10 7

                ♠ A J 10
                ♡ K 5
                ◇ 8 7 2
                ♣ A Q J 6 5

WEST	NORTH	EAST	SOUTH
	1NT	pass	3♣
pass	4♣	pass	6♣
all pass			

If both hearts and trumps break reasonably, you're safe. You can take the king and ace of trumps, and if both defenders follow, the king and ace of hearts and a heart ruff. Return to dummy with a trump, discard two diamonds on the good hearts and lose at most one spade. For an extra chance, though, lead the ♠Q at the second trick. If East doesn't cover, you'll go up with the ace and rely on the hearts; but if East is induced to play the king, your troubles are over.

Dlr: West
Vul: E-W

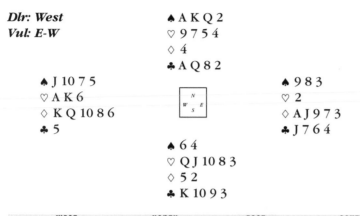

```
                    ♠ A K Q 2
                    ♡ 9 7 5 4
                    ◇ 4
                    ♣ A Q 8 2
    ♠ J 10 7 5                      ♠ 9 8 3
    ♡ A K 6                         ♡ 2
    ◇ K Q 10 8 6                    ◇ A J 9 7 3
    ♣ 5                             ♣ J 7 6 4
                    ♠ 6 4
                    ♡ Q J 10 8 3
                    ◇ 5 2
                    ♣ K 10 9 3
```

WEST	NORTH	EAST	SOUTH
1◇	dbl	3◇	3♡
4◇	4♡	all pass	

Opening lead: ♣5

South was sure West's club lead was a singleton, so he won with the king and tried to slide through the ♡10. West rose with the king and made a good play: he led the ◇Q, making sure East took the ace. East then returned a club, and West ruffed and cashed the ♡A for the setting trick.

South can't succeed against the best defense but can give himself a chance by starting spades at the second trick. He takes the ♠A-K-Q, throwing a diamond, and then leads the deuce. East should ruff; but any East with an ounce of fallibility may refuse to ruff a loser. South can then discard his last diamond: a loser on a loser. When West wins, he can't put East in for a club ruff, and South is safe.

Dlr: South
Vul: Both

♠ A K
♡ 10 9 3
◇ J 10 9 5
♣ A K J 7

```
      N
  W       E
      S
```

♠ Q J 5
♡ K Q J 2
◇ A Q 6 2
♣ Q 8

WEST	NORTH	EAST	SOUTH
			1NT
pass	4NT	pass	6NT
all pass			

West leads the ♠10. Plan the play.

♠ A K
♡ 10 9 3
◇ J 10 9 5
♣ A K J 7

♠ 10 9 8 6 3   ♠ 7 4 2
♡ 7 5   ♡ A 8 6 4
◇ K 8 3   ◇ 7 4
♣ 6 4 2   ♣ 10 9 5 3

```
      N
  W       E
      S
```

♠ Q J 5
♡ K Q J 2
◇ A Q 6 2
♣ Q 8

  South was an expert who wasn't satisfied to stake the slam on a finesse — even when there seemed to be no way to avoid it. At Trick 2, he led a low heart from dummy, winning with the queen when East ducked. South then returned a spade to dummy and led the ♡10.

  East would have beaten the contract by taking the ace but thought South might have a heart holding such as K-Q-5-2. Then East would save one trick by ducking again, and South might even let the ten ride and lose to West's jack. So East played low again — and the ♡10 won. South next let the ◇J ride. West took the king but had no more hearts; and South was home with three diamonds, three spades, four clubs and two hearts.

Dlr: South
Vul: Both

♠ 9 8 7
♡ A Q 10 8
◇ A 6 5
♣ 10 9 4

	N	
W		E
	S	

♠ A 5 2
♡ 9 2
◇ 9 7 3 2
♣ A K J 8

THE DISCARDS HAVE A MESSAGE

WEST	NORTH	EAST	SOUTH
			1♣
1♠	dbl	pass	1NT
all pass			

West leads the ♠K, winning, and continues with the queen. East discards a heart, and you take the ace and let the ♡9 ride. East wins with the jack and shifts to the ◇Q. You take dummy's ace, lead the ♣10 to your king and return a second heart toward dummy. West plays low. What do you do?

If West started with ♡K43, a second finesse will win three hearts, a diamond, a spade and at least two clubs. But that would mean East's hearts were J-7-6-5, and he wouldn't have pitched a heart from that holding. You should take the ♡A and finesse in clubs, hoping to win four clubs and one trick in each of the other suits.

♠ 9 8 7
♡ A Q 10 8
◇ A 6 5
♣ 10 9 4

♠ K Q J 10 6 4
♡ 6 4 3
◇ K 10 8
♣ 6

	N	
W		E
	S	

♠ 3
♡ K J 7 5
◇ Q J 4
♣ Q 7 5 3 2

♠ A 5 2
♡ 9 2
◇ 9 7 3 2
♣ A K J 8

Most declarers pay scant attention to the defenders' discards, yet they are a rich source of inference.

Dlr: North
Vul: N-S

	♠ K J 5 4	
	♡ A 10 6	
	◇ A 6 4	
	♣ K J 4	

♠ A 8 6 3	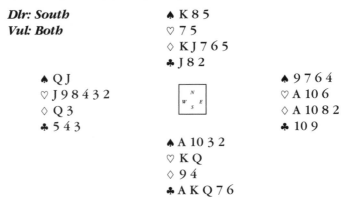	♠ Q 10 9
♡ 4		♡ 8 7 5 2
◇ J 10 9 7		◇ Q 8 2
♣ 10 7 5 2		♣ A 9 8

	♠ 7 2	
	♡ K Q J 9 3	
	◇ K 5 3	
	♣ Q 6 3	

WEST	NORTH	EAST	SOUTH
	1NT	pass	3♡
pass	4♡	all pass	

West leads the ◇J, and South wins in dummy and draws trumps. West, who must discard three times, lets go a spade, a club and another spade. South leads a club to the king and East's ace, wins the diamond return and leads a spade. When West plays low, South should put up the king. West might discard spades from A-8-6-3 but not from Q-8-6-3 (possibly giving away a trick).

Dlr: South
Vul: Both

	♠ K 8 5	
	♡ 7 5	
	◇ K J 7 6 5	
	♣ J 8 2	

♠ Q J		♠ 9 7 6 4
♡ J 9 8 4 3 2		♡ A 10 6
◇ Q 3		◇ A 10 8 2
♣ 5 4 3		♣ 10 9

	♠ A 10 3 2	
	♡ K Q	
	◇ 9 4	
	♣ A K Q 7 6	

WEST	NORTH	EAST	SOUTH
			1♣
pass	1◇	pass	1♠
pass	2♣	pass	2NT
pass	3NT	all pass	

In a Bermuda Bowl, West led a heart against 3NT, and East took the ace and returned the ten. The French declarer won and ran off five clubs. West threw a heart and a diamond, while East pitched diamonds. Declarer then led a spade: jack, king, four. On the next spade,

East played the six, and South... put up the ace, dropping the queen for nine tricks! More than likely, South based his play on East's failure to discard a spade; with five low spades, East might have spared one. In the same position, the U.S. declarer finessed the ♠10 and went down.

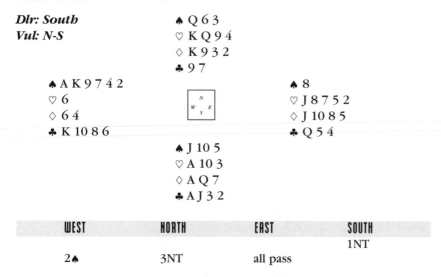

Dlr: South
Vul: N-S

	♠ Q 6 3	
	♡ K Q 9 4	
	◊ K 9 3 2	
	♣ 9 7	
♠ A K 9 7 4 2		♠ 8
♡ 6		♡ J 8 7 5 2
◊ 6 4		◊ J 10 8 5
♣ K 10 8 6		♣ Q 5 4
	♠ J 10 5	
	♡ A 10 3	
	◊ A Q 7	
	♣ A J 3 2	

WEST	NORTH	EAST	SOUTH
			1NT
2♠	3NT	all pass	

West led the ♠K and continued with the ♠A and a third spade to the queen. East threw a heart and then a club. South was sure that the heart discard was an 'idle fifth' card, which defenders often hasten to let go. So South took the ♡K and led a heart to his ten, winning four hearts, three diamonds, a club and a spade. East would have done better to throw two clubs on the spades.

Try this last example yourself:

Dlr: South
Vul: Both

        ♠ 7 2
        ♡ 8 7 4
        ◇ A K 5 3
        ♣ K Q 6 4

```
      N
   W     E
      S
```

        ♠ A Q 6 4
        ♡ A 10 6
        ◇ 6 4
        ♣ A J 7 2

WEST	NORTH	EAST	SOUTH
			1♣
pass	1◇	pass	1♠
pass	3♣	pass	3NT
all pass			

West leads the ♡5, East plays the queen, and you duck and win the heart return. When you run the clubs, East discards the ◇J and ♠5; West throws the ♠3. How do you continue?

East's discard of the ◇J denies the queen but also suggests five or more diamonds: East wouldn't discard a diamond from J-10-9-8. Cash the ◇AK and exit with a heart. After West takes three hearts, he must lead from the ♠K, giving you a ninth trick.

        ♠ 7 2
        ♡ 8 7 4
        ◇ A K 5 3
        ♣ K Q 6 4

♠ K 10 3   ♠ J 9 8 5
♡ K J 9 5 2   ♡ Q 3
◇ Q 7   ◇ J 10 9 8 2
♣ 9 8 3   ♣ 10 5

```
      N
   W     E
      S
```

        ♠ A Q 6 4
        ♡ A 10 6
        ◇ 6 4
        ♣ A J 7 2

COMPETITIVE BIDDING

③

Competitive bidding is the meat and gravy of bridge. It's distressing to watch the opponents make a game when you could have made a slam; but even the small swings born of misjudgment add up over the years. This section contains ideas to help you get better results in competitive auctions.

As in constructive bidding, a solid foundation is essential. Players who never make an error in a textbook sequence will have a big edge; so...

KNOW YOUR BASICS COLD

Here's another quiz. For each auction, pick the hand South is most likely to hold in Standard methods. Scoring is IMPs, with neither side vulnerable. The answer appears under each problem.

WEST	NORTH	EAST	SOUTH
			1◇
1♠	pass	pass	1NT

1

a) ♠ A 5
♡ A J 6 5
◇ A K 8 7 3
♣ Q 3

b) ♠ A K 8 5
♡ J 4
◇ A Q 6 5
♣ 7 6 5

c) ♠ A J 5
♡ 5
◇ A J 7 6 5
♣ A K 4 3

d) ♠ A J 4
♡ A 6
◇ A Q J 6 5
♣ Q 10 5

Hand (d) is correct: South promises a balanced hand too strong to open 1NT. Hand (a) would balance with a double; hand (b) wouldn't bid again; hand (c) would reopen with 2♣.

WEST	NORTH	EAST	SOUTH
			1NT
pass	pass	2♡	dbl

2

a) ♠ A K 5 4
♡ 7 6
◇ A Q 5 4
♣ A 5 4

b) ♠ K 4
♡ A Q 10 6
◇ J 9 8 3
♣ A K 4

c) ♠ K J 5
♡ K Q 9 8 3
◇ A 7 6
♣ Q J

d) ♠ A 7 6
♡ A J 6
◇ K J 8 3 2
♣ K J

Hand (b) is correct: the double *behind* the 2♡ bidder is for penalty. Hands (a) and (d) couldn't act again. Hand (c) would expect to beat 2♡ but is poor defensively for any alternative contract.

WEST	NORTH	EAST	SOUTH
			1NT
2♡	pass	pass	dbl

3

a) ♠ A Q 5 4
♡ 7 6
◇ A K 5 4
♣ A 5 4

b) ♠ A 5
♡ A J 9 5
◇ J 9 8 3
♣ A K 4

c) ♠ K 7
♡ K Q 9 8 3
◇ A J 6
♣ Q J 4

d) ♠ A 7 6
♡ A J 6
◇ K J 8 3 2
♣ K J

This time hand (a) is correct: this double *underneath* the 2♡ bidder is for takeout.

WEST	NORTH	EAST	SOUTH
			1♣
pass	1♡	1♠	2♣

4

a) ♠ 7 6
♡ K J 4
◇ A 7 6
♣ K Q 10 7 3

b) ♠ 7 6
♡ K 5
◇ A Q 5
♣ K 8 7 6 5 4

c) ♠ K J 4
♡ 8 7
◇ A 7 6
♣ A Q 9 7 5

d) ♠ 8 7
♡ A 6
◇ Q 6 3
♣ A K J 10 6 5

Hand (d) is correct: South's free rebid suggests a good suit. Hand (a) would raise to 2♡ or make a 'support double' if using that method; hand (b) would pass over 1♠ — few experts would rebid 2♣ freely with minimum values and a poor suit. Hand (c) would rebid 1NT.

	WEST	NORTH	EAST	SOUTH
			1♡	1♠
5	2♡	pass	pass	dbl

a) ♠ K Q 10 6 5   b) ♠ K Q 10 8 7   c) ♠ K Q 10 8 7   d) ♠ J 10 8 7 6
    ♡ 6 5   ♡ A K   ♡ A 6   ♡ A K J 9
    ◇ A 5 4   ◇ A Q 5   ◇ K 6 5   ◇ J 5
    ♣ Q 6 3   ♣ 6 5 4   ♣ Q J 5   ♣ A 6

Hands (a) and (d) couldn't act a second time; hand (b) would double 1♡ and bid spades next. Hand (c) is correct: South's double is for takeout, and his hand is limited by the failure to double earlier.

	WEST	NORTH	EAST	SOUTH
			1♠	dbl
6	pass	2♣	pass	2◇

a) ♠ 7 6   b) ♠ 7 6   c) ♠ 7 6   d) ♠ 8 7
    ♡ A J 7 6   ♡ A J 7   ♡ A Q 7   ♡ A J 7 6 5
    ◇ A K Q 10 5   ◇ A K 10 6 5   ◇ A K Q 8 7   ◇ A K Q 8 7
    ♣ 7 6   ♣ Q 6 5   ♣ K 6 5   ♣ 5

Hand (b) would overcall 2◇ or, having doubled, would pass 2♣. Hand (d) would overcall 2♡ instead of doubling or might use a convention such as Michaels to show both red suits. Experts who advocate 'equal-level conversion' might have hand (a), arguing that since 2◇ doesn't increase the level of the contract, it need not show extra strength. Hand (c) is what you could expect from me. Discuss this sequence with your partner.

	WEST	NORTH	EAST	SOUTH
			1♠	dbl
7	2♠	pass	pass	3◇

a) ♠ 8   b) ♠ 8   c) ♠ 4   d) ♠ 7 6
    ♡ A Q 5 4   ♡ A Q 5   ♡ A 5   ♡ A J 5
    ◇ A K 10 6 5 4   ◇ A K 10 6 5 4   ◇ K Q 10 7 6 5   ◇ K J 10 4 3
    ♣ Q 4   ♣ Q 4 2   ♣ A Q 5 4   ♣ K J 4

Hand (c) would overcall 2◇, and hand (d) couldn't act a second time. Let's assume South will have good support for the other major when he starts with a double and say that hand (a) is correct. See the next problem.

	WEST	NORTH	EAST	SOUTH
			1♠	2◇
⑧	2♠	pass	pass	dbl

a) ♠ 8
 ♡ A Q 5 4
 ◇ A K 10 6 5 4
 ♣ Q 4

b) ♠ 8
 ♡ A Q 5
 ◇ A K 10 6 5 4
 ♣ Q 4 2

c) ♠ 4
 ♡ A 5
 ◇ K Q 10 7 6 5
 ♣ A Q 5 4

d) ♠ 7 6
 ♡ A J 5
 ◇ K J 10 4 3
 ♣ K J 4

South's double is for takeout. Again, hands (c) and (d) are out. But if South would have a hand like (a) on Problem 7, North should expect a hand like (b) on this auction. Therefore, North had better not try 3♡ on a poor-four card suit. A good partnership should define these two auctions.

	WEST	NORTH	EAST	SOUTH
	1♡	pass	1NT	dbl
⑨				

a) ♠ A J 6
 ♡ A 6 5
 ◇ K J 6 5
 ♣ K J 6

b) ♠ K Q 7 6
 ♡ A 10 9 5
 ◇ 5
 ♣ A Q 7 6

c) ♠ A 5
 ♡ A 6
 ◇ 6 5 4
 ♣ K Q J 9 6 4

d) ♠ K Q 7 6
 ♡ 6
 ◇ A J 6 5 3
 ♣ K Q 5

It would be risky to act with hand (a) and foolish with hand (b). South might survive the double with hand (c), but hand (d) is correct: South's double is a takeout double of hearts.

	WEST	NORTH	EAST	SOUTH
			1◇	pass
⑩	1♡	pass	1♠	dbl

a) ♠ A Q 10 5
 ♡ A J 6 5
 ◇ K J 8 6
 ♣ 6

b) ♠ 7
 ♡ K Q 7 6
 ◇ A Q 9 5
 ♣ A J 5 4

c) ♠ 6
 ♡ K J 5 4
 ◇ A 9 5 4
 ♣ K J 6 5

d) ♠ A J 5
 ♡ 8 7 6 2
 ◇ A Q 5
 ♣ A Q 6

Hand (b) is correct: South's double promises a good hand with clubs and diamonds. Some experts would act over 1◇ with (a), but if they passed, they'd pass again over 1♠. Hand (c) isn't strong enough to climb in; hand (d) would bid 1NT over 1◇.

	WEST	NORTH	EAST	SOUTH
			1♡	pass
⑪	1♠	pass	2♣	2◇

a) ♠ 6 5
 ♡ A 7 6 5
 ◇ A Q 10 7 5
 ♣ 6 5

b) ♠ 6 5
 ♡ A Q 9 6 4
 ◇ K Q 10 8 7
 ♣ A

c) ♠ 3
 ♡ A J 7 6
 ◇ K Q 8 6 5 3
 ♣ A 4

d) ♠ 6
 ♡ K 10 7 5 4
 ◇ A Q J 5
 ♣ K 7 6

Hands (a) and (d) couldn't act safely; and hand (c) would overcall 2◊. Hand (b) is correct: South's delayed entry suggests long diamonds together with length and strength in hearts.

	WEST	NORTH	EAST	SOUTH
		1♡	1♠	pass
12	pass	dbl	pass	2♡

a) ♠ A J 9 5 3   b) ♠ 6 5 4 2   c) ♠ 7 6 5   d) ♠ K J 9 7 5
   ♡ Q 6 5   ♡ Q 6 5   ♡ K 4   ♡ Q 5
   ◊ 5 4   ◊ J 6 5   ◊ J 6 5   ◊ K 6
   ♣ 6 5 4   ♣ 6 5 4   ♣ 9 8 7 5 3 ♣ 7 6 4 3

Hand (a) would bid 2♡ over 1♠; it would be wrong to pass, intending to pass a reopening double for penalty, with undisclosed heart support. Hand (b) is correct. Hand (c) would bid 2♣ over the double; hand (d) would pass the double for penalty.

	WEST	NORTH	EAST	SOUTH
		1♠	1NT	2NT
13				

a) ♠ Q 7 6   b) ♠ 6   c) ♠ 5   d) ♠ Q 6
   ♡ 7 6   ♡ 5   ♡ K Q 10 7 5   ♡ A J 5
   ◊ A Q 7 6   ◊ Q 10 7 6 5   ◊ 7   ◊ K J 7 6
   ♣ Q 10 6 2   ♣ K J 8 7 6 5   ♣ A K J 7 6 5   ♣ Q 10 6 5

Hands (a) and (d) would double 1NT for penalty; hand (b) couldn't act. Hand (c) is correct: in my opinion, South suggests a freakish, game-going hand unsuitable for a penalty double of 1NT.

	WEST	NORTH	EAST	SOUTH
	1◊	1♡	pass	3♡
14				

a) ♠ 7 6   b) ♠ 7 6   c) ♠ 7 6 5 4   d) ♠ 7
   ♡ A K 6 5   ♡ K J 4   ♡ Q 10 7 6   ♡ Q 10 7 6 5
   ◊ A 5   ◊ A 7 6 5   ◊ 5   ◊ 7 6
   ♣ K 8 6 5   ♣ Q 7 6 5   ♣ K 6 5 4   ♣ K J 8 7 6

Hand (c) is correct: a jump raise of an overcall should be preemptive since other actions are available to show strength. Hand (a) would cuebid 2◊; hand (b) would cuebid 2◊ or raise to 2♡; hand (d) would jump to 4♡.

	WEST	NORTH	EAST	SOUTH
15	1♡	pass	pass	2NT

a) ♠ 7
♡ 6
◇ Q J 9 5 4
♣ K Q 8 4 3 2

b) ♠ A J 6 5
♡ A K
◇ Q 10 6 5
♣ K Q 6

c) ♠ 5 4
♡ K 6
◇ A 7 6
♣ A K Q 10 6 5

d) ♠ A J 7
♡ A K 3
◇ K Q 5 4
♣ A 10 6

Hand (a) would pass; hands (b) and (d) would start with a double. In my opinion, hand (c) is a likely hand for South.

	WEST	NORTH	EAST	SOUTH
16	1♡	dbl	1♠	dbl

a) ♠ A J 9 5
♡ Q J 9 5
◇ Q 5
♣ 7 6 5

b) ♠ 7 6
♡ A 7 6
◇ K 8 7 6
♣ Q 7 6 5

c) ♠ 7 6 5
♡ A J 10
◇ Q 9 5
♣ Q 9 4 3

d) ♠ Q J 9 6 5
♡ J 6
◇ 6 5 4
♣ J 5 4

South's double is for penalty in the absence of any partnership agreement. Hand (a) is correct. Hand (b) would bid 2◇. Hand (c) would bid 1NT; South doesn't promise spade strength for this bid since North has suggested spades. Hand (d) isn't strong enough to act.

	WEST	NORTH	EAST	SOUTH
17		1♡	dbl	pass
	2♣	pass	pass	2♡

a) ♠ K 7 6
♡ K 7 6
◇ 7 6 5
♣ 9 6 5 4

b) ♠ 8 7 6 5
♡ A 7
◇ J 8 7
♣ 9 7 6 5

c) ♠ 8 7 6 5 4
♡ K 10 7 6
◇ J 5
♣ 9 7

d) ♠ K 7 6
♡ A 6 5
◇ Q 8 7 6
♣ 6 5 4

Hand (a) would bid 2♡ directly over the double; hand (b) would never act; hand (c) would bid 3♡, preemptive, over the double. Hand (d) is correct: South promises the values for a maximum single raise. This is how he can distinguish between a maximum and a minimum raise over the double. This is admittedly an old treatment, but in my opinion effective.

	WEST	NORTH	EAST	SOUTH
18			1♠	dbl
	1NT	2◇	2♠	dbl

a) ♠ A J 9 4
♡ Q J 5 4
◇ A 5
♣ K J 4

b) ♠ K 6
♡ A K 5 4
◇ Q 4
♣ A J 9 6 5

c) ♠ 7
♡ A Q J 6 5
◇ Q 5
♣ A Q 8 7 6

d) ♠ A 4
♡ K 10 7 6
◇ Q 4
♣ A 9 7 6 4

Hand (b) is correct: South's second double shows extra strength, mediocre diamond support and something in spades. Hand (a) would overcall 1NT; hand (c), a two-suiter, would bid 2♡ over 1♠ instead of doubling. Hand (d) isn't strong enough to act a second time.

WEST	NORTH	EAST	SOUTH
		1NT	2♠

19

a) ♠ J 9 7 6 4 3
♡ 6
◇ K 8 5 2
♣ K 5

b) ♠ K Q J 10 6 5
♡ A Q
◇ A 7 6
♣ 5 4

c) ♠ K Q J 9 7 5
♡ 6 5
◇ A 8 7 6
♣ 6

d) ♠ K Q J 9 7 6 4
♡ 8
◇ J 10 6
♣ 6 4

Hand (c) is correct: South promises good spades and an average hand. Hand (a) would not overcall with such a ragged suit; hand (b) would double 1NT; hand (d) would jump to 3♠, preemptive.

WEST	NORTH	EAST	SOUTH
1◇	pass	pass	dbl
pass	1♡	pass	1♠

20

a) ♠ K Q 9 7 6
♡ K 6
◇ 7 6 5
♣ Q 5 4

b) ♠ K Q 9 7 4
♡ A K
◇ 6 5 4
♣ A Q 6

c) ♠ K J 8 7
♡ J 6 5
◇ A 10 6
♣ K 9 6

d) ♠ A Q 8 7 6
♡ A J 6
◇ 8 7
♣ A 9 5

Hand (a) would balance with 1♠; hand (b) would jump to 2♠ over 1♡; hand (c) would balance with 1NT. Hand (d) is correct: since South would balance with 1♠ on less strength, he must double and bid his suit with sound opening values.

WEST	NORTH	EAST	SOUTH
	1♡	1♠	dbl[1]
2♠	pass	pass	3♡

21

1. Negative.

a) ♠ 6 5
♡ Q 6 5
◇ K 7 6 5
♣ Q 6 5 4

b) ♠ 7 6
♡ Q 6 5
◇ A Q 7 6
♣ K Q 6 5

c) ♠ 7 6
♡ 10 7 6
◇ A J 6 3
♣ K Q 7 6

d) ♠ 7 6
♡ Q 5
◇ A Q 7 6
♣ K J 6 5 3

It's hard to construct a reasonable South hand, but maybe your partner is apt to torture you with new auctions. Hand (a) would bid 2♡ over 1♠; hand (b) might start with a double but would then bid 4♡; hand (d) would bid 2♣ over 1♠. The sequence suggests invitational values, but hand (c) is the best I can do for South; can you do better?

	WEST	NORTH	EAST	SOUTH
22	1◊	pass	1♡	pass
	1NT	pass	2◊	2♠

a) ♠ K Q 10 7 6
♡ A Q 5
◊ 6 5
♣ J 5 4

b) ♠ K J 10 7
♡ A 6
◊ 7 6 5 4
♣ 6 5 4

c) ♠ K J 10 6 5
♡ K 6
◊ 7 6 5
♣ 7 6 5

d) ♠ A J 9 6 5 4
♡ Q 8 7 6
◊ 6
♣ 6 5

Hand (a) would bid 1♠ over 1♡; a few experts might hold (b), but to act would be risky and might mislead partner. Hand (c) is correct: when East-West have found a fit but have announced limited values, South may climb in on a light hand with spade length; this is a sort of balancing action in the direct seat. Hand (d) would jump to 2♠ over 1♡.

	WEST	NORTH	EAST	SOUTH
			1◊	dbl
23	pass	1NT	pass	2♣

a) ♠ A J 5
♡ J 6 5 4
◊ —
♣ A J 9 6 5 3

b) ♠ A 6 5
♡ K 6 5 4
◊ 6
♣ A Q 8 6 4

c) ♠ A J 6
♡ K 7 6
◊ 8 7
♣ A K Q 8 6

d) ♠ A 7 6 5
♡ Q 7 6 5
◊ —
♣ A Q J 6 5

In my opinion, hand (a) would overcall 2♣, hand (b) would pass 1NT, and hand (c) would raise 1NT to 2NT. Hand (d) is a possible hand for South.

	WEST	NORTH	EAST	SOUTH
			1◊	dbl
24	pass	1NT	pass	2♡

a) ♠ A 5 4
♡ K Q 10 7 6
◊ 6
♣ A 7 6 5

b) ♠ Q 6 5 4
♡ K Q 10 7 6
◊ —
♣ A J 6 5

c) ♠ K Q 5
♡ A Q 10 7 6 5
◊ 6
♣ A Q 5

d) ♠ A 6 3
♡ Q 10 7 6 5
◊ A 7 6
♣ A K 5

Now South is more likely to have a strong hand; he could have overcalled 1♡ with a fair hand and heart length. Hand (c) is correct. Hand (a) would overcall, and hand (b) might overcall instead of doubling and risking a penalty pass by partner. Hand (d), a balanced hand with scattered values, might raise 1NT to 2NT.

	WEST	NORTH	EAST	SOUTH
				1♡
25	2♣	3♣	5♣	pass
	pass	dbl	pass	5♡

a) ♠ K 5 3   b) ♠ A 5 4   c) ♠ A 7   d) ♠ 8 7
   ♡ Q J 7 6 5   ♡ K 7 6 5 3   ♡ K J 10 7 5 3   ♡ A Q 8 6 5 4
   ◇ A K 3   ◇ A J 7 6 4   ◇ Q 7   ◇ A K J 5
   ♣ 6 5   ♣ —   ♣ J 5 3   ♣ 7

The question is whether South's 'pass-but-pull-a-double' sequence is stronger than a direct bid of 5♡ and hence encourages slam. If you think it is, give South a hand like (d); otherwise, expect a hand like (b). Talk it over with your partner. Neither (a) nor (c) would bid 5♡.

As in constructive bidding, a difference of opinion over whether a bid is forcing is a recipe for disaster. I was recently watching two experts, one a world champion, on OKbridge, when this auction occurred:

WEST	EXPERT #1	EAST	EXPERT #2
	1◇	dbl	redbl
1♠	pass	pass	2NT
pass	pass	pass	

TIP 2

IS IT
FORCING?

Expert #2 had only 12 points, but considered his 2NT forcing. Expert #1, who had opened with an unimpressive 12-count, disagreed. The result was a missed game, since nine tricks were cold.

Here are 25 sequences: decide whether South's last call is forcing. I'll tell you what I think, but the only 'correct' answers are the ones on which you and your partner agree.

	WEST	NORTH	EAST	SOUTH
(1)		1◇	1♡	2NT

	WEST	NORTH	EAST	SOUTH
(2)			1◇	pass
	pass	1♠	pass	3♣

	WEST	NORTH	EAST	SOUTH
(3)				1◇
	1♡	dbl[1]	pass	2♠

1.   Negative.

	WEST	NORTH	EAST	SOUTH
(4)				1♣
	1♠	dbl[1]	pass	2◇

1.   Negative.

	WEST	NORTH	EAST	SOUTH
(5)				
	1♡	1NT	pass	3◇

6

WEST	NORTH	EAST	SOUTH
	1♡	dbl	1♠

7

WEST	NORTH	EAST	SOUTH
			1♡
1♠	pass	pass	3♣

8

WEST	NORTH	EAST	SOUTH
	1♢	dbl	redbl
1♠	pass	pass	2♣

9

WEST	NORTH	EAST	SOUTH
			1♡
pass	2♡	pass	pass
dbl	redbl	3♣	pass

10

WEST	NORTH	EAST	SOUTH
	1♢	pass	2♣
2♠	pass	pass	3♢

11

WEST	NORTH	EAST	SOUTH
	1♢	pass	1♡
1♠	pass	pass	2♣

12

WEST	NORTH	EAST	SOUTH
	1♢	pass	1♠
2♣	pass	pass	3♢

13

WEST	NORTH	EAST	SOUTH
1♢	1♡	pass	1♠

14

WEST	NORTH	EAST	SOUTH
1♢	1♠	pass	1NT

15

WEST	NORTH	EAST	SOUTH
1♢	1♠	pass	2NT

16

WEST	NORTH	EAST	SOUTH
1♢	2♠	pass	2NT

	WEST	NORTH	EAST	SOUTH
17				1♥
	2♣	pass	pass	dbl
	pass	pass	2♦	pass

	WEST	NORTH	EAST	SOUTH
18				1♦
	dbl	redbl	pass	2♦

	WEST	NORTH	EAST	SOUTH
19				1♦
	dbl	redbl	pass	pass
	1♥	pass	pass	2♦

	WEST	NORTH	EAST	SOUTH
20			1♦	dbl
	pass	2♠	pass	3♣

	WEST	NORTH	EAST	SOUTH
21	1♥	dbl	pass	2♥
	pass	2♠	pass	2NT

	WEST	NORTH	EAST	SOUTH
22	1♥	dbl	pass	2♥
	pass	2♠	pass	3♠

	WEST	NORTH	EAST	SOUTH
23		1♣	1♠	2♦
	pass	2♥	pass	3♥

	WEST	NORTH	EAST	SOUTH
24				1♠
	dbl	2♠	3♥	4♠
	pass	pass	5♥	pass

	WEST	NORTH	EAST	SOUTH
25	3♠	pass	pass	dbl
	pass	4♥	4♠	pass

MY PREFERENCES

1. Not forcing. South has forcing actions available.

2. Strongly encouraging but not forcing. South could cuebid to force.

3. Not forcing. South promises four-card spade support but may have minimum values. He might bid 1♠ on a hand such as

♠ K Q 5 ♡ 6 5 3 ◇ A 7 6 3 ♣ K J 2

4. Not forcing. In my opinion, South has not 'reversed' to show strength but has merely suggested a contract. Find out what your partner thinks; else you may have a result like this:

	♠ 7 5 3			♠ J 2
	♡ A J 9 3			♡ 7 4 2
	◇ Q 10 8	N W E S		◇ A K 6 4
	♣ K 10 4			♣ A Q 7 3

WEST	NORTH	EAST	SOUTH
		1♣	2♠
dbl	pass	3◇	pass
5♣	dbl	all pass	

East thought he was merely placing the contract when he bid 3◇; West thought East had reversed and had long clubs and extra strength. A 1◇ opening instead of 1♣ would have let East-West stop at 3◇, but the result was mostly attributable to the fact that East-West hadn't discussed this sequence.

5. Not forcing. South can cuebid to force.

6. Forcing; but most experts would treat a 2♣ or 2◇ bid as not forcing.

7. Not forcing. The 1♡ bid wasn't forcing, so 3♣ can't be; South could cuebid to force.

8. Forcing. New suits after a redouble are forcing.

9. Not forcing. Although North's redouble announced a maximum raise and interest in penalizing the opponents, North may have many hands on which he isn't willing either to bid 3♡ or to double 3♣.

10. **Not forcing.** Auctions that begin 1◇-pass-2♣ are awkward, but here the 2♠ interference is beneficial. With a strong hand, South would have alternative calls.

11. **Forcing.** A new suit by responder is forcing. A case exists, however, for a non-forcing treatment here; consult your partner.

12. **Not forcing.**

13. My preference is to play a change of suit after an overcall as forcing, but many experts do otherwise.

14. **Not forcing,** although a few expert pairs extend the Forcing Notrump to this situation. More importantly, what kind of hand would you expect from South? Is his bid constructive or is he running for his life with a singleton spade and a poorish hand?

15. **Not forcing.** South has forcing alternatives.

16. **Forcing.** Most experts assign a conventional meaning to 2NT: for instance, it might ask partner to show a side singleton.

17. **Forcing.** It should be, at least, but I've seen North pass anyway because no other action was attractive.

18. **Not forcing.** Expert consensus is that the direct 2◇ rebid suggests a minimum distributional hand.

19. **Forcing,** assuming South would have rebid 2◇ at his second turn with weakness.

20. **Forcing.** Both North and South have made constructive bids.

21. **Forcing.** South doesn't like spades but could have jumped to 2NT directly to invite game.

22. **Not forcing.** South's 2♡ cuebid was forcing, but not to game.

23. **Not forcing.** North's 2♡ didn't promise a strong hand since it was the cheapest bid he had available, and South may have no extra strength.

24. **Forcing,** most likely, although the vulnerability may be a factor. Entire books have treated the subject of when a pass is forcing in similar auctions.

25. When I was North, my partner thought his pass was forcing. I didn't. This illustrates the complexity of the 'forcing pass' issue; no partnership can anticipate every situation it will face.

TIP 3

WHEN YOUR PARTNER STRAINS TO COMPETE, DON'T HANG HIM

Playing IMPs, neither side vulnerable, you hold as South,

♠ Q J 6   ♡ 8 5   ◇ A 9 6 5 2   ♣ K 7 4

WEST	NORTH	EAST	SOUTH
		2♡	pass
4♡	4♠	pass	?

What do you say?

Pass. Since you have ten working points, and North has bid 4♠ on his own, to raise to 5♠ is tempting. But North's hand is unknown; he may have taken a big gamble to come in. Give him room; the full deal may be

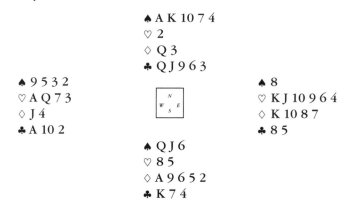

                ♠ A K 10 7 4
                ♡ 2
                ◇ Q 3
                ♣ Q J 9 6 3

♠ 9 5 3 2   ♠ 8
♡ A Q 7 3   ♡ K J 10 9 6 4
◇ J 4   ◇ K 10 8 7
♣ A 10 2   ♣ 8 5

                ♠ Q J 6
                ♡ 8 5
                ◇ A 9 6 5 2
                ♣ K 7 4

Not everyone would act on the North hand, but 4♠ is cold (if the defense leads two rounds of hearts, North can discard his diamond loser to keep control); and if North passes, East is likely to make 4♡.

Enemy preemption can force your partner to stretch to enter the auction; he must assume you have a few values — and bid them on your behalf — or the opponents will steal you blind. Don't punish him. Sometimes you'll miss a good slam, but even on occasions when your partner has a huge hand, it's wise not to try for perfection in a crowded auction. When your partner acts over a preempt, assume he has bid six of your points.

Look at this deal from a U.S. Team Trials:

Dlr: North
Vul: None

```
                    ♠ J 10 9 8 6 3
                    ♡ 7 2
                    ◇ —
                    ♣ K Q J 10 4
    ♠ A 4 2                           ♠ K 7
    ♡ J 10 8 5          N             ♡ A K Q 4 3
    ◇ Q 5 2         W       E         ◇ K 7 3
    ♣ A 6 5            S              ♣ 8 7 2
                    ♠ Q 5
                    ♡ 9 6
                    ◇ A J 10 9 8 6 4
                    ♣ 9 3
```

WEST	NORTH	EAST	SOUTH
Martel	Meckstroth	Stansby	Rodwell
	3♠	4♡	pass
pass(!)	pass		

West had four good trumps, two aces and a queen; yet he refused to punish East's bold overcall. Even 4♡ would have failed with the ◇A opening lead, but South led the ♠Q. East drew trumps, stripped the spades, cashed the ♣A and exited with a club, endplaying North.

Even low-level preemption can put you under pressure.

Dlr: East
Vul: None

```
                    ♠ K Q 10 9 4 3
                    ♡ 9
                    ◇ Q 8 2
                    ♣ 10 9 3
    ♠ 8 5 2                          ♠ A 6
    ♡ 10 7 6 3 2       N             ♡ K Q 8 4
    ◇ K 3          W       E         ◇ A J 7 4
    ♣ A 7 2           S              ♣ 8 5 4
                    ♠ J 7
                    ♡ A J 5
                    ◇ 10 9 6 5
                    ♣ K Q J 6
```

WEST	NORTH	EAST	SOUTH
		1◇	pass
1♡	2♠	3♡	pass
4♡	all pass		

North led the ♠K, and West went down one, losing two trumps, a spade and a club, even though he finessed in diamonds to get one club discard. West should have given East room by passing 3♡. East had to compete despite his minimum; if he passes, North will play 2♠ and make it.

North hand: ♠ 9 7 2 / ♥ A Q 8 2 / ◇ J 5 / ♣ 8 5 4 2

East hand: ♠ A 4 / ♥ K J 4 3 / ◇ A K Q 4 3 / ♣ 9 3

WEST	NORTH	EAST	SOUTH
		1◇	pass
1♡	2♠	3♡	all pass

West took eleven tricks. If North had passed, East would still have raised the 1♡ response to 3♡; over the interference he should have taken the pressure off West by jumping to game.

You can't always tell when your partner has stretched his values to get in, but some enemy auctions are almost a notarized affidavit that your side can make something. I watched this deal on OKbridge.

Dlr: North
Vul: Both

North: ♠ J 5 / ♥ 8 5 3 / ◇ Q 4 / ♣ K 10 9 6 3 2

West: ♠ K Q 8 3 / ♥ K 10 4 / ◇ J 9 3 / ♣ A 8 4

East: ♠ A 9 6 4 / ♥ Q / ◇ K 10 8 7 5 2 / ♣ J 7

South: ♠ 10 7 2 / ♥ A J 9 7 6 2 / ◇ A 6 / ♣ Q 5

WEST	NORTH	EAST	SOUTH
	pass	pass	2♡
pass	3♡	all pass	

East-West lost their way and let South get out for down one, -100, when they were on for 4♠. If you hear an opposing weak two-bid followed by a raise, treat it like a bull treats a red flag; get into the bidding with any excuse.

This deal came up in a Bermuda Bowl:

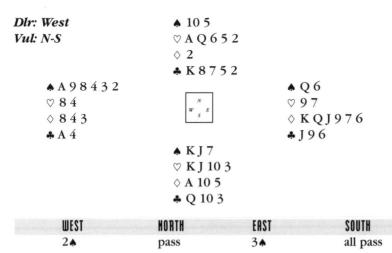

♠ 10 5
♡ A Q 6 5 2
♢ 2
♣ K 8 7 5 2

♠ A 9 8 4 3 2
♡ 8 4
♢ 8 4 3
♣ A 4

♠ Q 6
♡ 9 7
♢ K Q J 9 7 6
♣ J 9 6

♠ K J 7
♡ K J 10 3
♢ A 10 5
♣ Q 10 3

WEST	NORTH	EAST	SOUTH
2♠	pass	3♠	all pass

West's 3♠ went down four, -200. It seems either North or South should have felt spurred to act, though that's easier to say in hindsight. At the other table, West passed as dealer, and East opened 1♢ in third seat. South overcalled 1♡ and North raised to 4♡ for +650.

What do you think South should do on this next example? IMPs, neither side vulnerable, and South holds

♠ 6 4 3   ♡ A K 9 7 4   ♢ A K 9   ♣ 7 6

WEST	NORTH	EAST	SOUTH
2♠	pass	3♠	?

South should bid 4♡. A double is possible, but a pass, although it may be right, is defeatist. This is South's gamble to take. If North's hand is short in spades with a few values, South will have a play for game. The full deal may be

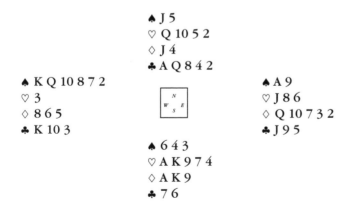

♠ J 5
♡ Q 10 5 2
♢ J 4
♣ A Q 8 4 2

♠ K Q 10 8 7 2
♡ 3
♢ 8 6 5
♣ K 10 3

♠ A 9
♡ J 8 6
♢ Q 10 7 3 2
♣ J 9 5

♠ 6 4 3
♡ A K 9 7 4
♢ A K 9
♣ 7 6

As East, playing for the U.S. in a Bermuda Bowl, you're the dealer with

♠ K J   ♡ 2   ◇ K Q 9 8 5   ♣ A 10 7 5 4

WEST	NORTH	EAST	SOUTH
		1◇	4♡
pass	pass	?	

Both sides are vulnerable. What do you say?

Pass. If you bid 5♣ now, when you'd have rebid only 2♣ without South's preempt, you're letting your opponents jerk you around. The full deal:

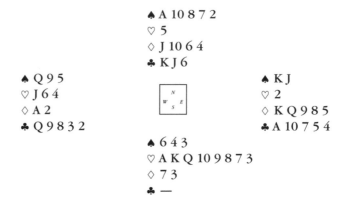

```
              ♠ A 10 8 7 2
              ♡ 5
              ◇ J 10 6 4
              ♣ K J 6
♠ Q 9 5                        ♠ K J
♡ J 6 4          N             ♡ 2
◇ A 2        W       E         ◇ K Q 9 8 5
♣ Q 9 8 3 2      S             ♣ A 10 7 5 4
              ♠ 6 4 3
              ♡ A K Q 10 9 8 7 3
              ◇ 7 3
              ♣ —
```

WEST	NORTH	EAST	SOUTH
		1◇	4♡
pass	pass	5♣	pass
pass	dbl	all pass	

West put down a magic dummy, but East still went down one in 5♣ doubled. In the other room, East passed 4♡ and went plus.

I just warned you against punishing partner for an aggressive action; but there is a subtle difference between taking a calculated risk and letting an opponent's bid push you over the line into unsoundness. I watched two famous experts bid these hands on OKbridge.

```
        ♠ Q J 7 3              ♠ A 8 5 4 2
        ♡ 7          ┌─────┐   ♡ 8 3
        ◇ K 6 2      │  N  │   ◇ A 8 5
        ♣ A J 8 4 2  │W   E│   ♣ K Q 3
                     │  S  │
                     └─────┘
```

WEST	NORTH	EAST	SOUTH
1♣	pass	1♠	4♡
4♠	pass	5♠	pass
6♠	all pass		

Down one. North, not surprisingly, had a trump trick. East's 5♠, which West interpreted (perhaps wrongly) as a demand for slam if West had a heart control, may have been too much; but West was more at fault for bidding 4♠ when he was worth only 2♠. If West refuses to be goaded and passes, East will double to show a good hand — and then West can try 4♠.

As South, both sides vulnerable at IMPs, you hold

$$♠ A 10 7 6 5 2 \quad ♡ J 4 \quad ◇ 10 4 \quad ♣ Q 10 4$$

West opens 3◇, and there are two passes. Do you bid or sell out?

You should pass and stay fixed. North is marked with some points, but if he has enough for you to make 3♠, he'll raise you to 4♠ when you bid. I balance as much as anyone, but you must draw the line somewhere.

```
Dlr: South           ♠ K Q 7 6
Vul: N-S             ♡ K 8 7 5
                     ◇ Q
                     ♣ K Q J 7
  ♠ A 5 4 3                        ♠ 10 9 8 2
  ♡ A J 9 2      ┌─────┐           ♡ 6
  ◇ A 10 2       │  N  │           ◇ K 3
  ♣ 5 4          │W   E│           ♣ A 10 9 8 3 2
                 │  S  │
                 └─────┘
                     ♠ J
                     ♡ Q 10 4 3
                     ◇ J 9 8 7 6 5 4
                     ♣ 6
```

WEST	NORTH	EAST	SOUTH
			pass
1♠	1NT	4♠	5◇
dbl	all pass		

North's 1NT overcall was no thing of beauty, but South's 5◇ was a wild stab that was punished for -1400. South has won several world titles, but this time he let East's pressure bid goad him into an indiscretion.

The opponents don't have to jack the bidding up high to tempt you into an undisciplined action. As South, both sides vulnerable at IMPs, you hold

♠ A J   ♡ Q 3   ◊ 9 6 4 2   ♣ J 8 7 4 2

WEST	NORTH	EAST	SOUTH
	1♠	2◊	?

Pass. I often see players try 2♠ in this situation, but it's wrong to raise when North, who is likely short in diamonds, won't sell out to 2◊. Yes, 2♠ might make — but the auction might not end there. North might try for game and get too high; or if East-West compete, North might make a losing competitive decision.

A questionable trump holding is always a warning to avoid aggressive tactics.

Dlr: South
Vul: E-W

```
                  ♠ 10 9 4
                  ♡ K 6 3
                  ◊ 10 9 8 7 5
                  ♣ Q 2
♠ A K J 2                        ♠ 6
♡ Q J 10 9 4        N            ♡ A 8 7 5
◊ J 6           W     E          ◊ A 4 3 2
♣ 8 6               S            ♣ K 7 4 3
                  ♠ Q 8 7 5 3
                  ♡ 2
                  ◊ K Q
                  ♣ A J 10 9 5
```

WEST	NORTH	EAST	SOUTH
			1♠
2♡	2♠	3♠	4♠
dbl	all pass		

North's raise to 2♠ was merely shaky — his ♡K looked like a winner, and it was then-or-never — but I can't begin to defend South's 4♠ with weak trumps. He ruffed the second heart and led the ♣A and a club to East's king. When East returned a trump, West took the jack, king and ace and forced out South's last trump with another heart lead, leaving the defense in control. The penalty came to -1700!

In a high-level competitive auction, it's easy to get carried away.

Dlr: East
Vul: N-S
IMPs

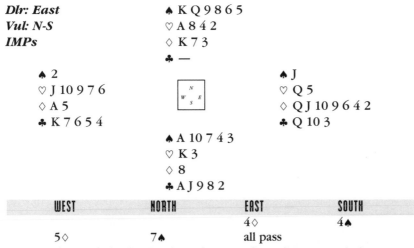

	♠ K Q 9 8 6 5	
	♡ A 8 4 2	
	◇ K 7 3	
	♣ —	
♠ 2		♠ J
♡ J 10 9 7 6		♡ Q 5
◇ A 5		◇ Q J 10 9 6 4 2
♣ K 7 6 5 4		♣ Q 10 3
	♠ A 10 7 4 3	
	♡ K 3	
	◇ 8	
	♣ A J 9 8 2	

WEST	NORTH	EAST	SOUTH
		4◇	4♠
5◇	7♠	all pass	

North-South had a lead in the match and expected their counterparts to bid the grand slam. Still, the 4♠ overcall was questionable, and 7♠ was a wild shot. Even if South were void in diamonds, a grand slam was not assured. When West led the ♡J, South could have made 7♠ on a squeeze but actually went down one. The contract in the other room was 6♠.

Playing IMPs, North-South vulnerable, you hold as West

♠ Q 10 9 7 5 ♡ K 9 ◇ K 9 6 2 ♣ 10 8

WEST	NORTH	EAST	SOUTH
pass	pass	1◇	4♡
?			

What do you say?

Pass. You wouldn't have bid beyond the two-level without the interference. Don't be goaded without an attractive reason.

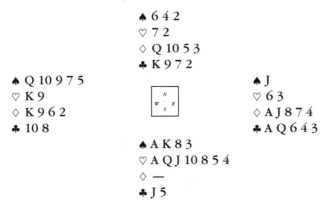

	♠ 6 4 2	
	♡ 7 2	
	◇ Q 10 5 3	
	♣ K 9 7 2	
♠ Q 10 9 7 5		♠ J
♡ K 9		♡ 6 3
◇ K 9 6 2		◇ A J 8 7 4
♣ 10 8		♣ A Q 6 4 3
	♠ A K 8 3	
	♡ A Q J 10 8 5 4	
	◇ —	
	♣ J 5	

In a U.S. Team Trials, only Billy Eisenberg passed 4♡ for +300. Every other West acted and went minus.

3 · COMPETITIVE BIDDING

At IMPs, with North-South vulnerable, you hold as South

♠ — ♡ A K 4 ◊ Q J 8 4 ♣ A K J 8 5 3

WEST	NORTH	EAST	SOUTH
			1♣
1♠	pass	pass	dbl
2♡	pass	2♠	?

What do you say?

Bid 3♣ (or perhaps 3◊). Since there may be more bidding, tell partner you have extra length in clubs. Another double would suggest strength, but 3♣ is not a weak action and is more descriptive.

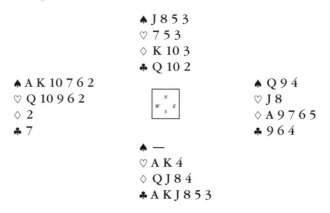

♠ J 8 5 3
♡ 7 5 3
◊ K 10 3
♣ Q 10 2

♠ A K 10 7 6 2
♡ Q 10 9 6 2
◊ 2
♣ 7

♠ Q 9 4
♡ J 8
◊ A 9 7 6 5
♣ 9 6 4

♠ —
♡ A K 4
◊ Q J 8 4
♣ A K J 8 5 3

WEST	NORTH	EAST	SOUTH
			1♣
1♠	pass	pass	dbl
2♡	pass	2♠	dbl
4♠	dbl	all pass	

The actual South doubled again — and induced North to misjudge. Since North didn't know South had long clubs, he doubled 4♠ and led a club. West ruffed the second club and started the hearts. South won, forced in clubs, won the next heart and led a fourth club (best), which West ruffed in his hand. When North declined to overruff, declarer diagnosed the trump position. He took the ◊A, ruffed a diamond and ran hearts through North to make the contract.

At the other table:

WEST	NORTH	EAST	SOUTH
			1♣
1♠	pass	pass	dbl
2♡	pass	2♠	3◇
4♠	5♣	all pass	

This time South showed long clubs by implication, and North preferred 5♣ with his minor-suit honors. West led his singleton diamond and got a ruff, but South took the rest; he ruffed West's spade return, took two trumps, ran the diamonds to pitch a heart from dummy and ruffed a heart.

Just as a computer can't solve a problem if it's fed wrong data, partners can't make good decisions without good information. In a competitive auction, describe your hand.

Matchpoints, East-West vulnerable:

♠ J 8 5   ♡ 10   ◇ A Q 10 7 6   ♣ 7 5 3 2

WEST	NORTH	EAST	SOUTH
1♡	2♠	3♡	?

A save at 4♠ will usually be correct; but bid 4◇ to direct the lead and help partner judge the situation if East-West push on to 5♡. The full deal may be

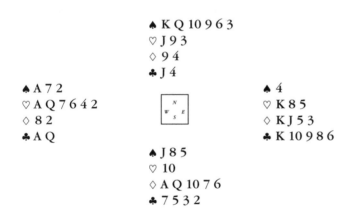

3 · COMPETITIVE BIDDING

Dlr: East
Vul: E-W

```
                          ♠ Q
                          ♡ 10 9 5 4
                          ◇ Q 5
                          ♣ K 9 8 6 4 2
      ♠ A K J 6 4 3                        ♠ 9 7 5 2
      ♡ 6 3            ┌─────────┐         ♡ J
      ◇ K 6 4 3 2      │    N    │         ◇ 10 9 8
      ♣ —              │  W   E  │         ♣ A Q 10 7 5
                       │    S    │
                       └─────────┘
                          ♠ 10 8
                          ♡ A K Q 8 7 2
                          ◇ A J 7
                          ♣ J 3
```

Table 1

WEST	NORTH	EAST	SOUTH
		pass	1♡
2♠	3♠	4♠	5♡
5♠	all pass		

Table 2

WEST	NORTH	EAST	SOUTH
		pass	1♡
1♠	2♡	4♠	5♡
5♠	all pass		

At both tables 5♠ went down one, and 5♡ would have been down two. If either West had known about East's clubs, he'd have defended 5♡; as it was, each West bid one more for luck. This deal from the 1974 Bermuda Bowl did not pass unnoticed. In 2001, East would bid clubs before raising spades, or jump in clubs, conventionally promising club values and a spade fit.

In a constructive auction, a bid of a new suit above game is a slam try; but when the opponents are threatening to sacrifice, it's better to use a new-suit bid to help partner make a competitive decision.

Dlr: West
Vul: E-W

```
                          ♠ A
                          ♡ 10 6 5
                          ◇ A J 10 3
                          ♣ 9 6 4 3 2
      ♠ 8 7 3                               ♠ J 5 2
      ♡ A J 9 7 2      ┌─────────┐          ♡ K Q 4 3
      ◇ —              │    N    │          ◇ 8 7 4 2
      ♣ A J 10 8 7     │  W   E  │          ♣ K Q
                       │    S    │
                       └─────────┘
                          ♠ K Q 10 9 6 4
                          ♡ 8
                          ◇ K Q 9 6 5
                          ♣ 5
```

BECOMING A BRIDGE EXPERT

When this deal arose in a Bermuda Bowl round-robin, some Souths were doubled in 4♠, usually making. When the U.S. sat East-West in their match against China, the auction was

WEST	NORTH	EAST	SOUTH
1♡	pass	3♡	3♠
4♣	pass	4♡	4♠
pass	pass	5♡	pass
pass	dbl	all pass	

Making five. South might have done better to leap directly to 4♠, as the U.S. player did in the other room. The actual 3♠ bid gave West a chance to bid 4♣, and after that, there was no chance East would let the opponents play 4♠.

A free bid once promised extra values. Modern players realize it's more dangerous to suppress a suit that may be a competitive vehicle than to overstate high-card strength slightly.

IMPs, neither side vulnerable:

♠ K 6   ♡ 7 4   ◇ A K 10 8 6 2   ♣ Q 5 3

WEST	NORTH	EAST	SOUTH
			1◇
pass	1♡	1♠	?

Bid 2◇. As long as North won't expect more in high cards, it is wise to show your long diamonds immediately. A possible deal:

```
              ♠ 8 7
              ♡ A 9 6 2
              ◇ Q 9 3
              ♣ K J 9 4
♠ J 9 4 3                    ♠ A Q 10 5 2
♡ Q 10          N            ♡ K J 8 5 3
◇ 7 5        W     E         ◇ J 4
♣ A 10 8 6 2     S           ♣ 7
              ♠ K 6
              ♡ 7 4
              ◇ A K 10 8 6 2
              ♣ Q 5 3
```

Table 1

WEST	NORTH	EAST	SOUTH
			1◇
pass	1♡	1♠	pass
3♠	all pass		

Table 2

WEST	NORTH	EAST	SOUTH
			1♦
pass	1♡	1♠	2♦
3♠	4♦	all pass	

Both 3♠ bids are preemptive. Both 4♦ and 3♠ are icy.

When your partner's opening bid is doubled, you must prepare for a competitive auction. A descriptive bid will help him make a correct decision.

♠ Q 7 4   ♡ Q 10 7 3   ♦ K 8 4   ♣ J 7 3

WEST	NORTH	EAST	SOUTH
	1♦	dbl	?

East suggests length and strength in hearts. South should give up on the hearts and show his hand with 1NT.

♠ 7   ♡ 10 8 5 4 3   ♦ A Q 7 6   ♣ 7 6 5

WEST	NORTH	EAST	SOUTH
	1♦	dbl	?

Certainly 1♡ might work out here, but a weak jump to 3♦ is more descriptive. If partner has hearts and minimum values, the opponents may own the deal at spades.

```
        ♠ 4                      ♠ 9 7 2
        ♡ K Q 8        N         ♡ A 10 7 5 2
        ♦ A 10 9 5 3  W   E      ♦ K 4
        ♣ A J 7 3      S         ♣ Q 10 4
```

WEST	NORTH	EAST	SOUTH
1♦	pass	1♡	1♠
2♣	3♠	all pass	

Although 3♠ went down, East-West could make 5♡. Perhaps East should have bid over 3♠, but West certainly should have supported the hearts when he had the chance.

Try this last example yourself. At IMPs, both sides vulnerable, you are South, playing in a U.S. Team Trials. You deal, holding:

♠ K J   ♡ A K 8 7 6   ♦ Q 10 9 8 5   ♣ J

WEST	NORTH	EAST	SOUTH
			1♡
1♠	2♡	2♠	?

What do you say?

Bid 3◇. More bidding is certain, and if you show your second suit, you may help partner judge. The full deal was

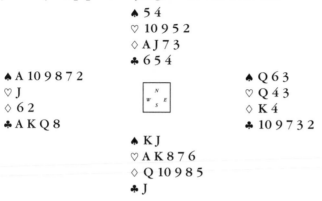

```
                        ♠ 5 4
                        ♡ 10 9 5 2
                        ◇ A J 7 3
                        ♣ 6 5 4
   ♠ A 10 9 8 7 2                          ♠ Q 6 3
   ♡ J                                     ♡ Q 4 3
   ◇ 6 2                                   ◇ K 4
   ♣ A K Q 8                               ♣ 10 9 7 3 2
                        ♠ K J
                        ♡ A K 8 7 6
                        ◇ Q 10 9 8 5
                        ♣ J
```

Table 1

WEST	NORTH	EAST	SOUTH
			1♡
1♠	2♡	2♠	3◇
4♠	5♡	pass	pass
dbl	all pass		

Table 2

WEST	NORTH	EAST	SOUTH
			1♡
1♠	2♡	2♠	3♡
4♠	all pass		

The 3◇ bid gains 9 IMPs; when you bid diamonds, North, with a diamond fit, saves in 5♡ over 4♠. You'll guess the trumps to get out for down one, -200. In the replay, South bid 3♡ at his second turn, and 4♠ made against him for +620.

MAKE YOUR BIDDING FARSIGHTED

Playing matchpoints, both sides vulnerable, you hold as South,

♠ 10 7 4 2   ♡ K 9 5 2   ◇ 6 3   ♣ A 5 2

WEST	NORTH	EAST	SOUTH
1♣	dbl	1◇	?

What do you say?

Suppose you respond 1♡. After two passes, East bids two of a minor. You have enough strength to compete at the two level, but if you bid 2♡, you may miss a superior spade fit; if you try 2♠, you may find you were better off in hearts. Since you are strong enough to bid twice, start with 1♠ and bid 2♡ next. You can play in two of either major. North's hand may be

♠ A 8 5 3   ♡ Q 7 4   ◇ A J 7 5   ♣ K 6

or

♠ A 8 3   ♡ Q 7 4 3   ◇ A J 7 5   ♣ K 6

Planning in the auction is as important as counting your tricks and forming a plan as declarer. Effective bidders anticipate competition. At IMPs, neither side vulnerable, you hold as South:

♠ 6 5   ♡ K Q 8 5 3   ◇ 8 6   ♣ A J 9 4

North opens 1♣, East doubles. Bid 1♡, planning to support clubs next. Although you have 10 HCP (plus distribution), a redouble would be shortsighted. You want to show a fair hand with good hearts and club support; but the auction will get crowded if the opponents bid and raise spades. If you don't start to describe your hand quickly, you may have to go to the four-level to finish.

Here's another case where you must think about how the auction may develop before choosing your first call. At IMPs, with neither side vulnerable, you hold as South:

♠ A Q J 5 2   ♡ —   ◇ 9 5 2   ♣ A K J 9 2

East opens 1♡. Bid 2♣, expecting competition in the red suits. In the worst case, West will raise to 4♡; but after two passes, you can try 4♠ and play in the black suit North prefers. If you overcall 1♠, you may have to choose between missing game or missing clubs.

Similarly, at IMPs, with neither side vulnerable, you hold as South:

♠ 6   ♡ A Q J 10 3   ◇ A Q J 7 3 2   ♣ 9

West opens 4♠, passed round to you. Bid 4NT for takeout. This is a 'two-step' action: you can bet North will bid 5♣, but then you'll convert to 5◇, suggesting diamonds and hearts.

At IMPs, with neither side vulnerable, you hold as South:

♠ Q 7 5 2 ♡ — ◇ A Q 3 ♣ A Q J 7 4 2

East opens 1♡. Bid 2♣: when the opponents threaten to compete in hearts, it's better to get your long suit into the picture immediately. Look what happened to an expert on this deal:

Dlr: South
Vul: E-W

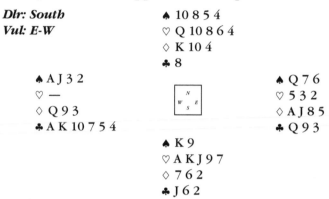

♠ 10 8 5 4
♡ Q 10 8 6 4
◇ K 10 4
♣ 8

♠ A J 3 2   ♠ Q 7 6
♡ —   ♡ 5 3 2
◇ Q 9 3   ◇ A J 8 5
♣ A K 10 7 5 4   ♣ Q 9 3

♠ K 9
♡ A K J 9 7
◇ 7 6 2
♣ J 6 2

Table 1

WEST	NORTH	EAST	SOUTH
			1♡
dbl	4♡	all pass	

Table 2

WEST	NORTH	EAST	SOUTH
			1♡
2♣	4♡	pass	pass
dbl	pass	5♣	all pass

The cards lay well for East-West, so though 4♡ went down three, 5♣ made seven. The first West couldn't bid 5♣ or double again over 4♡; but at the other table, where West showed his long suit before doubling, East knew what to do.

Players who overcall light may feel they must double with a one-suited hand and only 15 points. But even with more strength, a player may do better to mention his long suit quickly. In a Spingold match...

Dlr: North
Vul: N-S

<pre>
                        ♠ 9 3
                        ♡ J 8
                        ◇ 10 9 8 6
                        ♣ K J 7 6 5
   ♠ Q J 8 7 2   ♠ 5
   ♡ 9 5 3   ┌─────┐   ♡ A K Q 10 7 6
   ◇ 5 3 2   │ N │   ◇ A Q 4
   ♣ 9 4   │ W E │   ♣ 10 3 2
                        │ S │
                        └─────┘
                        ♠ A K 10 6 4
                        ♡ 4 2
                        ◇ K J 7
                        ♣ A Q 8
</pre>

WEST	NORTH	EAST	SOUTH
	pass	1♡	dbl
pass	2♣	2♡	2♠
all pass			

South suppressed his five-card major in favor of a takeout double. As a result, he went down in 2♠ when a club partial would have produced ten tricks.

At IMPs, with neither side vulnerable, you hold as South:

♠ K Q 6   ♡ 4 2   ◇ A 2   ♣ A Q 9 7 4 2

WEST	NORTH	EAST	SOUTH
			1♣
1♡	1♠	2♡	?

Bid 3♣. If East-West compete to 3♡, you can bid 3♠ and play 3♠ or 4♣. If you raise spades now, you may miss a better spot in clubs.

Again at IMPs, with neither side vulnerable, you hold as South:

WEST	NORTH	EAST	SOUTH
			1♣
pass	1♠	dbl	?

♠ A Q 3   ♡ 9 6   ◇ K 2   ♣ K Q 10 9 4 2

Bid 2♣, planning to support spades later.

You're East, playing for the U.S. in a Bermuda Bowl. East-West are vulnerable, and you hold

♠ J 10 7 5   ♡ Q J 9 7   ◇ Q 7   ♣ Q J 2

WEST	NORTH	EAST	SOUTH
	pass	pass	1♡
dbl	pass	?	

What do you say now?

Bid 1NT. You may have a 4-4 spade fit, but 1NT may be a good contract (look at all those 'quacks'), and if North-South compete, you can introduce the spades later. The full deal:

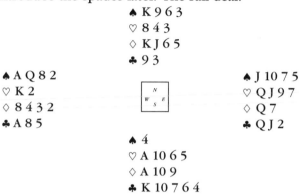

```
                    ♠ K 9 6 3
                    ♡ 8 4 3
                    ◇ K J 6 5
                    ♣ 9 3
   ♠ A Q 8 2                         ♠ J 10 7 5
   ♡ K 2                             ♡ Q J 9 7
   ◇ 8 4 3 2          N              ◇ Q 7
   ♣ A 8 5         W       E         ♣ Q J 2
                      S
                    ♠ 4
                    ♡ A 10 6 5
                    ◇ A 10 9
                    ♣ K 10 7 6 4
```

WEST	NORTH	EAST	SOUTH
	pass	pass	1♡
dbl	pass	1♠	2♣
pass	pass	2NT	all pass

The U.S. East could have survived by bidding 2♠ over 2♣ but unwisely branched out into notrump. He went down in 2NT, losing IMPs, when 2♠ would have made. East mistimed his bids: 1NT first, then 2♠ would let him play in either 2♠ or 2NT.

TIP 7

SUPPORT YOUR PARTNER

You're East, playing for the U.S. in a Bermuda Bowl. Neither side is vulnerable, and you hold

♠ Q J 10 5   ♡ 10 9   ◇ A Q J 5   ♣ Q J 2

WEST	NORTH	EAST	SOUTH
	pass	1◇	2♡
2♠	4♡	?	

What do you say here?

Bid 4♠. Your opening bid wasn't the strongest; but since you've opened, it won't help to suppress your fit for spades. The U.S. East actually passed and wound up regretting it. The full deal:

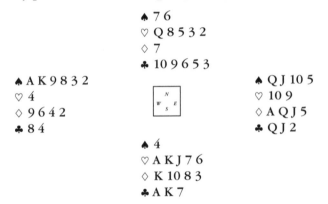

```
                    ♠ 7 6
                    ♡ Q 8 5 3 2
                    ◇ 7
                    ♣ 10 9 6 5 3
♠ A K 9 8 3 2                        ♠ Q J 10 5
♡ 4                 N                ♡ 10 9
◇ 9 6 4 2        W     E             ◇ A Q J 5
♣ 8 4               S                ♣ Q J 2
                    ♠ 4
                    ♡ A K J 7 6
                    ◇ K 10 8 3
                    ♣ A K 7
```

WEST	NORTH	EAST	SOUTH
	pass	1◇	2♡
2♠	4♡	pass	pass
4♠	5♡	5♠	dbl
all pass			

If East had bid 4♠, he could have doubled 5♡, presumably for +100. (That was the result in the other room, where East supported spades early.) But after East passed and heard West bid 4♠ and North try 5♡, he belatedly showed his support at the five-level and took a minus.

Somehow, it never turns out well to suppress a fit for your partner — no matter whether you have extra values, a minimum or a dog.

Dlr: South
Vul: Both

	♠ Q 5 2	
	♡ K 9 6 2	
	◇ 9 5 4	
	♣ 9 8 2	

♠ 4 3		♠ 10 9 8 6
♡ J 3		♡ 10 8
◇ A Q J 2		◇ K 8 6
♣ K Q 10 5 4		♣ J 7 6 3

	♠ A K J 7	
	♡ A Q 7 5 4	
	◇ 10 7 3	
	♣ A	

WEST	NORTH	EAST	SOUTH
			1♡
2♣	pass	pass	dbl
pass	2♡	all pass	

After North passed over 2♣, North-South never got on track. At the other table, North raised directly to 2♡, and South bid 4♡, making five.

A 'free raise' has no special significance. Show a fit even with minimum high-card strength; otherwise, competition may stop you from ever showing your support.

Dlr: South
Vul: N-S

	♠ 9 7 2	
	♡ A 10 7 5 2	
	◇ A 4	
	♣ J 10 4	

♠ K J 8 6		♠ A Q 10 5 3
♡ J 9 3		♡ 6 4
◇ 6 2		◇ Q J 9 8
♣ 7 6 5 2		♣ K 8

	♠ 4	
	♡ K Q 8	
	◇ K 10 7 5 3	
	♣ A Q 9 3	

WEST	NORTH	EAST	SOUTH
			1◇
pass	1♡	1♠	2♣
3♠	all pass		

East was happy to be -100 in 3♠, since North-South could take twelve tricks in hearts. South should have supported with 2♡ (or used a conventional support double) while he could.

Playing IMPs, neither side vulnerable:

WEST	NORTH	EAST	SOUTH
			1♢
pass	1♡	2♠	?

South holds

♠ 7 6   ♡ K J 5 4   ♢ A K Q 4   ♣ J 5 4

If East had passed or bid 1♠, South would bid 2♡. He must stretch to bid 3♡ here; he can't afford to lose the fit. North must allow for South to have minimum values (see Tip 3, this section).

In a Bermuda Bowl. . .

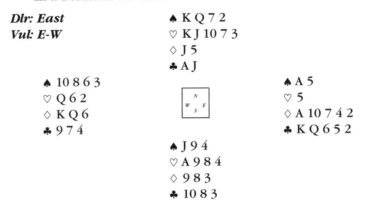

Dlr: East
Vul: E-W

North:
♠ K Q 7 2
♡ K J 10 7 3
♢ J 5
♣ A J

West:
♠ 10 8 6 3
♡ Q 6 2
♢ K Q 6
♣ 9 7 4

East:
♠ A 5
♡ 5
♢ A 10 7 4 2
♣ K Q 6 5 2

South:
♠ J 9 4
♡ A 9 8 4
♢ 9 8 3
♣ 10 8 3

WEST	NORTH	EAST	SOUTH
		1♢	pass
1♠	2♡	3♣	all pass

South thought he was too weak to raise hearts; but 3♣ made four; and at the other table, North-South were +140 in 3♡.

At IMPs, neither side vulnerable, you hold as South:

♠ K 10 6   ♡ 8 6   ♢ A Q 9 3   ♣ 10 7 4 2

WEST	NORTH	EAST	SOUTH
	1♠	2♢	?

What do you say?

Bid 2♠. It's wrong to go head-hunting for a penalty before you delve into the chances for game in spades. The full deal:

$\spadesuit$ A Q J 9 3
$\heartsuit$ A K 2
$\diamond$ 2
$\clubsuit$ Q J 9 3

$\spadesuit$ 7 5 4 2
$\heartsuit$ Q 10 7 5 4
$\diamond$ 8 5
$\clubsuit$ 8 5

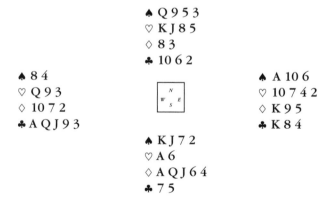

$\spadesuit$ 8
$\heartsuit$ J 9 3
$\diamond$ K J 10 7 6 4
$\clubsuit$ A K 6

$\spadesuit$ K 10 6
$\heartsuit$ 8 6
$\diamond$ A Q 9 3
$\clubsuit$ 10 7 4 2

WEST	NORTH	EAST	SOUTH
	1$\spadesuit$	2$\diamond$	dbl
all pass			

Perfect defense (three rounds of hearts, South ruffing, a spade to North's ace and a trump shift) would have beaten 2$\diamond$ doubled two; but East actually got out for down one. At the other table, where South raised to 2$\spadesuit$ over 2$\diamond$, North bid 4$\spadesuit$ and made it.

Matchpoints, neither side vulnerable, and South opens 1$\diamond$. As West, you hold

$\spadesuit$ 8 4 $\heartsuit$ Q 9 3 $\diamond$ 10 7 2 $\clubsuit$ A Q J 9 3

Do you act?

The actual West tried 2$\clubsuit$. The full deal:

$\spadesuit$ Q 9 5 3
$\heartsuit$ K J 8 5
$\diamond$ 8 3
$\clubsuit$ 10 6 2

$\spadesuit$ 8 4
$\heartsuit$ Q 9 3
$\diamond$ 10 7 2
$\clubsuit$ A Q J 9 3

$\spadesuit$ A 10 6
$\heartsuit$ 10 7 4 2
$\diamond$ K 9 5
$\clubsuit$ K 8 4

$\spadesuit$ K J 7 2
$\heartsuit$ A 6
$\diamond$ A Q J 6 4
$\clubsuit$ 7 5

WHEN YOU OVERCALL, WEIGH WHAT YOU HAVE TO GAIN AND TO LOSE

WEST	NORTH	EAST	SOUTH
			1$\diamond$
2$\clubsuit$	pass	2NT	all pass

South led a spade, and East went down two; but East-West got a good score for -100 since North-South could make a big spade partial. West's overcall was dangerous but had something to gain: a 2♣ overcall of a 1◇ opening has obstructive value.

Overcall with a goal in mind. It may be preemption, lead direction, the prospect of competing for the partscore, finding a save or looking for game. But an overcall with no clear purpose can help only the opponents. Playing IMPs, neither side vulnerable, East deals and opens 1♣. South should pass with

♠ K 5   ♡ K 5 4   ◇ K J 6 3 2   ♣ 6 3 2

A 1◇ overcall isn't preemptive or lead-directing. North-South aren't likely to have a game, South can't expect to compete successfully and doesn't want to encourage a save. If South acts, he may get doubled or give away information the opponents can use.

If you're willing to overcall light, the degree of preemption is a major factor. A 2♡ overcall of 1♠ consumes space, as does 1♠ over 1♣. Other overcalls, however, suggest soundness: 2♣ over 1♠ isn't preemptive, and the club suit offers little hope of competing for the partscore, much less of making game.

Never forget that intervention can help the opponents. I was playing on OKbridge when my partner and I held these cards:

♠ 7 6 4
♡ K J 2   [N W E S]   ♠ 3
◇ K 5   ♡ A 10 6 4
♣ A K 9 7 5   ◇ A Q 7
           ♣ Q J 10 3 2

WEST	NORTH	EAST	SOUTH
1♣	1♠	dbl	2♠
pass	pass	3♠	pass
4♡	pass	5♣	pass
6♣	all pass		

My partner, West, knew from the North-South bidding that I had a spade control and useful values. He made a fine bid of 6♣.

Featherweight overcalls may do nothing but steer the opponents to a good contract. In a Bermuda Bowl...

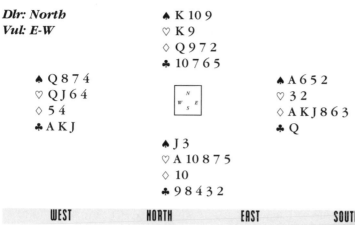

Dlr: North
Vul: E-W

North: ♠ K 10 9 ♡ K 9 ◇ Q 9 7 2 ♣ 10 7 6 5

West: ♠ Q 8 7 4 ♡ Q J 6 4 ◇ 5 4 ♣ A K J

East: ♠ A 6 5 2 ♡ 3 2 ◇ A K J 8 6 3 ♣ Q

South: ♠ J 3 ♡ A 10 8 7 5 ◇ 10 ♣ 9 8 4 3 2

WEST	NORTH	EAST	SOUTH
	pass	1◇	1♡(!)
3NT	all pass		

After the 1♡ overcall, West didn't bother to look for a spade fit; he blasted into 3NT. North led the ♡K — South's light overcall did the defense no good — and West had no trouble making his game. However, 4♠ could have been beaten.

An obvious drawback to a light overcall is the danger of a penalty. In an Olympiad final ...

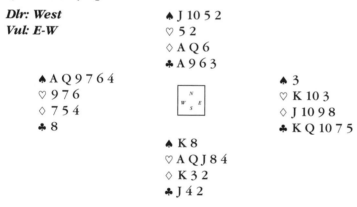

Dlr: West
Vul: E-W

North: ♠ J 10 5 2 ♡ 5 2 ◇ A Q 6 ♣ A 9 6 3

West: ♠ A Q 9 7 6 4 ♡ 9 7 6 ◇ 7 5 4 ♣ 8

East: ♠ 3 ♡ K 10 3 ◇ J 10 9 8 ♣ K Q 10 7 5

South: ♠ K 8 ♡ A Q J 8 4 ◇ K 3 2 ♣ J 4 2

WEST	NORTH	EAST	SOUTH
pass	pass	pass	1♡
1♠	dbl	1NT	pass
pass	dbl	2♣	pass
pass	dbl	all pass	

East's 2♣ doubled went down three. What did West think he had to gain by bidding?

At IMPs, both sides vulnerable, you hold as South:

♠ K Q 10 2 ♡ 10 3 ◇ A K J 10 3 ♣ Q 5

The dealer, on your right, opens 1♠. Do you act?

Nobody can say for sure whether overcalling with — or despite — length in the opening bidder's suit is a winning tactic. The actual South was an optimist: he tried 2◊, suspecting that North didn't have many spades and hence had some diamonds.

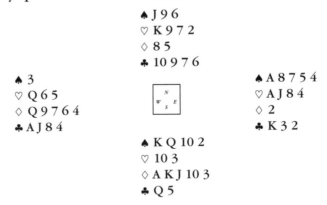

                    ♠ J 9 6
                    ♡ K 9 7 2
                    ◊ 8 5
                    ♣ 10 9 7 6

♠ 3   ♠ A 8 7 5 4
♡ Q 6 5   ♡ A J 8 4
◊ Q 9 7 6 4   ◊ 2
♣ A J 8 4   ♣ K 3 2

                    ♠ K Q 10 2
                    ♡ 10 3
                    ◊ A K J 10 3
                    ♣ Q 5

WEST	NORTH	EAST	SOUTH
		1♠	2◊
pass	pass	dbl	all pass

They picked declarer clean: spade to the ace, spade ruff, heart to the jack, spade ruff, ♡A, spade ruff with the ◊9. West cashed the ♣A and led a club to East's king; and when East led his last spade, South couldn't shut out West's ◊Q. Down four.

If the West and North hands had been reversed, North would indeed have been short in spades, long in diamonds. Well, suppose they are:

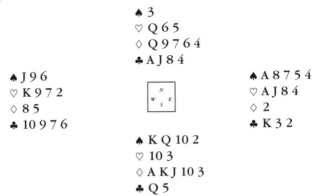

                    ♠ 3
                    ♡ Q 6 5
                    ◊ Q 9 7 6 4
                    ♣ A J 8 4

♠ J 9 6   ♠ A 8 7 5 4
♡ K 9 7 2   ♡ A J 8 4
◊ 8 5   ◊ 2
♣ 10 9 7 6   ♣ K 3 2

                    ♠ K Q 10 2
                    ♡ 10 3
                    ◊ A K J 10 3
                    ♣ Q 5

South finds his diamond fit if he bids but loses nothing if he passes. West would pass also, and North would balance with a double. North-South would probably land in a diamond or notrump partscore for a modest plus. In any case, no -1100. If South overcalls 2◊ on those cards, he has much to lose but nebulous prospect of gain. Sit me South, and I'm a passer.*

At IMPs, your prospects for game are a factor in the decision to enter the auction. In a U.S. Team Trials, Edgar Kaplan overcalled a 1♠ opening with 2♡, vulnerable, on

♠ K 8 3   ♡ A J 9 6 5   ◊ Q 5   ♣ A 9 8.

Kaplan wrote that he hated to overcall but felt passing was more dangerous. He weighed the risk — the ragged suit — against his high cards and controls and judged that the chance of game justified taking action. But if you hold

♠ A 9 5   ♡ A 7 3   ◊ K 10 8 6 3   ♣ Q 5,

a 2◊ overcall is unattractive. Game in diamonds is less likely, and the threat of disaster is real.

What about overcalls for a lead? On some deals, you'll become the opening leader yourself. On others, partner's lead will be clearly indicated, so he may lead the right suit without help; sometimes the lead will not matter. A lead-directing overcall misfired here:

Dlr: West	♠ A 4
Vul: N-S	♡ A K 5 2
	◊ 4 3
	♣ Q 8 7 4 3

```
          ♠ A 4
          ♡ A K 5 2
          ◊ 4 3
          ♣ Q 8 7 4 3
♠ J 8 5 3              ♠ Q 10
♡ 9 8 7        N       ♡ Q J 10 6 4
◊ A 6 5      W   E     ◊ 10 9
♣ J 10 9       S       ♣ A 6 5 2
          ♠ K 9 7 6 2
          ♡ 3
          ◊ K Q J 8 7 2
          ♣ K
```

*When I wrote about this deal in the OKbridge *Spectator*, some readers argued for a 1NT overcall; they contended that 1NT is safer, may make and aims toward the most likely game. It wouldn't occur to me to bid 1NT with skimpy high-card values, the wrong pattern and no stopper in two suits. It seems to me that a 1NT overcall ignores a bidding principle: any action, but especially a competitive action, can have long-term consequences. If you overcall 1NT, you may occasionally snatch a plus there when you were headed for a minus, but the auction will seldom end in 1NT. Will partner stay out of 3NT with

♠ J 9 3   ♡ A K 5 4   ◊ Q 4 2   ♣ 6 4 2

or avoid 4♡ with

♠ 4   ♡ A 9 7 5 4 2   ◊ 8 6   ♣ K J 4 2

At IMPs, he might blast into game with even less; after all, he thinks you'll have tenaces behind the opening bidder and expects the play to be easy when the location of most of the missing honors is known. Surely a pass is the soundest action over 1♠.

North opened 1♣, and East overcalled 1♡ for the lead. After North-South reached 4♠, West duly led a heart. Away went South's ♣K on a high heart. South then took the ace and king of spades, knocked out the ◇A and claimed when diamonds split 3-2. If you overcall strictly for the lead, you'd better be right!

You're playing IMPs, East-West vulnerable; East deals and opens 1◇. Would you act as South with:

♠ K 8 7 3 2   ♡ 8   ◇ A J 10 5 2   ♣ 10 9

Bid 1♠. It's not safe to overcall, but it's not safe to pass at favorable vulnerability with so much offensive potential. The full deal may be

♠ Q J 6 5
♡ 6 3 2
◇ 9 4
♣ A K J 3

♠ 10 4		♠ A 9
♡ A K Q 10 9 7 4	N W E S	♡ J 5
◇ 8 6		◇ K Q 7 3
♣ 7 5		♣ Q 10 8 6 2

♠ K 8 7 3 2
♡ 8
◇ A J 10 5 2
♣ 9 4

WEST	NORTH	EAST	SOUTH
		1◇	1♠
2♡	4♣	dbl	pass
pass	4♠	pass	pass
dbl	all pass		

It turns out that 4♠ doubled makes for +590. I'm biased in favor of sound overcalls, but not blind: if you always wait for sound values, you'll occasionally miss a good save or a distributional game.

You're West, playing for the U.S. in a Bermuda Bowl match against Argentina, neither side vulnerable.

♠ J 3   ♡ 7 4 3 2   ◇ K Q 9 4 3   ♣ A 2

WEST	NORTH	EAST	SOUTH
	1♡	pass	1♠
?			

BEWARE THE 'DEATH SEAT'

Would you act?

Pass, pass, pass. But the U.S. player chose a 2◇ overcall and caused an embarrassing disaster.

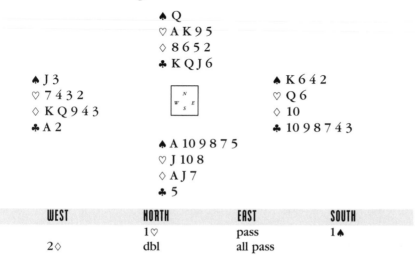

```
                    ♠ Q
                    ♡ A K 9 5
                    ◇ 8 6 5 2
                    ♣ K Q J 6
  ♠ J 3                              ♠ K 6 4 2
  ♡ 7 4 3 2          N               ♡ Q 6
  ◇ K Q 9 4 3      W   E             ◇ 10
  ♣ A 2              S               ♣ 10 9 8 7 4 3
                    ♠ A 10 9 8 7 5
                    ♡ J 10 8
                    ◇ A J 7
                    ♣ 5
```

WEST	NORTH	EAST	SOUTH
	1♡	pass	1♠
2◇	dbl	all pass	

North led the ♡K and shifted to the ♠Q: king, ace. West took the club shift with the ace and tried to cash the ♠J, which was ruffed. North cashed a club, on which South threw a heart, took the ♡A and led a third heart. South overruffed dummy's ◇10 with the jack and led the ♠10, winning as West pitched a heart. West ruffed the next spade with the ◇Q and led the ◇9 to South's ace. Another spade promoted a trump for North for down five.

A player who has heard an opening bid on his left and an unlimited response on his right sits in the 'death seat'. The opening bidder's hand is unknown — he may have strength — and responder may have a good hand. To act is now more dangerous and entering the auction has less to gain. On an auction such as

WEST	NORTH	EAST	SOUTH
1♡	pass	1♠	

East-West already know whether they have a trump fit in either major. If South bids, say, 2♣, he won't obstruct the opponents and is unlikely to buy the contract.

The 2◇ doubled deal took place in 1961. You'd think players would learn, but fifteen years later, another U.S. Bermuda Bowler stuck out his neck in almost the same position.

Dlr: East
Vul: Both

	♠ A K Q 6 4 2	
	♡ 10	
	◇ 7 6	
	♣ J 9 7 2	
♠ J 9 5 3		♠ 8
♡ A 6 2		♡ 9 8 5 4
◇ 10 5 4		◇ A Q 9 8 3
♣ 10 8 4		♣ K Q 3
	♠ 10 7	
	♡ K Q J 7 3	
	◇ K J 2	
	♣ A 6 5	

WEST	NORTH	EAST	SOUTH
		pass	1♡
pass	1♠	2◇	dbl
all pass			

Dummy produced three trumps and an ace, so East went down only two, -500. At the other table, East opened 1◇, not the soundest opening bid, but safer than passing and then overcalling in the death seat. North-South reached 4♠, down one.

Dlr: West
Vul: N-S

	♠ 7 3	
	♡ 6 4 3	
	◇ 9 5 4 3	
	♣ 10 9 5 3	
♠ Q 8 2		♠ K 10 9 6 4
♡ A Q 10 7 2		♡ 9 8
◇ A Q 10		◇ 7 6 2
♣ 4 2		♣ A Q 8
	♠ A J 5	
	♡ K J 5	
	◇ K J 8	
	♣ K J 7 6	

WEST	NORTH	EAST	SOUTH
1♡	pass	1♠	1NT
dbl	all pass		

BECOMING A BRIDGE EXPERT

South counted his 17 points and climbed in with 1NT. Since West had a good opening lead and knew his A-Q's lay behind South's kings, he doubled, and the massacre was on.

The defense was good. West led the ♠2 to East's king, and South took the ace and tried the ♣K. East won and led the ♠10, winning, and then a heart: jack, queen. West next cashed the ♠Q and the ◇A. When East signaled low, West led a club; and East won, ran the spades and led another heart. Down six! South's bid was foolhardy; he could gain a little or lose a lot. If he passes quietly, East-West may stop in 2♠ for +170 points, not +1700.

As South, playing in a U.S. Team Trials, you hold

♠ A Q 10 6 5 ♡ J 6 3 ◇ 10 4 ♣ A K J

West opens 1◇, North passes, East responds 1♡. Both sides are vulnerable. Would you act?

If you'd overcall 1♠, you're in the vast majority (which includes me, I suppose). But even harmless-looking overcalls can come to grief in the death seat. A world champion tried 1♠; West had four good spades and a good hand, and the penalty was 500. Beware!

Let's see how you feel about preemption. At IMPs, neither vulnerable, you deal as West, and hold

♠ 8 4 ♡ K Q J 10 5 ◇ J 3 ♣ 10 6 3 2

What do you say?

Pass. Resist the temptation to open an unsound weak two-bid when your partner is yet to speak. The actual West opened 2♡, and East jumped to 3NT on

♠ K 7 3 ♡ A 9 3 ◇ A K 6 2 ♣ Q J 4

He got a spade lead and was ready to claim nine tricks — until the dummy appeared with no sixth heart.

Many experts have adopted a random, destructive preemptive style. I believe in sticking to the textbook. If you open 3◇ on

♠ 4 ♡ 8 5 ◇ K J 10 8 6 5 3 ♣ J 10 7

your preempt is descriptive as well as obstructive, and your partner can make an informed competitive decision. If you might have

♠ J 6 4 ♡ 8 ◇ K 10 7 5 4 3 ♣ 10 7 6

you'll give the opponents problems occasionally, but your partner will be a non-participant.

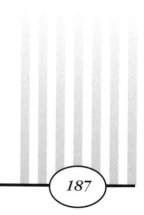

PREEMPT SENSIBLY

I watched a pair of former world champions — and they really are that good — on OKbridge, playing IMPs against a pair that was good but not expert. The champs seemed to be advocates of the modern style: preempt first, worry about it later.

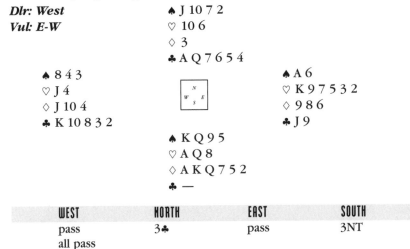

Dlr: West
Vul: E-W

```
                    ♠ J 10 7 2
                    ♡ 10 6
                    ◇ 3
                    ♣ A Q 7 6 5 4
♠ 8 4 3                             ♠ A 6
♡ J 4                               ♡ K 9 7 5 3 2
◇ J 10 4                            ◇ 9 8 6
♣ K 10 8 3 2                        ♣ J 9
                    ♠ K Q 9 5
                    ♡ A Q 8
                    ◇ A K Q 7 5 2
                    ♣ —
```

WEST	NORTH	EAST	SOUTH
pass	3♣	pass	3NT
all pass			

If I had to construct a North hand not to preempt on, that might have been it: six broken clubs, a trick and a half on defense and four spades to two honors. Moreover, one opponent had passed. But then I'm a curmudgeon. I expected South to force with 3◇; but in North-South's system, a new-suit response wasn't forcing, so South had to bid what he thought he might make. West led the ◇J, and South contrived to lose three tricks for +430; but 6♠ would have a been a good spot and would have made easily.

Next...

Dlr: West
Vul: N-S

```
                    ♠ K
                    ♡ J 8 6
                    ◇ Q 10 7 6 5 4 2
                    ♣ 9 5
♠ Q 9 7 6 4                         ♠ 10 8 5 3 2
♡ K 4                               ♡ A 9 7
◇ J 8                               ◇ A 9
♣ A Q 10 4                          ♣ 8 6 2
                    ♠ A J
                    ♡ Q 10 5 3 2
                    ◇ K 3
                    ♣ K J 7 3
```

WEST	NORTH	EAST	SOUTH
pass	3◇	pass	3NT
all pass			

BECOMING A BRIDGE EXPERT

North's 3◇ at unfavorable vulnerability is an eye-blinker. South guessed — I emphasize 'guessed' — to try 3NT, reasonably enough, but the dummy wasn't what he'd hoped for. The defense was thoroughly confused but still beat the contract one (it seems down six was more likely).

Watching these deals made me wonder: why do some experts feel compelled to turn bridge into a lottery? I can understand a loose preemptive style in a one-session pair game — but at IMPs, when a 51% game is a winner, and one has teammates to account to. What are our top players afraid of? Don't they have enough self-esteem to believe they can outclass their opposition through steady, flawless effort?

Another preemptive woe involves lack of discipline: preempting, then bidding again. The literature is full of deals where a player saved after the opponents had bid game or slam under pressure. Such actions invariably come to grief. In a Spingold. . .

Dlr: West
Vul: Both

	♠ J 10 7	
	♡ A J 7	
	◇ Q 9 8 6 2	
	♣ Q 9	

♠ Q 2		♠ K 9 8 6 5 4
♡ 10 5 3 2		♡ Q
◇ K J 3		◇ 10 4
♣ 10 7 5 3		♣ A 8 6 4

	♠ A 3	
	♡ K 9 8 6 4	
	◇ A 7 5	
	♣ K J 2	

WEST	NORTH	EAST	SOUTH
pass	pass	2♠	dbl
3♠	dbl	pass	4♡
pass	pass	4♠	dbl
all pass			

East's 4♠ doubled went down 800 when 4♡ was going down at least one. East should have passed; he had good defense, and the enemy auction to 4♡ had been anything but comfortable.

In another Spingold. . .

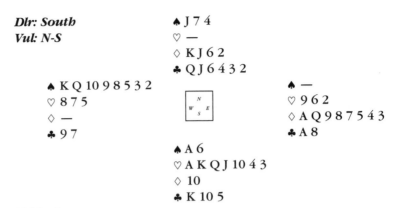

Dlr: South
Vul: N-S

North:
♠ J 7 4
♡ —
◇ K J 6 2
♣ Q J 6 4 3 2

West:
♠ K Q 10 9 8 5 3 2
♡ 8 7 5
◇ —
♣ 9 7

East:
♠ —
♡ 9 6 2
◇ A Q 9 8 7 5 4 3
♣ A 8

South:
♠ A 6
♡ A K Q J 10 4 3
◇ 10
♣ K 10 5

Table 1

WEST	NORTH	EAST	SOUTH
			1♡
4♠	pass	pass	5♡
pass	pass	dbl	all pass

Table 2

WEST	NORTH	EAST	SOUTH
			1♡
4♠	dbl	pass	6♡
6♠(!)	dbl	all pass	

At the first table, 5♡ doubled went down two. In the replay, West's bid of 6♠, which went down four doubled, was too horrible for words.

Back to undisciplined preemption. In a U.S. Team Trials final …

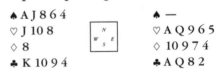

West:
♠ A J 8 6 4
♡ J 10 8
◇ 8
♣ K 10 9 4

East:
♠ —
♡ A Q 9 6 5
◇ 10 9 7 4
♣ A Q 8 2

WEST	NORTH	EAST	SOUTH
			pass
2◇ [1]	pass	2♠	all pass

1. Usually a weak two-bid in a major.

At the other table, East-West unimaginatively bid 4♡ and made an overtrick. If West's 'weak two-bid' is what bridge is coming to, you can include me out.

You're East, playing for the U.S. in a Bermuda Bowl, East-West vulnerable. You hold:

BECOMING A BRIDGE EXPERT

♠ A 7 4 ♡ K Q J 10 7 6 4 3 ◇ — ♣ K 3

North, playing Precision, deals and opens 1♣, strong. What do you say?

Assume you jump to 4♡. South bids 4♠, and there are two passes. What do you say now?

```
                    ♠ 5 3
                    ♡ A
                    ◇ A Q J 8 2
                    ♣ A Q J 8 6
    ♠ K 10 2                           ♠ A 7 4
    ♡ 8              ┌─────┐           ♡ K Q J 10 7 6 4 3
    ◇ 9 7 4 3        │ N   │           ◇ —
    ♣ 10 9 7 5 2     │W   E│           ♣ K 3
                     │  S  │
                     └─────┘
                    ♠ Q J 9 8 6
                    ♡ 9 5 2
                    ◇ K 10 6 5
                    ♣ 4
```

WEST	NORTH	EAST	SOUTH
	1♣[1]	4♡	4♠
pass	pass	5♡	dbl
all pass			

1. Strong.

East's 4♡ preempt with thirteen high-card points and controls in all four suits wouldn't have been everyone's choice. His 5♡, after South had been obliged to stab at 4♠, was more questionable. As it was, 5♡ doubled went down 500, and 4♠ would have failed.

As it happened, the U.S. still gained on the deal. At the other table, North-South were +550 in 5◇ doubled.

TIP 11

DON'T SELL OUT TOO SOON

IMPs, neither side vulnerable. West deals and opens 1♡, and there are two passes. What do you say as South with each of these hands?

1)
a) ♠ K Q 10 7 6
♡ 8 7 6
◊ K 5
♣ 7 6 5

b) ♠ K Q 10 7
♡ 5 4
◊ A 7 6
♣ J 6 5 4

c) ♠ K 7 4
♡ A 10 4
◊ Q 10 6 5
♣ K 5 3

d) ♠ K Q 10 6 5
♡ A 5
◊ K 7 6
♣ A 9 4

IMPs, neither side vulnerable. East deals and opens 1♡, you pass, West raises to 2♡ and there are two passes. What do you say as South with each of these hands?

2)
a) ♠ K J 9 7 6
♡ 8 7 6
◊ K 5
♣ 7 6 5

b) ♠ K Q 10 7
♡ 5 4
◊ A 7 6
♣ J 6 5 4

c) ♠ A 4
♡ 6
◊ J 10 8 6 5
♣ K J 9 6 4

d) ♠ 7 6
♡ K Q J 10 8
◊ A K 5
♣ J 6 5

SOLUTIONS

1)
a) 1♠
b) Double
c) 1NT
d) Double

In these examples, South can assume North has some points, else East-West would still be bidding. To stop East-West from buying the deal for a song, South must stretch to act. Balancing overcalls and doubles may be based on shaded values. In (d), South would overcall 1♠ in the direct position; in the balancing seat, he must double before bidding his suit to suggest a sound hand.

2)
a) 2♠
b) Double
c) 2NT[1]
d) Pass

1.   (Unusual, length in both minors)

Since East-West have found a fit but have stopped low, South can expect points from North, and North-South are also likely to have a fit somewhere. South's action on (c) is risky, but to sell out at the two-level is losing tactics. On (d), South would like to say "I double for penalty"; but since the Laws of Bridge don't allow that call, he must go quietly.

When the opponents find a fit but advertise limited values, don't sell out: back in and fight for the partscore. This is a typical balancing deal from a U.S. Team Trials.

BECOMING A BRIDGE EXPERT

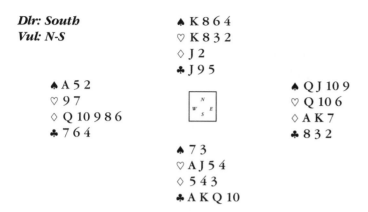

Dlr: South
Vul: N-S

```
                    ♠ K 8 6 4
                    ♡ K 8 3 2
                    ◇ J 2
                    ♣ J 9 5
♠ A 5 2                              ♠ Q J 10 9
♡ 9 7                                ♡ Q 10 6
◇ Q 10 9 8 6                         ◇ A K 7
♣ 7 6 4                              ♣ 8 3 2
                    ♠ 7 3
                    ♡ A J 5 4
                    ◇ 5 4 3
                    ♣ A K Q 10
```

WEST	NORTH	EAST	SOUTH
			1♣
pass	1♡	pass	2♡
pass	pass	2♠	all pass

East went down two, -100, but his action gained 2 IMPs when North-South played 2♡, +170, at the other table.

Balancing decisions can be nerve-racking, but 'When in doubt, act' is a sound approach. You'll give the opponents the last guess, and you'll enjoy declarer's advantage if they let you have the contract: more pitfalls loom on defense than in dummy play.

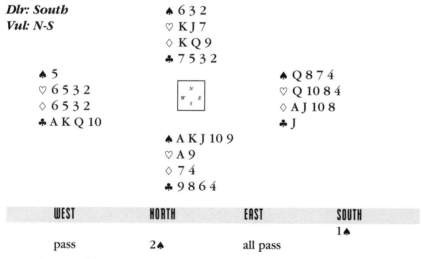

Dlr: South
Vul: N-S

```
                    ♠ 6 3 2
                    ♡ K J 7
                    ◇ K Q 9
                    ♣ 7 5 3 2
♠ 5                                  ♠ Q 8 7 4
♡ 6 5 3 2                            ♡ Q 10 8 4
◇ 6 5 3 2                            ◇ A J 10 8
♣ A K Q 10                           ♣ J
                    ♠ A K J 10 9
                    ♡ A 9
                    ◇ 7 4
                    ♣ 9 8 6 4
```

WEST	NORTH	EAST	SOUTH
			1♠
pass	2♠	all pass	

West couldn't act over 1♠; but when North-South stopped in 2♠, West should have balanced with a double: East might have made 3♡. Against 2♠, West cashed four club tricks. East let go a diamond, a heart and another heart. West then led a diamond to the king and ace, and East returned the jack to dummy's queen. South finessed with the ♠J, led a heart to the king, drew trumps with another finesse and claimed. West's timid pass shouldn't have cost much, since 2♠ can be defeated. On the clubs, East must discard three diamonds, baring his ace. If West leads a diamond next, East wins and leads a heart. South takes the jack and finesses in trumps but can't get back for another trump finesse.

An apparent misfit should discourage you from balancing. In a U.S. Team Trials ...

Dlr: South
Vul: N-S

```
                    ♠ 8 4
                    ♡ 6 3
                    ◇ A Q 9 7 3
                    ♣ 9 8 6 3
  ♠ J 7                              ♠ A 9 5 3 2
  ♡ J 10 5 2          N              ♡ K 4
  ◇ K J 5 2        W     E           ◇ 10 8 4
  ♣ Q J 5             S              ♣ A 10 2
                    ♠ K Q 10 6
                    ♡ A Q 9 8 7
                    ◇ 6
                    ♣ K 7 4
```

WEST	NORTH	EAST	SOUTH
			1♡
pass	1NT	pass	2♣
pass	2♡	2♠	dbl
all pass			

East's 2♠ was a 'pre-balance', as it's called; he judged that South was about to pass. But East's ♡K was under the gun, and North's 2♡ preference didn't confirm true heart support, only a tolerance. South led the ♡A, which softened the blow a little; but East was still down two, -300.

Not all balancing actions are low-level. Here's a remarkable deal from the 1968 Olympiad final, U.S. vs. Italy:

Dlr: East
Vul: E-W

```
                    ♠ K Q 7 2
                    ♡ K J 8 5 4 3 2
                    ◇ 7
                    ♣ 2
  ♠ 8 6 4 3                          ♠ —
  ♡ 10               N               ♡ Q 6
  ◇ A K 6 3       W     E            ◇ J 10 9 5 4 2
  ♣ A Q 9 8          S               ♣ K 10 7 6 5
                    ♠ A J 10 9 5
                    ♡ A 9 7
                    ◇ Q 8
                    ♣ J 4 3
```

BECOMING A BRIDGE EXPERT

WEST	NORTH	EAST	SOUTH
		pass	1♠
pass	4NT	pass	5♡
pass	5♠	all pass	

After North-South for Italy blasted to the five-level, the U.S. West thought for a long time before passing. He suspected East had a spade void, length in at least one minor and a few values. Sure enough, the winning action was to balance with 5NT, since 5♠ was cold, and East-West were cold for 6◇ (or 7◇ if South led the ♠A!).

Would you balance on this next deal? At IMPs, neither side vulnerable, you hold as South:

♠ Q 6   ♡ 6   ◇ A Q 8 7 5   ♣ K 8 6 4 3

WEST	NORTH	EAST	SOUTH
1♠	pass	pass	?

Balancing is unattractive. One reason is that you have no good action: if you bid one minor, you may belong in the other. A second reason is that the opponents could have a heart fit and may even be cold for game; hence balancing has much to lose.

Whatever you do, don't punish your partner for balancing. You must realize that he has bid your cards.

Dlr: South
Vul: Both

♠ A Q J 5 2
♡ J 6 2
◇ Q 7
♣ Q 10 8

♠ 9 8 6 3		♠ 10 7 4
♡ 10 5		♡ K Q 9 4 3
◇ A J 9 4		◇ –
♣ A 6 3		♣ K J 9 7 2

♠ K
♡ A 8 7
◇ K 10 8 6 5 3 2
♣ 5 4

WEST	NORTH	EAST	SOUTH
			pass
pass	1♠	pass	2◇
pass	pass	2♡	3◇
dbl	all pass		

In a major U.S. team event West led the ♡10. South took the ace, cashed three spades to discard clubs, ruffed a club and led the ◇10, limiting West to two trump tricks. Result: +670 to North-South. West must have thought his double was a sure thing; but East's balancing 2♡ didn't promise a defensive trick, and the double told South how to play the trumps.

How about this one? At IMPs, East-West vulnerable, playing in a U.S. Team Trials, you hold as East:

♠ K 10 5 4　♡ A 2　◇ 7 5 3 2　♣ A 8 5

WEST	NORTH	EAST	SOUTH
			pass
pass	1◇	pass	1♡
pass	2◇	pass	pass
2♠	3◇	?	

What do you say now?

Bid 4♠. If ever there was a time to 'hang' partner for balancing, it's now. He backed in on an auction that didn't suggest balancing (North-South haven't confirmed a fit) and is likely to have at most one diamond. The hands fit well, and a vulnerable game is at stake. Bobby Goldman actually did leap to 4♠. The full deal:

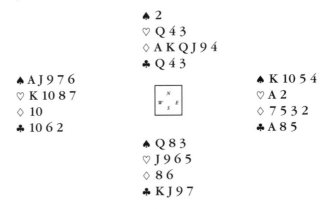

West ruffed the second diamond, ducked a club, won the club return and crossruffed for ten tricks.

You are playing IMPs, neither side vulnerable, and you hold as South:

♠ K Q 10 9 8 5 3 ♡ – ◇ Q 10 5 4 ♣ 4 3

WEST	NORTH	EAST	SOUTH
			3♠
dbl	pass	4♡	?

What do you say?

You might have opened 4♠; but now the only issue is that your partner is in the better position to judge. Pass. If North also passes, trust him to have made a reasonable decision. The full deal may be

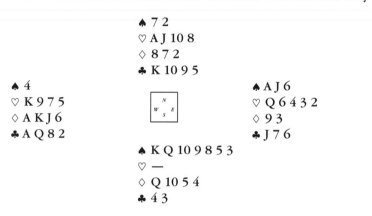

♠ 7 2
♡ A J 10 8
◇ 8 7 2
♣ K 10 9 5

♠ 4   ♠ A J 6
♡ K 9 7 5   ♡ Q 6 4 3 2
◇ A K J 6   ◇ 9 3
♣ A Q 8 2   ♣ J 7 6

♠ K Q 10 9 8 5 3
♡ —
◇ Q 10 5 4
♣ 4 3

On this layout, both 4♡ and 4♠ are going down.

If you're driving on a winding two-lane road, 'Do Not Pass' is good advice. 'Trust Your Partner' is the best advice at bridge, but many players are guilty of masterminding: they refuse to defer to partner and let him use his judgment.

WEST	NORTH	EAST	SOUTH
			1♠
pass	3♠[1]	4♡	?

1. Forcing.

Playing IMPs, with neither side vulnerable, South should pass with

♠ K Q 8 6 2 ♡ 7 6 ◇ A Q 4 ♣ K J 4

If North doubles 4♡, South should be happy to play for the penalty.

In partscore competitive auctions, leave the last say to partner when you have no clear action.

WEST	NORTH	EAST	SOUTH
	1♠	dbl	2♠
pass	pass	3◇	?

At IMPs, neither side vulnerable, South had a normal raise and has a routine pass with

♠ Q 10 6   ♡ A 8 5 2   ◇ 9 8   ♣ J 7 4 2

But with

♠ Q 10 6 4   ♡ A 8 5 2   ◇ 9 8   ♣ Q 7 5

South has four trumps and sound values; he would consider bidding 3♠ in front of his partner.

In a Bermuda Bowl match ...

Dlr: West
Vul: None

```
                    ♠ Q 10 6 2
                    ♡ Q J 7 6
                    ◇ 10 9 8
                    ♣ Q 4
   ♠ K 7 4 3                          ♠ J
   ♡ 9 3 2              N             ♡ A K 10 8 4
   ◇ A K 3 2        W       E         ◇ Q J 7
   ♣ 7 6                S             ♣ J 8 3 2
                    ♠ A 9 8 5
                    ♡ 5
                    ◇ 6 5 4
                    ♣ A K 10 9 5
```

WEST	NORTH	EAST	SOUTH
pass	pass	1♡	dbl
pass	1♠	pass	pass
2♡	2♠	3♡	3♠
dbl	all pass		

North-South's 3♠ went down one doubled, and East-West went down one in 3♡ at the other table. South erred by charging on with 3♠ after North had pushed East-West to the three-level. Since North was marked with length in hearts, he could better assess the chances of going plus on defense.

As that deal shows, when the opponents compete, the player with length in their suit can usually make better competitive decisions. It's the same at higher levels.

Dlr: East
Vul: E-W

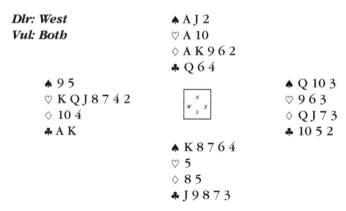

North: ♠ J 7 2 ♡ Q 3 ◇ A 10 8 7 6 2 ♣ K Q

West: ♠ K Q 6 5 ♡ 9 8 5 2 ◇ K J 5 3 ♣ 4

East: ♠ 9 ♡ A K 10 7 6 4 ◇ 9 4 ♣ A J 8 2

South: ♠ A 10 8 4 3 ♡ J ◇ Q ♣ 10 9 7 6 5 3

WEST	NORTH	EAST	SOUTH
		1♡	1♠
3♡	4♠	5♡	pass
pass	dbl	all pass	

East's 5♡ doubled went down one; but he could have passed over 4♠, and West would have doubled for +300 at least. If instead West had:

$$♠ \ 865 \quad ♡ \ QJ52 \quad ◇ \ A852 \quad ♣ \ K4$$

he would bid 5♡ himself.

In a U.S. Women's Team Trials ...

Dlr: West
Vul: Both

North: ♠ A J 2 ♡ A 10 ◇ A K 9 6 2 ♣ Q 6 4

West: ♠ 9 5 ♡ K Q J 8 7 4 2 ◇ 10 4 ♣ A K

East: ♠ Q 10 3 ♡ 9 6 3 ◇ Q J 7 3 ♣ 10 5 2

South: ♠ K 8 7 6 4 ♡ 5 ◇ 8 5 ♣ J 9 8 7 3

Table 1

WEST	NORTH	EAST	SOUTH
4♣[1]	pass	4◇[2]	pass
4♡	dbl	all pass	

1. Good 4♡ opening.
2. Relay to 4♡.

Table 2

WEST	NORTH	EAST	SOUTH
4♡	dbl	pass	4♠
pass	pass	5♡	5♠
dbl	all pass		

At the first table, 4♡ doubled went down two for +500, a reasonable result for North-South, after South guessed to pass instead of bidding 4♠ on slim values. In the replay, South unwisely pushed on to the five-level in front of partner despite those same values. Of course, 5♠ went down.

Now try this example. You're East, North-South vulnerable, with

♠ A 8 6 ♡ Q 9 8 ◇ 3 2 ♣ Q 10 8 5 3

WEST	NORTH	EAST	SOUTH
1♠	pass	2♠	dbl
pass	3♡	?	

What do you say?

Pass. Since you have only three-card spade support and a possible defensive trick in hearts, let West decide. If he's willing to defend, so are you. The full deal:

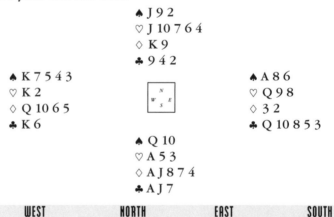

```
                    ♠ J 9 2
                    ♡ J 10 7 6 4
                    ◇ K 9
                    ♣ 9 4 2
    ♠ K 7 5 4 3                    ♠ A 8 6
    ♡ K 2              N           ♡ Q 9 8
    ◇ Q 10 6 5     W     E         ◇ 3 2
    ♣ K 6              S           ♣ Q 10 8 5 3
                    ♠ Q 10
                    ♡ A 5 3
                    ◇ A J 8 7 4
                    ♣ A J 7
```

WEST	NORTH	EAST	SOUTH
1♠	pass	2♠	dbl
pass	3♡	3♠	all pass

West's 3♠ went down one, while 3♡ would have been down at least one. It looks like East muffed a routine decision, but even world-class players can lose their hold on discipline: the deal is from a Bermuda Bowl final!

You're West, playing in a Spingold final. With North-South vulnerable, you hold

♠ 9 4 2   ♡ 9 8 7 6   ◇ Q 8 3   ♣ A K 8

WEST	NORTH	EAST	SOUTH
pass	pass	1♡	1♠
3♡	3♠	4♡	4♠
?			

What do you say now?

Pass, don't double. An expert South who bids game at this vulnerability, after both you and East have suggested strength, knows something about the distribution you don't. The full deal was

	♠ Q 6 3	
	♡ 10 5 4 2	
	◇ A J 10 7 4	
	♣ 9	

♠ 9 4 2		♠ 5
♡ 9 8 7 6		♡ A K Q J 3
◇ Q 8 3		◇ K 9 2
♣ A K 8		♣ J 7 3 2

	♠ A K J 10 8 7	
	♡ —	
	◇ 6 5	
	♣ Q 10 6 5 4	

WEST	NORTH	EAST	SOUTH
pass	pass	1♡	1♠
3♡	3♠	4♡	4♠
dbl	all pass		

West led a heart, which was ruffed. South gave up a club, won the trump return, ruffed a club, ruffed a heart and ruffed another club, setting up his clubs. He lost one diamond, making five, for +990.

The other West did a little better:

WEST	NORTH	EAST	SOUTH
pass	pass	1♡	3♠
4♡	4♠	pass	pass
dbl	all pass		

This West led a trump, so South went after the diamonds and took six spade tricks and four diamonds. Making four, +790. Both Wests, incidentally, were world champions.

Many losing penalty doubles are based on the speculation that the opponents don't know what they're doing. That is a poor basis for doubling capable players.

Dlr: East
Vul: Both

```
                     ♠ J 10 6 2
                     ♡ Q J 9 5
                     ◇ A K J 9 6
                     ♣ —
    ♠ 7                            ♠ A K
    ♡ 10 2              N          ♡ K 8 7 6
    ◇ Q 8 7 5 2     W     E        ◇ 10 4 3
    ♣ K Q J 9 6        S           ♣ A 10 8 3
                     ♠ Q 9 8 5 4 3
                     ♡ A 4 3
                     ◇ —
                     ♣ 7 5 4 2
```

WEST	NORTH	EAST	SOUTH
		1♡	1♠
dbl	4♠	dbl	all pass

Making five; and at the other table:

WEST	NORTH	EAST	SOUTH
		1NT[1]	pass
2♠[2]	pass	2NT	pass
3♣[3]	dbl	pass	4♠
pass	pass	dbl	all pass

1. 12-14 HCP.
2. Transfer to 2NT.
3. Mildly encouraging, presumably.

Making five again for a push. North-South knew they lacked the top trumps when they bid game, so East's double was an insult.

It is a mistake to double the only contract you are confident of defeating. Consider this auction, at IMPs, neither side vulnerable:

WEST	NORTH	EAST	SOUTH
	1♡	2♣	?

Even if his double would be for penalty, South should pass with

♠ 7 6   ♡ J 5   ◇ 7 5 4   ♣ Q J 9 7 5 3.

East might fail in 2♣ doubled, but if East-West run, South lacks the high-card values to defend against another contract.

Opponents seem to bid a lot at favorable vulnerability. Still, that doesn't compel you to double without trump tricks or a stack in one of their key suits. In a Bermuda Bowl final …

Dlr: East
Vul: N-S

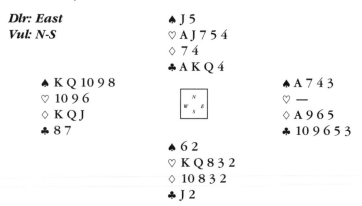

```
                    ♠ J 5
                    ♡ A J 7 5 4
                    ◇ 7 4
                    ♣ A K Q 4
  ♠ K Q 10 9 8                        ♠ A 7 4 3
  ♡ 10 9 6          ┌─────────┐       ♡ —
  ◇ K Q J          │ N       │        ◇ A 9 6 5
  ♣ 8 7            │ W     E │        ♣ 10 9 6 5 3
                   │    S    │
                   └─────────┘
                    ♠ 6 2
                    ♡ K Q 8 3 2
                    ◇ 10 8 3 2
                    ♣ J 2
```

Table 1

WEST	NORTH	EAST	SOUTH
		pass	pass
2♠	dbl	4♠	pass
pass	dbl	pass	5♡
pass	pass	5♠	dbl
all pass			

Table 2

WEST	NORTH	EAST	SOUTH
		pass	pass
2♠	dbl	4♠	dbl
all pass			

At the first table North mistakenly thought East-West were stealing and doubled twice despite sub-minimum values. That induced South to double 5♠ for -650. In the replay, it's a mystery how South expected to beat 4♠ doubled. West made five again, for +690.

If your opponents reach 3NT with skinny high-card values, they'll often have a long suit to make up the difference. A defender with discarding problems may fall victim to a squeeze or endplay.

Dlr: North
Vul: Both

```
                    ♠ J 2
                    ♡ K 9 3
                    ◊ Q 6
                    ♣ A Q J 10 7 2
    ♠ 8 6                             ♠ A K 10 9 5 3
    ♡ 8 7 5 2          N              ♡ A Q J
    ◊ 7 5 4 3       W     E           ◊ K J 9
    ♣ 6 5 3            S              ♣ 4
                    ♠ Q 7 4
                    ♡ 10 6 4
                    ◊ A 10 8 2
                    ♣ K 9 8
```

WEST	NORTH	EAST	SOUTH
	1♣	dbl	1NT
pass	2♣	2♠	2NT
pass	3NT	dbl	all pass

West led a spade, and East established his suit; but South then ran the clubs. When East kept a good spade and the guarded ◊K, blanking the ♡A, South led a low heart from dummy next, setting up the king for his ninth trick. Despite East's massive hand, 3NT was unbeatable.

Lead-directing doubles of fourth-suit bids are not without risk. In a Vanderbilt semifinal, South held

♠ A J 7   ♡ K 9 8   ◊ K Q 8 5   ♣ 8 6 3

WEST	NORTH	EAST	SOUTH
1♠	pass	2♡	pass
3♣	pass	3◊	?

South doubled, but East had 0-6-5-2 distribution, and the ♡AQ and diamond support turned up in dummy. Making five!

It's also risky to pass a low-level negative or responsive double. This is a unilateral and dangerous action.

Dlr: North
Vul: None

```
                    ♠ A 10 9 4 3
                    ♡ Q
                    ◇ J 10 2
                    ♣ A J 5 3
  ♠ K J 8                             ♠ Q 6 5 2
  ♡ 7 6              N                ♡ A J 10 8
  ◇ K 8 7 5 4      W   E              ◇ A Q 6
  ♣ K 4 2            S                ♣ 9 7
                    ♠ 7
                    ♡ K 9 5 4 3 2
                    ◇ 9 3
                    ♣ Q 10 8 6
```

WEST	NORTH	EAST	SOUTH
	pass	1NT	2♡
dbl[1]	all pass		

1.   Negative.

East's pass with three trump tricks looked reasonable, and West certainly had his values. But South had shape, and dummy had a fit for his second suit. Result: +470 to North-South.

Try this next example yourself. At IMPs, neither side vulnerable, you hold as West:

♠ K Q 4 ♡ J 8 5 ◇ 10 8 6 5 ♣ J 8 2

WEST	NORTH	EAST	SOUTH
		pass	1◇
pass	1♡	pass	1♠
pass	3♣	pass	4♣
pass	4♠	pass	5◇
pass	5♡	pass	6♠
?			

At this point, South flashes his hand, and you see the ♠A. Do you double?

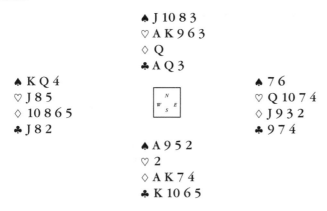

```
                    ♠ J 10 8 3
                    ♡ A K 9 6 3
                    ◇ Q
                    ♣ A Q 3
  ♠ K Q 4                             ♠ 7 6
  ♡ J 8 5             N               ♡ Q 10 7 4
  ◇ 10 8 6 5        W   E             ◇ J 9 3 2
  ♣ J 8 2             S               ♣ 9 7 4
                    ♠ A 9 5 2
                    ♡ 2
                    ◇ A K 7 4
                    ♣ K 10 6 5
```

The worst doubles are those that help declarer make a contract that would fail undoubled. If you double, South won't double-finesse in trumps and may adopt this line: club opening lead to the ten, two more high clubs, ◊Q, ♡A, ♡K, heart ruff, ◊A, ◊K, diamond ruff. With three cards left, declarer lets the ♠J ride, and West is endplayed. West's double stands to gain 50 points; it may cost more than 1000 points. Those aren't good odds.

TIP 14

MAKE INFEREN-TIAL PENALTY DOUBLES

Playing IMPs, neither side vulnerable, you hold as East:

♠ A J 9 7   ♡ 9 2   ◊ 9 4   ♣ K J 10 5 2

WEST	NORTH	EAST	SOUTH
	1♣	pass	1♡
pass	1♠	pass	1NT
pass	2NT	pass	3NT
pass	pass	?	

What do you do now?

Double. The chance of multiple undertricks is ten times greater than the chance 3NT will make. North-South had a labored auction to game and have no extra high-card strength; you know that no suit will break well for them. The full deal may be

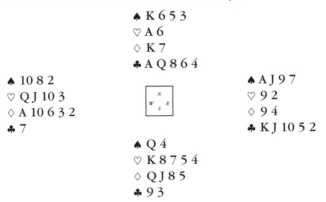

<pre>
                    ♠ K 6 5 3
                    ♡ A 6
                    ◊ K 7
                    ♣ A Q 8 6 4
    ♠ 10 8 2   ♠ A J 9 7
    ♡ Q J 10 3   N   ♡ 9 2
    ◊ A 10 6 3 2   W   E   ◊ 9 4
    ♣ 7   S   ♣ K J 10 5 2
                    ♠ Q 4
                    ♡ K 8 7 5 4
                    ◊ Q J 8 5
                    ♣ 9 3
</pre>

Since your double suggests strength in dummy's suits, West might start with a club opening lead; but only seven tricks are probable on any lead.

In the previous section, we saw players making speculative penalty doubles that backfired when declarer had better information. Good penalty doubles are based on a big surprise for declarer.

WEST	NORTH	EAST	SOUTH
		1♠	pass
2♠	pass	2NT	pass
3♣	pass	3♠	pass
4♠	pass	pass	?

South should double with

♠ Q J 10 8   ♡ J 10 9   ◇ 8 6 4 3   ♣ 7 3

East is hoping for no trump losers, and South knows he has two. South has a good opening lead, and the double may fool declarer into placing South with high cards that North holds.

On this auction:

WEST	NORTH	EAST	SOUTH
		1♡	pass
2◇	pass	3◇	pass
3♡	pass	4♡	?

South should double and lead a diamond with

♠ 10 9 7 3   ♡ A   ◇ J 8 6 5 3   ♣ A 8 5 3

He can expect to give North at least two diamond ruffs.

Players often strain to bid vulnerable games. When the cards lie well, they succeed; when the cards are foul, you can double and collect a number.

Dlr: South
Vul: Both

```
                    ♠ K 8 5 4 2
                    ♡ Q 7 5
                    ◇ Q 5 2
                    ♣ Q 6
  ♠ Q 6 3                            ♠ A J 9 7
  ♡ K 10 6 2          N             ♡ 9 8 4
  ◇ 9 6            W     E          ◇ 10 7 3
  ♣ J 8 7 2           S             ♣ A 9 3
                    ♠ 10
                    ♡ A J 3
                    ◇ A K J 8 4
                    ♣ K 10 5 4
```

WEST	NORTH	EAST	SOUTH
			1◇
pass	1♠	pass	2♣
pass	2◇	pass	2NT
pass	3NT	dbl	all pass

Since the auction marked East with spade length and strength and South with shortness, West led the ♠Q. The defense collected four spades, a heart and a club for +500. If East doesn't double, West will lead a heart, and South will at worst go down one undoubled.

Dlr: South
Vul: Both

```
                    ♠ A J 6 3
                    ♡ J 8 7 2
                    ◇ 8 7 4
                    ♣ Q 6
    ♠ 7                            ♠ Q 9 8 4
    ♡ K Q 9 5          N           ♡ 10 4
    ◇ K 10 6 3     W       E       ◇ J 9 2
    ♣ J 10 9 4         S           ♣ K 8 7 2
                    ♠ K 10 5 2
                    ♡ A 6 3
                    ◇ A Q 5
                    ♣ A 5 3
```

WEST	NORTH	EAST	SOUTH
			1NT
pass	2♣	pass	2♠
pass	3♠	pass	4♠
dbl	all pass		

West led the ♣J, and South went down three. All the conditions for a winning penalty double were present: West had a good opening lead and knew the trumps weren't breaking, and North-South had conducted a tentative auction to game.

Experts often try this kind of 'short-side' double, where the player without the trump stack doubles. In a U.S. Women's Team Trials...

Dlr: West
Vul: Both

```
                    ♠ A K 9
                    ♡ A Q 10 9 4
                    ◇ 10 6
                    ♣ K J 7
    ♠ Q J 10 8 5                  ♠ 4
    ♡ —                N           ♡ J 6 5 3 2
    ◇ A K 9 8 3    W       E       ◇ 7 5 4
    ♣ Q 10 9           S           ♣ 8 6 4 3
                    ♠ 7 6 3 2
                    ♡ K 8 7
                    ◇ Q J 2
                    ♣ A 5 2
```

WEST	NORTH	EAST	SOUTH
1♠	2♡	pass	4♡
pass	pass	dbl	all pass

Tipped off by the questionable double, North won the ♠A at trick one and ran the ♡10 through East, picking up the suit. The club finesse was good for the tenth trick and +790.

At another table, however, the auction was

WEST	NORTH	EAST	SOUTH
1♠	dbl	pass	2♡
3◇	4♡	pass	pass
dbl!	all pass		

Here a short-side double fooled declarer, who did not take a first-round heart finesse against East and lost her contract.

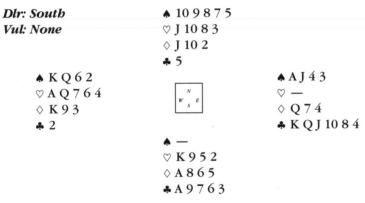

Dlr: South
Vul: None

```
              ♠ 10 9 8 7 5
              ♡ J 10 8 3
              ◇ J 10 2
              ♣ 5
♠ K Q 6 2                      ♠ A J 4 3
♡ A Q 7 6 4       N            ♡ —
◇ K 9 3        W     E         ◇ Q 7 4
♣ 2               S            ♣ K Q J 10 8 4
              ♠ —
              ♡ K 9 5 2
              ◇ A 8 6 5
              ♣ A 9 7 6 3
```

WEST	NORTH	EAST	SOUTH
			pass
1♡	pass	2♣	pass
2♡	pass	2♠	pass
3♠	pass	4♠	dbl
all pass			

South doubled because he had good defensive values and knew North had long trumps. South also got off to a good opening lead — a tricky ♡9 — and East went down two after he played dummy's ace.

Now try this one yourself. You're East, playing in an IMP Pairs event. With East-West vulnerable, you hold

♠ Q J 8 6 3　♡ 10 9　◇ —　♣ K J 8 5 4 2

WEST	NORTH	EAST	SOUTH
			2♡
pass	4NT	pass	5♣
pass	5♡	?	

What do you say now?

Double. West has a couple of aces, and you'll have a chance for a diamond ruff, especially if you double to alert him. The full deal:

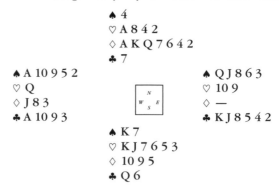

```
                      ♠ 4
                      ♡ A 8 4 2
                      ◇ A K Q 7 6 4 2
                      ♣ 7
    ♠ A 10 9 5 2                          ♠ Q J 8 6 3
    ♡ Q                                   ♡ 10 9
    ◇ J 8 3                               ◇ —
    ♣ A 10 9 3                            ♣ K J 8 5 4 2
                      ♠ K 7
                      ♡ K J 7 6 5 3
                      ◇ 10 9 5
                      ♣ Q 6
```

West led the ♣A, East signaled with the deuce and West shifted to a diamond. East ruffed and put partner in with the ♠A for another ruff; down two. Yes, your best call over 5♡ was 6♠! It's cold. But +300 against 5♡ doubled still gets you a good result.

TIP 15

DIRECT THE DEFENSE

You are East, playing IMPs, and North-South are vulnerable. You hold

♠ 8 5   ♡ Q J 10 9 8 5 3 2   ◇ J 8 4   ♣ —

WEST	NORTH	EAST	SOUTH
			1♣
pass	1◇	4♡	4♠
6♡	6♠	?	

What do you do now?

East judged to save at 7♡, a questionable move since North-South had been forced to guess; but the auction didn't end. South passed, and North tried 7♠. The full deal:

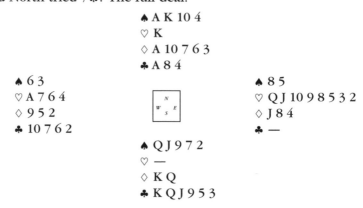

```
                      ♠ A K 10 4
                      ♡ K
                      ◇ A 10 7 6 3
                      ♣ A 8 4
    ♠ 6 3                                 ♠ 8 5
    ♡ A 7 6 4                             ♡ Q J 10 9 8 5 3 2
    ◇ 9 5 2                               ◇ J 8 4
    ♣ 10 7 6 2                            ♣ —
                      ♠ Q J 9 7 2
                      ♡ —
                      ◇ K Q
                      ♣ K Q J 9 5 3
```

WEST	NORTH	EAST	SOUTH
			1♣
pass	1♢	4♡	4♠
6♡	6♠	7♡	pass
pass	7♠	dbl	all pass

East's double asked for an unusual opening lead. West knew enough not to lead the ♡A but unfortunately tried a diamond. South claimed for +2470. If East was going to save over 6♠, he could have tried 7♣ on the way. North-South would collect only 1100 points against 7♡ doubled; and if they bid 7♠, West would know what to do.

Good players have the presence of mind to make lead-directing bids that will guide partner to the best defense. I can recall the first time I found a lead-director that worked; it was in a major knockout event.

Dlr: North
Vul: E-W

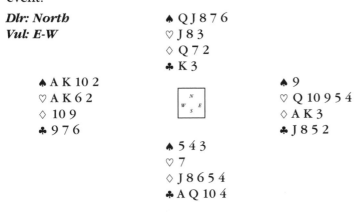

```
              ♠ Q J 8 7 6
              ♡ J 8 3
              ♢ Q 7 2
              ♣ K 3
♠ A K 10 2                    ♠ 9
♡ A K 6 2                     ♡ Q 10 9 5 4
♢ 10 9          N             ♢ A K 3
♣ 9 7 6       W   E           ♣ J 8 5 2
                S
              ♠ 5 4 3
              ♡ 7
              ♢ J 8 6 5 4
              ♣ A Q 10 4
```

WEST	NORTH	EAST	SOUTH
	pass	pass	pass
1♡	1♠	2♠	3♣
pass	pass	4♡	all pass

After my 3♣ bid, North led the ♣K and another club. On the fourth round of clubs, declarer misguessed by ruffing high and cashing the ♡KQ. Down one.

Suppose as South, with neither side vulnerable at IMPs, you hold

♠ A 7 3   ♡ 9 7 6 4 2   ♢ 4   ♣ K J 9 4

WEST	NORTH	EAST	SOUTH
1♠	3♣	3♠	?

West is about to bid 4♠. You know 5♣ will be a good save, but you can set up the defense against 5♠, if they push on, by bidding 4♢ now. Partner will lead a diamond against 5♠; and when you take the ♠A, you can hope to put him in with the ♣A to get a diamond ruff.

(It helps if your partner knows you're capable of making bids such as this.)

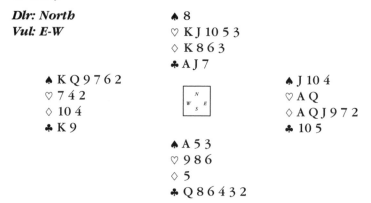

Dlr: North
Vul: E-W

North
♠ 8
♡ K J 10 5 3
♢ K 8 6 3
♣ A J 7

West
♠ K Q 9 7 6 2
♡ 7 4 2
♢ 10 4
♣ K 9

East
♠ J 10 4
♡ A Q
♢ A Q J 9 7 2
♣ 10 5

South
♠ A 5 3
♡ 9 8 6
♢ 5
♣ Q 8 6 4 3 2

WEST	NORTH	EAST	SOUTH
	1♡	2♢	2♡
2♠	pass	3♠	4♢
4♠	all pass		

South's lead-directing 4♢ worked like magic. When North led a diamond, West guessed well to finesse; but when he led a trump next, South won, led a club to North, ruffed the next diamond and cashed the ♣Q for the setting trick.

At matchpoints, every trick counts. Lynn Deas found a good lead-directing bid in a major pairs event at the 1999 Fall NABC.

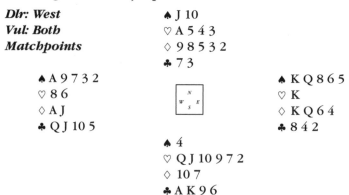

Dlr: West
Vul: Both
Matchpoints

North
♠ J 10
♡ A 5 4 3
♢ 9 8 5 3 2
♣ 7 3

West
♠ A 9 7 3 2
♡ 8 6
♢ A J
♣ Q J 10 5

East
♠ K Q 8 6 5
♡ K
♢ K Q 6 4
♣ 8 4 2

South
♠ 4
♡ Q J 10 9 7 2
♢ 10 7
♣ A K 9 6

West opened 1♠, and East responded 2NT, an artificial forcing spade raise. Deas, South, bid 3♣! East-West proceeded to their spade game, but North now led the ♣7. The resulting ruff held West to nine tricks and gave North-South a fine matchpoint result.

At IMPs, with neither side vulnerable, you hold as South:

♠ 9 5   ♡ 10 8 6 3 2   ◇ K J 9 2   ♣ 9 7

WEST	NORTH	EAST	SOUTH
1♠	dbl	redbl	?

What do you say?

Since partner is marked short in spades, East-West probably have you outgunned. Nine times out of ten, you'll end up defending a spade contract. Bid 2◇ to get partner off to a good opening lead. The full deal might be

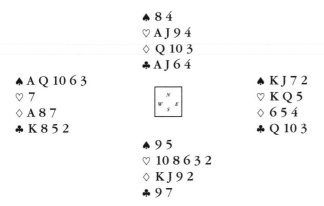

          ♠ 8 4
          ♡ A J 9 4
          ◇ Q 10 3
          ♣ A J 6 4

♠ A Q 10 6 3   ♠ K J 7 2
♡ 7   ♡ K Q 5
◇ A 8 7   ◇ 6 5 4
♣ K 8 5 2   ♣ Q 10 3

          ♠ 9 5
          ♡ 10 8 6 3 2
          ◇ K J 9 2
          ♣ 9 7

North might find the diamond lead on his own, but he'll appreciate your making it easy for him.

DEFENSE

④

Most authorities contend that defense is the hardest part of the game. It's true that a defender who neglects to count and doesn't think logically can run into trouble; but I'll try to show that good thought processes and a knowledge of basic principles are enough to defend most hands accurately.

TIP 1

OPENING LEADS: LET THE BIDDING GUIDE YOU

With both sides vulnerable, you're West. You have to lead from this sterling collection:

♠ 6 5 3   ♡ 7 4 2   ♢ 9 7 4 2   ♣ 6 5 3

WEST	NORTH	EAST	SOUTH
			1♢
pass	1♡	pass	1NT
pass	3NT	all pass	

What's your lead?

```
                    ♠ K J 8 4
                    ♡ A K 10 5
                    ♢ Q J 8
                    ♣ J 8
  ♠ 6 5 3                              ♠ 10 7 2
  ♡ 7 4 2          ┌─────┐             ♡ Q 8 3
  ♢ 9 7 4 2        │  N  │             ♢ A 5
  ♣ 6 5 3          │W   E│             ♣ K Q 10 4 2
                   │  S  │
                   └─────┘
                    ♠ A Q 9
                    ♡ J 9 6
                    ♢ K 10 6 3
                    ♣ A 9 7
```

The actual West chose a heart 'through dummy'. South took the ace, forced out the ♢A, won East's club switch and ran the spades and diamonds. At the end, South endplayed East and took eleven tricks.

Since West needs a miracle to beat 3NT, he must decide what miracle is most likely. West can assume East has a few high cards — and must also assume East has a long suit. If East has a decent hand and five spades, he might have bid 1♠ at his first turn; but East might be unwilling to risk bidding 2♣ even with fair values. If West leads a club, South takes no more than eight tricks.

To choose an opening lead, review the bidding, visualize the dummy and imagine how declarer will play the hand.

West should lead a heart from

WEST	NORTH	EAST	SOUTH
			1♠
pass	2♣	pass	2♠
pass	4♠	all pass	

♠ 6 5 3   ♡ K J 5   ♢ 10 9 8 3   ♣ K 5 3

Dummy will have a good hand with a club suit, and West can see that declarer may easily establish the clubs for discards. Since West needs fast tricks, he must make an aggressive lead.

♠ 6 5 3   ♡ K J 5   ◇ 10 9 8 3   ♣ K 5 3

WEST	NORTH	EAST	SOUTH
			1♠
pass	1NT	pass	2♣
pass	2♠	all pass	

Now West should lead the ◇ 10. Dummy will have skimpy values and may have a distribution such as 2-4-4-3. A safe, passive lead is in order.

♠ 6 5 3   ♡ K J 5   ◇ 10 9 8 3   ♣ K 5 3

WEST	NORTH	EAST	SOUTH
			1♠
pass	1NT	pass	2♣
all pass			

West should lead a trump. Dummy will have club support and usually a singleton spade. Since dummy may provide some spade ruffs but little else, the defense must try to stop the ruffs.

In this deal from a Bermuda Bowl, the winning lead would have saved more than 2000 points.

Dlr: South
Vul: None

```
                    ♠ 6
                    ♡ K Q 10 8 5 3
                    ◇ 2
                    ♣ J 9 6 3 2
  ♠ K Q J 10 9 2                      ♠ 8 5 3
  ♡ —                                 ♡ A 6
  ◇ K J 4             N               ◇ Q 10 7 3
  ♣ A K Q 4        W     E            ♣ 10 8 7 5
                     S
                    ♠ A 7 4
                    ♡ J 9 7 4 2
                    ◇ A 9 8 6 5
                    ♣ —
```

At one table, South for Argentina opened 1♡, West for North America cuebid 2♡ and North leaped to 5♡. East doubled, West passed and led a high club, and South crossruffed for twelve tricks, +750.

In the replay, with North America sitting North-South:

WEST	NORTH	EAST	SOUTH
			pass
2♠	3♡	3♠	4♡
5◇	6♣	pass	6♡
pass	pass	dbl	all pass

East led a spade, and North raced off twelve tricks for +1210. Since East had an ace and a queen, and West had promised great strength, North-South had to be bidding on distribution. If East leads the ace and another trump, he holds North to five trumps in his hand, three club ruffs in dummy, the ◇A, a long diamond and the ♠A. Down one.

At the Fall 1999 NABC in Boston, Mark Itabashi found a good opening lead by listening to the bidding.

Dlr: East
Vul: Both

	♠ A K Q 3	
	♡ A K J 4	
	◇ A 4	
	♣ J 10 5	
♠ 7 4		♠ J 5
♡ 7		♡ 10 6 5 3 2
◇ 10 9 5 3		◇ J 8 6 2
♣ A 8 6 4 3 2		♣ K 9
	♠ 10 9 8 6 2	
	♡ Q 9 8	
	◇ K Q 7	
	♣ Q 7	

WEST	NORTH	EAST	SOUTH
		pass	pass
3♣	dbl	pass	4♠
pass	5♠	all pass	

The auction painted Itabashi a clear picture of the North-South hands. He figured North had a solid hand with losing clubs; North's 5♠ asked South to go to slam if he controlled the clubs. South hadn't obliged, so he also held club losers. Since it seemed neither North nor South had the ♣K, Itabashi tried a low club — and he found a magic lie of the cards. East took the king and had a club to return. Itabashi won and led a third club, and when dummy followed, East ruffed with the ♠J to beat the contract.

Try this one yourself. At IMPs, with both sides vulnerable, you hold as West:

♠ Q J 7 6 ♡ Q 8 7 ◇ A K 10 ♣ A Q 10

WEST	NORTH	EAST	SOUTH
1NT	pass	2♣	2◇
2♠	3◇	4♠	5◇
dbl	all pass		

What do you lead?

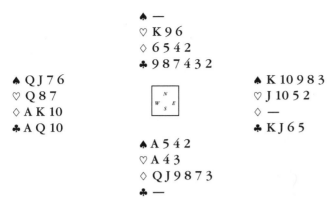

```
                          ♠ —
                          ♡ K 9 6
                          ◇ 6 5 4 2
                          ♣ 9 8 7 4 3 2
♠ Q J 7 6                                      ♠ K 10 9 8 3
♡ Q 8 7                    ┌─────┐             ♡ J 10 5 2
◇ A K 10                   │  N  │             ◇ —
♣ A Q 10                   │ W E │             ♣ K J 6 5
                           │  S  │
                           └─────┘
                          ♠ A 5 4 2
                          ♡ A 4 3
                          ◇ Q J 9 8 7 3
                          ♣ —
```

If you lead the ♠Q, you're -750. South discards a heart from dummy on the ♠A and crossruffs three spades and three clubs. He takes the ♡AK, ruffs a heart for his tenth trick and leads another club, ruffing with the ◇Q. You overruff but must give him the ◇J at the end. If instead you start correctly with the ◇K, as the bidding demands, you can continue with the ace and ten, and South goes down three!

Playing IMPs, both sides vulnerable, you hold as West:

♠ J 9 4 2   ♡ A 5 4 2   ◇ 7 4 3   ♣ 6 5

WEST	NORTH	EAST	SOUTH
	1◇	1♠	2♡
2♠	2NT	pass	3♡
pass	4♡	all pass	

What do you lead?

Since you have four trumps, a forcing defense may be effective; but after North has suggested spade strength, and South shortness, it's no time for fourth-best. Lead the ♠J through dummy.

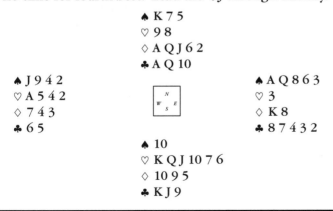

```
                          ♠ K 7 5
                          ♡ 9 8
                          ◇ A Q J 6 2
                          ♣ A Q 10
♠ J 9 4 2                                      ♠ A Q 8 6 3
♡ A 5 4 2                  ┌─────┐             ♡ 3
◇ 7 4 3                    │  N  │             ◇ K 8
♣ 6 5                      │ W E │             ♣ 8 7 4 3 2
                           │  S  │
                           └─────┘
                          ♠ 10
                          ♡ K Q J 10 7 6
                          ◇ 10 9 5
                          ♣ K J 9
```

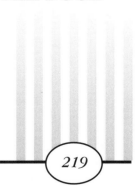

South ruffs the second spade and starts the trumps. You win the second trump and force with another spade. South must use up all his trumps to draw trumps, and East can cash spades when he gets in with the ◊K. If you start with the ♠2, the contract is unbeatable.

The table of preferred opening leads found in most texts is doubly worthless to any player past the novice stage. The taxing part of picking a lead is choosing a suit; and even then, picking which card to lead may require imagination. I seldom catch the New York Times syndrome on defense (the overwhelming desire to try for a brilliancy); but a few years ago on OKbridge I picked up as West

♠ Q 10 4 ♡ Q 10 9 6 5 2 ◊ 7 4 ♣ 8 3

WEST	NORTH	EAST	SOUTH
	1♣	pass	1◊
pass	1♠	pass	1NT
pass	3♣	pass	3NT
all pass			

Prospects looked desperate — the opponents surely had the material for nine tricks — so I tried a desperate lead: the ♠Q. It was my lucky day since the full deal was

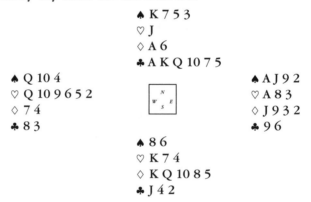

```
                    ♠ K 7 5 3
                    ♡ J
                    ◊ A 6
                    ♣ A K Q 10 7 5
♠ Q 10 4                            ♠ A J 9 2
♡ Q 10 9 6 5 2         N            ♡ A 8 3
◊ 7 4              W       E        ◊ J 9 3 2
♣ 8 3                 S             ♣ 9 6
                    ♠ 8 6
                    ♡ K 7 4
                    ◊ K Q 10 8 5
                    ♣ J 4 2
```

We took four spades and East's ♡A. The lead of the ♠10 would have been good enough, but the queen also catered to a singleton jack in South.

Most players have tried leading the king from Kx against a suit contract, hoping for a ruff, or the king from KJ109x against notrump, hoping to smother the bare queen in dummy. How about this situation?

```
                    ♠ K J 10 7 2
                    ♡ 8 4
                    ◇ 5 2
                    ♣ K J 9 6
♠ 8 5                                      ♠ A Q 6 3
♡ 10 6 5 2          ┌─────┐                ♡ 7 3
◇ K 10 7 6 3        │  N  │                ◇ A Q J 8 4
♣ 7 2               │ W E │                ♣ 5 4
                    │  S  │
                    └─────┘
                    ♠ 9 4
                    ♡ A K Q J 9
                    ◇ 9
                    ♣ A Q 10 8 3
```

WEST	NORTH	EAST	SOUTH
		1◇	1♡
3◇[1]	dbl[2]	pass	4♡
all pass			

1.   Preemptive.
2.   Responsive.

Since West could see he might never be on lead after the first
trick, he started with the king of diamonds. This lead might deceive
declarer or, more likely, let West stay on lead to make a helpful shift.
Sure enough, East signaled with the ◇Q, and West shifted to a spade.
East took the queen and ace and led a third spade, and South could-
n't shut out West's ♡10 and went down.

At IMPs, neither side vulnerable, you hold as West:

♠ J 7 3   ♡ A 9 4 2   ◇ 9 3   ♣ A J 8 2

WEST	NORTH	EAST	SOUTH
			1◇
pass	1♡	pass	1♠
pass	2◇	pass	2NT
pass	3NT	all pass	

What do you lead?

You're unlikely to beat this contract with the clubs, and since
North-South had a 'slow' auction to game and own little if any extra
strength, a club lead may give up a vital trick. South is marked short
in hearts, and if North has good hearts behind your ace, your chances
of success decrease toward zero. Lead the ♡A. The full deal might
be

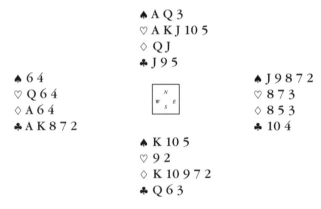

♠ A 6
♥ J 8 5 3
♦ K 6 5
♣ 7 6 5 4

♠ J 7 3
♥ A 9 4 2
♦ 9 3
♣ A J 8 2

♠ 9 8 4 2
♥ Q 10 7 6
♦ J 8 7
♣ Q 9

♠ K Q 10 5
♥ K
♦ A Q 10 4 2
♣ K 10 3

Don't be afraid to go against the book!

TIP 3

OPENING LEADS: WHEN YOUR PARTNER IS WEAK, ALL BETS ARE OFF

You are West, playing IMPs, with both sides vulnerable. You hold

♠ 6 4 ♥ Q 6 4 ♦ A 6 4 ♣ A K 8 7 2

WEST	NORTH	EAST	SOUTH
	1♥	pass	1NT
pass	3NT	all pass	

What do you lead?

A high club might be right since it's barely possible you can run the suit; but if you prefer to lead low, start with the deuce, not the fourth-highest seven.

♠ A Q 3
♥ A K J 10 5
♦ Q J
♣ J 9 5

♠ 6 4
♥ Q 6 4
♦ A 6 4
♣ A K 8 7 2

♠ J 9 8 7 2
♥ 8 7 3
♦ 8 5 3
♣ 10 4

♠ K 10 5
♥ 9 2
♦ K 10 9 7 2
♣ Q 6 3

If West leads the seven, South will fear that West has a five-card suit. Instead of forcing out the ♦A for nine tricks, South will finesse in hearts and win five hearts, three spades and a club. But if West leads the ♣2, South will start the diamonds next and go down.

When your partner will play no role in the defense, you can wage guerrilla warfare: you need not adhere to lead conventions that may put him in the picture — but may also help declarer.

WEST	NORTH	EAST	SOUTH
			1NT
pass	4NT	pass	6NT
all pass			

Since East is busted, West should lead the ♣10 from

♠ A 7 5   ♡ Q 10 6 5 3   ◇ 6 5   ♣ J 10 9

When your partner can have no strength, you can alter your opening leads for tactical reasons.

Dlr: South
Vul: None

```
                    ♠ Q
                    ♡ A 8 6 4
                    ◇ Q 5
                    ♣ A Q 10 5 4 2
♠ A J 10 9 4                          ♠ 7 3 2
♡ K J 3            N                   ♡ 10 9 7 2
◇ A 3 2         W     E                ◇ 8 4
♣ 8 6              S                   ♣ J 9 7 3
                    ♠ K 8 6 5
                    ♡ Q 5
                    ◇ K J 10 9 7 6
                    ♣ K
```

WEST	NORTH	EAST	SOUTH
			1◇
1♠	2♣	pass	2◇
pass	2♡	pass	2NT
pass	3NT	all pass	

West should lead the ♠A. He has no reason to lead the jack to preserve communication since East will never get in.

Dlr: North
Vul: Both

```
                    ♠ Q 9 3
                    ♡ A Q 9 5 4
                    ◇ A Q 6 4
                    ♣ K
♠ A K 2                               ♠ 7 4
♡ 7 2              N                   ♡ J 10 8 6
◇ K J 9 8 5     W     E                ◇ 7 2
♣ 9 6 4            S                   ♣ Q 8 7 5 2
                    ♠ J 10 8 6 5
                    ♡ K 3
                    ◇ 10 3
                    ♣ A J 10 3
```

WEST	NORTH	EAST	SOUTH
	1♡	pass	1♠
pass	2◇	pass	2♡
pass	2♠	pass	3NT
all pass			

North-South would have been better off in 4♠, but hindsight is always 20-20. North's bidding suggested extra strength, so West suspected dummy would have the ◇AQ. West therefore led the ◇J — a *surrounding* play on opening lead! South won with the queen and tried the spades, but West took the king and continued with the ◇K, forcing the ace and consigning South to defeat.

Both sides are vulnerable. The opponents bid 1NT-3NT, and as West, you hold

♠ J 9 7 2   ♡ A 9 7 2   ◇ A 10 8   ♣ A 4

What is your lead?

At the table, the winning lead was the ♡7. The full deal:

```
                   ♠ K 6 3
                   ♡ K J 3
                   ◇ Q 6 4
                   ♣ J 10 9 5
     ♠ J 9 7 2                        ♠ 8 4
     ♡ A 9 7 2          N             ♡ 10 8 6 5
     ◇ A 10 8       W       E         ◇ J 9 7 2
     ♣ A 4              S             ♣ 8 7 6
                   ♠ A Q 10 5
                   ♡ Q 4
                   ◇ K 5 3
                   ♣ K Q 3 2
```

South took the queen and forced out the ♣A, and West then led the ♡2, masquerading as a man with a five-card suit. South had eight tricks: three clubs, two hearts and three spades. He could force out the ◇A but would go down if West could then cash three hearts. So South instead tried the three top spades, hoping to drop the jack. When East showed out, South led a diamond — and West won and cashed two hearts and the ♠J to beat the contract.

Dlr: South
Vul: N-S

♠ K J 10 8 5
♡ K 9 5
◇ A J 3
♣ 7 3

♠ 9 7 4
♡ 7 3
◇ K 10 2
♣ A 9 8 5 4

WEST	NORTH	EAST	SOUTH
			1♡
pass	1♠	pass	2♡
pass	4♡	all pass	

West leads the ♣Q, and you take the ace. South plays low. What next?

If declarer has the ♠A and solid trumps, he'll take the rest; so East must assume West has a major-suit trick. To expect two from him, though, is unreasonable on the bidding; so besides the ♣A, the defense needs two tricks in diamonds. Since dummy's spades will provide diamond discards eventually, East must assume West has the ◇Q and shift promptly to a low diamond, hoping the full deal is something like

♠ K J 10 8 5
♡ K 9 5
◇ A J 3
♣ 7 3

♠ A 3 2
♡ 8 2
◇ Q 8 6 5
♣ Q J 10 2

♠ 9 7 4
♡ 7 3
◇ K 10 2
♣ A 9 8 5 4

♠ Q 6
♡ A Q J 10 6 4
◇ 9 7 4
♣ K 6

Defenders must make assumptions on every deal. Some may be based on evidence; others, though speculative, are necessary because the alternative is to concede that the contract is cold.

TIP 4

GIVE YOURSELF A CHANCE

Dlr: *South*
Vul: *N-S*

```
                        ♠ Q 5
                        ♡ 10 9 8 4 3
                        ◇ K Q 3
                        ♣ A J 2
     ♠ 10 8 4 2                              ♠ A 9 6 3
     ♡ A Q 2               N                 ♡ 7 6 5
     ◇ 10 7 4          W       E             ◇ 8 6 5
     ♣ K 10 9              S                 ♣ Q 4 3
                        ♠ K J 7
                        ♡ K J
                        ◇ A J 9 2
                        ♣ 8 7 6 5
```

WEST	NORTH	EAST	SOUTH
			1◇
pass	1♡	pass	1NT
pass	3NT	all pass	

West leads the ♠2, and East takes the ace and returns a spade. South wins with the queen in dummy and leads a heart to his jack and West's queen. West knows a spade continuation can win only four tricks for the defense; and since South must have the ♡K on the bidding, he can set up nine winners eventually. West must shift to the ♣10, assuming East has the queen. If South takes the ace, the defense has two hearts, two clubs and a spade; if South ducks, West can continue clubs or shift back to spades effectively.

You can't give yourself a chance if you forget how many tricks you need:

Dlr: *East*
Vul: *E-W*

```
                        ♠ Q 9 5 3
                        ♡ A Q
                        ◇ K J 10 6
                        ♣ Q 9 2
     ♠ 7 6 2                                 ♠ A 4
     ♡ K 9 6 4             N                 ♡ 10 7 5 3 2
     ◇ 8 7 5 4          W       E            ◇ A 2
     ♣ K 6                  S                ♣ A 5 4 3
                        ♠ K J 10 8
                        ♡ J 8
                        ◇ Q 9 3
                        ♣ J 10 8 7
```

WEST	NORTH	EAST	SOUTH
		1♡	pass
2♡	dbl	pass	2♠
all pass			

BECOMING A BRIDGE EXPERT

Against 2♠, West found the good lead of the ♣K, but when East won the next club, he gave West a club ruff immediately. The defense got the ♠A and ◇A, but South made his contract. East could count six defensive tricks if West had the ♠K; but if he had the ♡K instead, only a diamond ruff would beat the contract. Since East had the ♠A, he could wait to give West a ruff; East should lead the ◇A at the third trick, then another diamond. When he took the ♠A, he could give West a club ruff and get a diamond ruff in return.

Dlr: North
Vul: N-S

```
                  ♠ A K J 9 3
                  ♡ 5
                  ◇ 10 8 6 3
                  ♣ A K 3
  ♠ 10 7 6                        ♠ 8 5 2
  ♡ J 10 8 7 4        N           ♡ A 9 3
  ◇ Q 7           W       E       ◇ A K J 2
  ♣ 9 5 2             S           ♣ J 7 6
                  ♠ Q 4
                  ♡ K Q 6 2
                  ◇ 9 5 4
                  ♣ Q 10 8 4
```

WEST	NORTH	EAST	SOUTH
	1♠	pass	1NT
pass	2◇	pass	2NT
pass	3NT	all pass	

West leads the ♡J. East knows he can't run the hearts: West can't have ♡KJ108x, since then South would have only eight points, and his bidding promises nine or ten. But East can't afford to duck the first trick since South may run the spades and the clubs for nine tricks. East should take the ♡A and shift to a low diamond, hoping West has the queen. If South has the ◇Q instead of the ♠Q, the defense is helpless.

Try this last example yourself.

Dlr: North
Vul: None

♠ 7 6 5 4
♡ Q 10 4
◇ K Q
♣ K Q 3 2

♠ A K 10 2
♡ 6 5 3
◇ A 4 3
♣ J 10 8

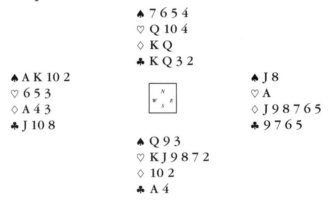

WEST	NORTH	EAST	SOUTH
	1♣	pass	1♡
pass	1NT	pass	3♡[1]
all pass			

1.   Invitational.

You lead the ♠K, and East plays the jack. How do you continue?

You can see three spade tricks and the ◇A. To beat the contract, East must have an ace. If East has the ♣A, he'll always get it in time to lead a spade, giving you two more spade tricks; so you should shift to a trump in case he has the ace of hearts.

♠ 7 6 5 4
♡ Q 10 4
◇ K Q
♣ K Q 3 2

♠ A K 10 2
♡ 6 5 3
◇ A 4 3
♣ J 10 8

♠ J 8
♡ A
◇ J 9 8 7 6 5
♣ 9 7 6 5

♠ Q 9 3
♡ K J 9 8 7 2
◇ 10 2
♣ A 4

A club shift lets South take a fast spade pitch on the clubs. Nor will East be happy if you continue spades, giving him a ruff.

Dlr: North
Vul: N-S

♠ A Q J 7 3
♡ 8 6
◇ J 3
♣ A Q J 2

♠ 8 5 2
♡ A J 5 2
◇ A 10 5 2
♣ 7 6

WEST	NORTH	EAST	SOUTH
	1♠	pass	1NT
pass	2♣	pass	2NT
pass	3NT	all pass	

You lead the ♡2. East takes the king and returns the ♡9: ten, jack. How do you continue?

If East has the ♠K, South is surely going down, so you should assume East has either the ◇K or the ♣K. If you lead a club at the third trick and find South with that king plus the ♠K, he'll have nine tricks. So the right shift is a low diamond. Even if South has strong diamonds such as K-Q-9-x, he can't succeed. If he continues diamonds, you'll duck, and South can get only five spades, two diamonds and a club. In fact, the full deal is

♠ A Q J 7 3
♡ 8 6
◇ J 3
♣ A Q J 2

♠ 8 5 2
♡ A J 5 2
◇ A 10 5 2
♣ 7 6

♠ 10 6 4
♡ K 9 3
◇ K 8 4
♣ 10 9 8 3

♠ K 9
♡ Q 10 7 4
◇ Q 9 7 6
♣ K 5 4

If a defender sees two chances to prevail, he mustn't commit to the line of defense that will, if it fails, forego his second chance. Here's another example:

Dlr: North
Vul: Both

```
                    ♠ K J 10 4 3
                    ♡ Q 9 6 2
                    ◇ 6 5 3
                    ♣ K
♠ 8 7 5 2                          ♠ A 9
♡ A 5                              ♡ 8 4
◇ A K           [N W E S]          ◇ J 10 9 7 2
♣ J 10 9 6 2                       ♣ 8 7 5 4
                    ♠ Q 6
                    ♡ K J 10 7 3
                    ◇ Q 8 4
                    ♣ A Q 3
```

WEST	NORTH	EAST	SOUTH
	pass	pass	1♡
pass	3♡	all pass	

West starts with the ◇AK. An expert East would play the jack on the second diamond, suit preference for spades; but West should shift to a spade no matter what. East needs an ace to beat the contract. A spade shift loses nothing if South has that ace; but if South has the ♣AQ, a club shift lets him discard dummy's last diamond.

Dlr: North
Vul: Both

```
                    ♠ K J 9
                    ♡ Q 4
                    ◇ K 9 7 5 2
                    ♣ A J 6
♠ 6 3                             ♠ A 4
♡ A 8 7 3                         ♡ K 10 9 6 2
◇ 6 4           [N W E S]         ◇ J 8 3
♣ K Q 10 7 2                      ♣ 9 5 4
                    ♠ Q 10 8 7 5 2
                    ♡ J 5
                    ◇ A Q 10
                    ♣ 8 3
```

WEST	NORTH	EAST	SOUTH
	1◇	pass	1♠
pass	2♠	pass	4♠
all pass			

West leads the ♣K: six, four, three. A diamond shift may be right but puts all his eggs in one leaky basket. Instead, West should cash the ♡A. If East signaled low, West would try a diamond; when East encourages in hearts, a heart continuation defeats the contract.

Basic technique can let a defender preserve his options.

Dlr: West
Vul: N-S

♠ Q J 9 7 3
♡ A Q 6 4
◇ 9 5
♣ J 10

♠ 6 5 4
♡ 7 2
◇ 10 8 7 2
♣ A 8 5 2

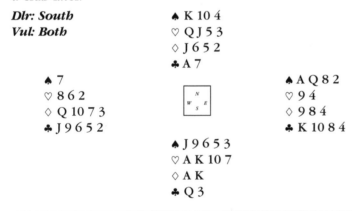

♠ 8 2
♡ K 3
◇ K J 6 4
♣ 9 7 6 4 3

♠ A K 10
♡ J 10 9 8 5
◇ A Q 3
♣ K Q

WEST	NORTH	EAST	SOUTH
pass	pass	pass	1♡
pass	3♡	pass	6♡
all pass			

West led the ◇2, and East played the king, losing to South's ace. When South lost the trump finesse next, East returned a diamond; and South produced the queen, drew trumps and threw his clubs on dummy's spades. West might have led a higher diamond; but since South was marked with the ◇A, East should have tried the ◇J at the first trick. When South won with the queen, East would know to lead a club later.

Dlr: South
Vul: Both

♠ K 10 4
♡ Q J 5 3
◇ J 6 5 2
♣ A 7

♠ 7
♡ 8 6 2
◇ Q 10 7 3
♣ J 9 6 5 2

♠ A Q 8 2
♡ 9 4
◇ 9 8 4
♣ K 10 8 4

♠ J 9 6 5 3
♡ A K 10 7
◇ A K
♣ Q 3

WEST	NORTH	EAST	SOUTH
			1♠
pass	2◇	pass	2♡
pass	3♡	pass	4♡
all pass			

West leads the ♠7. East can see two spades and a ruff; and if West has the ◇A or ◇K, it'll always win a trick; so East must seek a club trick. After East takes the ♠Q, he should return the ♠2 (suit preference for clubs) without cashing the ace. West can ruff and shift to a club, establishing the setting trick. But if East cashes the ♠A before giving West a ruff, South can win the club shift, draw trumps and throw dummy's club loser on a good spade.

Try this last example yourself.

Dlr: South
Vul: N-S

```
              ♠ Q J 3
              ♡ K 4
              ◊ 9 6 5
              ♣ K Q J 5 4

    ♠ K 5
    ♡ Q 10 9 5         N
    ◊ A Q 10 2       W   E
    ♣ 10 8 7           S
```

WEST	NORTH	EAST	SOUTH
			1♠
pass	2♣	pass	2◊
pass	3♠	pass	4♠
all pass			

You lead the ♡10. Declarer wins with dummy's king and lets the ♠Q ride to your king. What do you lead next?

You need to find East with either the ♣A or the ◊K. If you lead a club and find South with the ace, he makes an overtrick. Shift to a low diamond.

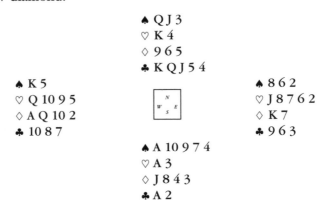

```
              ♠ Q J 3
              ♡ K 4
              ◊ 9 6 5
              ♣ K Q J 5 4

    ♠ K 5                              ♠ 8 6 2
    ♡ Q 10 9 5        N               ♡ J 8 7 6 2
    ◊ A Q 10 2      W   E             ◊ K 7
    ♣ 10 8 7          S               ♣ 9 6 3
              ♠ A 10 9 7 4
              ♡ A 3
              ◊ J 8 4 3
              ♣ A 2
```

You'd defeat the contract even if the South hand were

♠ A 10 9 7 4   ♡ A 3   ◊ K J 8 4 3   ♣ 2

Dlr: South
Vul: Both

```
            ♠ J 5
            ♡ 8 5 3
            ◇ A 6 5 4
            ♣ J 7 6 5
♠ Q 10 7 4 3
♡ A 6 2          ┌─────┐
◇ K 10 7         │  N  │
♣ Q 3            │W   E│
                 │  S  │
                 └─────┘
```

WEST	NORTH	EAST	SOUTH
			1♡
pass	2♡	pass	4♡
all pass			

CHERISH THE ACE OF TRUMPS

Things start badly when dummy's jack wins your spade opening lead, East following with the nine. South next leads a trump to his king. How do you defend?

Duck. When you have A-x-x of trumps, it is often correct to refuse the first trump lead.

```
                ♠ J 5
                ♡ 8 5 3
                ◇ A 6 5 4
                ♣ J 7 6 5
♠ Q 10 7 4 3                      ♠ 9 8
♡ A 6 2          ┌─────┐          ♡ 9 7
◇ K 10 7         │  N  │          ◇ Q J 9 3
♣ Q 3           │W   E│          ♣ K 10 9 8 4
                 │  S  │
                 └─────┘
                ♠ A K 6 2
                ♡ K Q J 10 4
                ◇ 8 2
                ♣ A 2
```

If you let the ♡K win, South is in bad shape. If he leads another trump, you take the ace and lead a third trump. South can't ruff his last low spade in dummy and loses a trick in each suit. If instead South tries to ruff a spade next, East scores the ♡9 on an overruff. South would get home if you won the first trump. If you returned the ♠Q, he could win, cash one high trump and then ruff a spade in dummy safely.

It's wrong to part with the ace of trumps, the most potent card in the deck, on a whim. Players often lead the ace of trumps, or some other ace, 'to see dummy'. But you get to see dummy no matter what you lead, and to release an ace often costs a vital tempo. Too often, what you'll see is what lead would have been better.

Possession of the boss trump can help you conduct a forcing

defense — if you take your ace at the right moment.

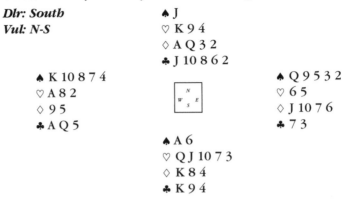

Dlr: South
Vul: N-S

```
                    ♠ J
                    ♡ K 9 4
                    ◇ A Q 3 2
                    ♣ J 10 8 6 2
  ♠ K 10 8 7 4                        ♠ Q 9 5 3 2
  ♡ A 8 2                             ♡ 6 5
  ◇ 9 5                              ◇ J 10 7 6
  ♣ A Q 5                            ♣ 7 3
                    ♠ A 6
                    ♡ Q J 10 7 3
                    ◇ K 8 4
                    ♣ K 9 4
```

WEST	NORTH	EAST	SOUTH
			1♡
1♠	2♣	3♠	pass
pass	4♡	all pass	

West leads a spade, and South takes the ace, ruffs his last spade in dummy and leads a trump. If West wins immediately, South is safe. He can win any return, draw trumps (leaving him with two) and play clubs. He has time to establish a club for his tenth trick.

Now suppose West ducks the first trump. When he wins the next trump, he forces South to ruff a spade in his hand; dummy has no more trumps. When West takes the ♣Q, he forces out South's last trump with another spade; and when West takes the ♣A, he can cash a spade for the setting trick.

When the opponents play in a 4-3 fit (or a 4-2 fit; stranger things have happened), be reluctant to part with the ace of trumps.

Dlr: North
Vul: Both

```
                    ♠ 7 4 2
                    ♡ K 7 6
                    ◇ A K 10 4 2
                    ♣ K 3
  ♠ K J 8 5 3                         ♠ A Q 9
  ♡ A 3 2                             ♡ 9 8 5
  ◇ 8 7 5                            ◇ 9 6
  ♣ 9 5                              ♣ 10 8 7 6 4
                    ♠ 10 6
                    ♡ Q J 10 4
                    ◇ Q J 3
                    ♣ A Q J 2
```

WEST	NORTH	EAST	SOUTH
	1◇	pass	1♡
pass	2♡	pass	4♡
all pass			

West leads a spade, and three rounds force South to ruff. When South leads the ♡Q next, he succeeds if West takes his ace; but if West ducks and ducks again if declarer continues with the ♡J, South is finished. If South leads a third trump, West cashes spades; if instead South abandons trumps, East eventually scores his low trump.

Try this one yourself.

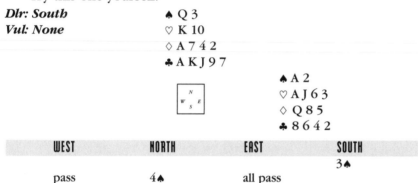

Dlr: South
Vul: None

♠ Q 3
♡ K 10
◇ A 7 4 2
♣ A K J 9 7

♠ A 2
♡ A J 6 3
◇ Q 8 5
♣ 8 6 4 2

WEST	NORTH	EAST	SOUTH
			3♠
pass	4♠	all pass	

West leads the ♡2. Dummy plays the ten, and your jack wins. Plan your defense.

South is marked with three low hearts. If you lead the ace and a low trump, you can stop a heart ruff in dummy but won't beat the contract: dummy's clubs will give South all the tricks he needs. Instead, you must switch to a low trump without releasing the ace.

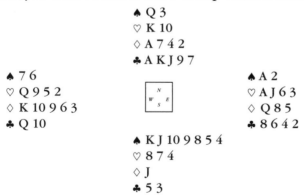

♠ Q 3
♡ K 10
◇ A 7 4 2
♣ A K J 9 7

♠ 7 6
♡ Q 9 5 2
◇ K 10 9 6 3
♣ Q 10

♠ A 2
♡ A J 6 3
◇ Q 8 5
♣ 8 6 4 2

♠ K J 10 9 8 5 4
♡ 8 7 4
◇ J
♣ 5 3

South is stuck. If he leads another heart, you win and cash the ace of trumps and a heart. If instead South tries for a heart discard on the clubs, West will get a ruff.

Dlr: South
Vul: N-S

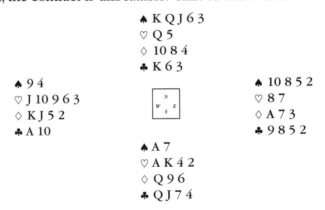

♠ K Q J 6 3
♡ Q 5
◇ 10 8 4
♣ K 6 3

♠ 9 4
♡ J 10 9 6 3
◇ K J 5 2
♣ A 10

WEST	NORTH	EAST	SOUTH
			1NT
pass	3♠	pass	3NT
all pass			

COUNT, COUNT, COUNT!

You lead the ♡J. Dummy's queen wins, and South next leads a club to his queen and your ace. How do you continue?

You know South has the ♡AK and the ♣Q. He surely has the ♠A, otherwise he'd be attacking spades, his best suit. So South can't have the ◇AQ, which would give him at least 19 points; and if he has the ◇A, the contract is unbeatable. Shift to a low diamond.

♠ K Q J 6 3
♡ Q 5
◇ 10 8 4
♣ K 6 3

♠ 9 4
♡ J 10 9 6 3
◇ K J 5 2
♣ A 10

♠ 10 8 5 2
♡ 8 7
◇ A 7 3
♣ 9 8 5 2

♠ A 7
♡ A K 4 2
◇ Q 9 6
♣ Q J 7 4

East will take the ace and return a diamond (your lead of a low diamond suggests strength in diamonds; if you wanted a heart return, you'd lead a higher diamond), and the defense will get four diamonds and a club.

Effective defense without counting is impossible. In the problem above, West can't succeed unless he counts declarer's playing tricks and high-card points. On most deals, the defenders also need to form a picture of declarer's distribution; and it all starts with a count of their possible defensive tricks.

Dlr: South
Vul: E-W

	♠ 5 4	
	♡ A Q 10 4	
	◊ 6 5 4	
	♣ Q 9 4 3	

♠ 10 9	N	♠ J 8 6
♡ 9 8 7 2	W E	♡ J 3
◊ J 8 7	S	◊ A K 9 3
♣ J 10 8 5		♣ A 7 6 2

	♠ A K Q 7 3 2	
	♡ K 6 5	
	◊ Q 10 2	
	♣ K	

WEST	NORTH	EAST	SOUTH
			1♠
pass	1NT	pass	3♠
all pass			

West leads the ♣J, and East puts up the ace, dropping South's king. The defense has no heart tricks, and two trump tricks from West is too much to ask. East must therefore try for three diamonds and a trump; he may as well shift to a low diamond at the second trick. If South plays the ten, West wins with the jack and returns a diamond. After East takes the king and ace, the lead of the thirteenth diamond promotes the setting trick in trumps.

Dlr: South
Vul: N-S

	♠ A 8 6 4 3	
	♡ A 5	
	◊ J 9 6 4	
	♣ 3 2	

♠ 10 9 5 2	N	♠ K J 7
♡ J 9 7 4	W E	♡ K 8 3 2
◊ K 8 2	S	◊ 7 5
♣ 7 5		♣ Q 10 9 8

	♠ Q	
	♡ Q 10 6	
	◊ A Q 10 3	
	♣ A K J 6 4	

WEST	NORTH	EAST	SOUTH
			1♣
pass	1♠	pass	2◊
pass	3◊	pass	3NT
all pass			

West leads the ♡4, and South ducks to East's king. Before 'automatically' returning a heart, East should automatically try to count South's distribution. West's lead marks South with three hearts, probably with the queen to justify his 3NT bid. South reversed and hence suggests longer clubs than diamonds; if his pattern were 2-3-4-4, he'd jump to 2NT at his second turn or open 1NT. So East can place South with a singleton spade — and shift to the ♠K. When the diamond finesse loses, South goes down.

Counting tricks can determine whether an active or a passive defense is better.

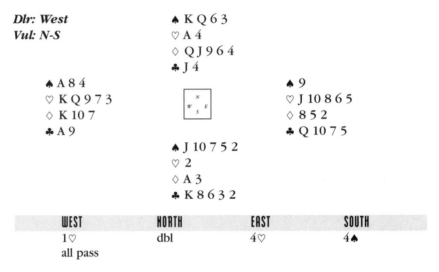

Dlr: West
Vul: N-S

```
                    ♠ K Q 6 3
                    ♡ A 4
                    ◇ Q J 9 6 4
                    ♣ J 4
 ♠ A 8 4                             ♠ 9
 ♡ K Q 9 7 3                         ♡ J 10 8 6 5
 ◇ K 10 7           N                ◇ 8 5 2
 ♣ A 9           W     E             ♣ Q 10 7 5
                    S
                    ♠ J 10 7 5 2
                    ♡ 2
                    ◇ A 3
                    ♣ K 8 6 3 2
```

WEST	NORTH	EAST	SOUTH
1♡	dbl	4♡	4♠
all pass			

West leads the ♡K. South takes the ace and leads the ♠K, and West wins and tries to cash the ♡Q. South ruffs, draws trumps and leads the ◇A and another diamond. When West takes the king, he must resist the urge to lay down the ♣A. West knows South has four spade tricks, a heart and four diamonds. Since South can't make his contract without a club trick, West can afford to exit passively with his last diamond and let South break the clubs.

BECOMING A BRIDGE EXPERT

Dlr: South
Vul: E-W
Matchpoints

```
                    ♠ A K J
                    ♡ K 6 3
                    ♢ 8 6 3
                    ♣ Q 10 7 3
  ♠ 10 9 8 5 3                      ♠ Q 7 2
  ♡ 7              N                ♡ Q 10 9
  ♢ A J 7 5 2    W   E              ♢ K 9
  ♣ K 8            S                ♣ J 9 6 5 4
                    ♠ 6 4
                    ♡ A J 8 5 4 2
                    ♢ Q 10 4
                    ♣ A 2
```

WEST	NORTH	EAST	SOUTH
			pass
pass	1♣	pass	1♡
pass	1NT	pass	3♡
all pass			

West leads the ♠10, and South wins in dummy and cashes the ♡KA, shrugging when West shows out. South then leads the ♣A and a club to West's king. West knows South had the ♡AJ8542 and the ♣A. The ♢K would give him an opening bid; so West shifts to a low diamond, and the defense wins three diamonds, a club and a trump.

Try this last example yourself.

Dlr: North
Vul: None

```
                    ♠ A Q 7 6
                    ♡ Q 8
                    ♢ Q 8 5 3
                    ♣ K 5 4
  ♠ J 3
  ♡ K J 5 2          N
  ♢ J 10 6         W   E
  ♣ Q J 10 7         S
```

WEST	NORTH	EAST	SOUTH
	1♢	pass	1♠
pass	2♠	pass	4♠
all pass			

You lead the ♣Q, winning, and continue clubs. Declarer ruffs and cashes the king and ace of trumps, East discarding a club. South then ruffs dummy's last club, cashes the ♡A and exits with the ♡10 to your king. What do you lead?

To beat the contract, you need two diamond tricks. You know South had six spades and one club. If he had three diamonds and three hearts, you can exit safely with a heart. Even if South's pattern was 6-2-4-1, a heart return will be safe: South will get a ruff-sluff, but he'll be sluffing his fourth diamond that would be a winner anyway.

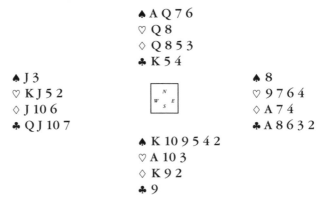

```
                        ♠ A Q 7 6
                        ♡ Q 8
                        ◇ Q 8 5 3
                        ♣ K 5 4
    ♠ J 3                                      ♠ 8
    ♡ K J 5 2              N                   ♡ 9 7 6 4
    ◇ J 10 6           W       E               ◇ A 7 4
    ♣ Q J 10 7             S                   ♣ A 8 6 3 2
                        ♠ K 10 9 5 4 2
                        ♡ A 10 3
                        ◇ K 9 2
                        ♣ 9
```

A diamond return gives South a chance; a heart beats him.

TIP 8

ASSUME DECLARER IS OPERATING CORRECTLY

Dlr: North
Vul: Both
Matchpoints

```
                        ♠ K Q J 5
                        ♡ 8 5 3
                        ◇ A K Q 2
                        ♣ J 3
    ♠ A 2
    ♡ K 10 6 2              N
    ◇ 10 8 7 4 3        W       E
    ♣ K 2                  S
```

WEST	NORTH	EAST	SOUTH
	1◇	pass	2♣
pass	2♠	pass	4♣
pass	5♣	all pass	

You lead the ♡2. South takes East's jack with the ace, leads the ◇9 to dummy — East plays the six — and lets the ♣J ride to your king. How do you defend?

To try to cash the ♡K can't be right. South can't have a losing heart unless he also has three diamonds; if he had, say, 2-2-2-7 distribution, he'd try to discard his losing heart on the diamonds before taking the trump finesse. You should return a diamond.

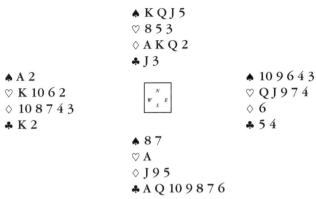

```
              ♠ K Q J 5
              ♡ 8 5 3
              ◇ A K Q 2
              ♣ J 3
♠ A 2                              ♠ 10 9 6 4 3
♡ K 10 6 2        N               ♡ Q J 9 7 4
◇ 10 8 7 4 3    W   E             ◇ 6
♣ K 2             S               ♣ 5 4
              ♠ 8 7
              ♡ A
              ◇ J 9 5
              ♣ A Q 10 9 8 7 6
```

South wouldn't have bothered with the trump finesse at IMPs, but at matchpoints he succumbed to the lure of an overtrick.

As a defender, base your play on the premise that declarer knows what he's doing. If you do, and he doesn't, you'll have few regrets. But if you assume your opponent has erred when he hasn't, you'll be like the snake in Eden: without a leg to stand on.

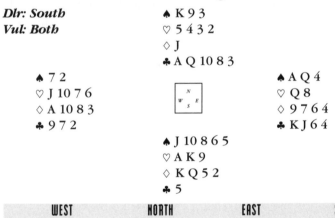

```
Dlr: South        ♠ K 9 3
Vul: Both         ♡ 5 4 3 2
                  ◇ J
                  ♣ A Q 10 8 3
♠ 7 2                              ♠ A Q 4
♡ J 10 7 6        N               ♡ Q 8
◇ A 10 8 3      W   E             ◇ 9 7 6 4
♣ 9 7 2           S               ♣ K J 6 4
                  ♠ J 10 8 6 5
                  ♡ A K 9
                  ◇ K Q 5 2
                  ♣ 5
```

WEST	NORTH	EAST	SOUTH
			1♠
pass	2♣	pass	2◇
pass	2♠	pass	3♠
all pass			

West leads a low heart to the queen and ace, and South tables a low diamond. West should grab the ◇A and shift to a trump. South's play suggests he's looking for diamond ruffs in dummy. If South is good enough to lead a diamond when he has the ♣KJ but needs help with a guess in trumps, West must compliment South on his subtlety and pay off.

I used this deal in my column in the ACBL *Bulletin*:

Dlr: North
Vul: Both

```
                    ♠ A 8 3
                    ♡ A 9 8
                    ◇ K 8
                    ♣ Q J 10 5 4
  ♠ K 9 7 6                           ♠ J 10 4 2
  ♡ 6 4 3          ┌─────┐            ♡ K 5
  ◇ Q 6 5 4 3      │ N   │            ◇ J 9
  ♣ 2              │W   E│            ♣ A 9 8 7 6
                   │  S  │
                   └─────┘
                    ♠ Q 5
                    ♡ Q J 10 7 2
                    ◇ A 10 7 2
                    ♣ K 3
```

WEST	NORTH	EAST	SOUTH
	1♣	pass	1♡
pass	1NT	pass	3◇
pass	3♡	pass	4♡
all pass			

When West leads his singleton club, East must win and shift to the ♠J. East can wait to give West a club ruff; and if West has the ♠K, East must lead a spade from his side to establish the setting trick. The *Bulletin*, which seems to delight in publishing questionable submissions by unknown contributors, let a reader present this hypothetical deal in response:

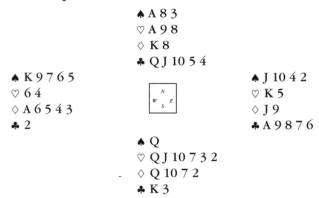

```
                    ♠ A 8 3
                    ♡ A 9 8
                    ◇ K 8
                    ♣ Q J 10 5 4
  ♠ K 9 7 6 5                         ♠ J 10 4 2
  ♡ 6 4            ┌─────┐            ♡ K 5
  ◇ A 6 5 4 3     │ N   │            ◇ J 9
  ♣ 2             │W   E│            ♣ A 9 8 7 6
                  │  S  │
                  └─────┘
                    ♠ Q
                    ♡ Q J 10 7 3 2
                    ◇ Q 10 7 2
                    ♣ K 3
```

After the same bidding and lead, the reader said he took the ♣A and duly returned the ♠J — not a success. An unimaginative club return would defeat the contract, and he was chastised by West.

Put the second deal into a decent game, and no South would choose the daisy-picking 3◇ bid. Since South knows hearts is the proper strain, he would bid 3♡ (invitational), 2♡ if in a timid mood, or perhaps, in some styles, a 'new minor forcing' 2◇; but nobody would bid 3◇. East should assume South has only five hearts to explain his effort to get a heart preference.

Dlr: South
Vul: E-W

		♠ A Q 6	
		♡ A Q J 9 5	
		◇ 10 4	
		♣ J 10 2	

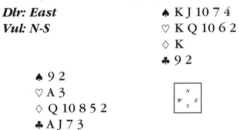

♠ 8 7 2
♡ 7 6 3
◇ Q 9 8 3
♣ K 7 4

♠ K J 10 5
♡ 10 8 4
◇ K J 2
♣ 8 6 5

♠ 9 4 3
♡ K 2
◇ A 7 6 5
♣ A Q 9 3

WEST	NORTH	EAST	SOUTH
			1♣
pass	1♡	pass	1NT
pass	3NT	all pass	

West leads the ♠8. South considers taking the ace but fears East may have five spades; so South instead plays the queen from dummy, losing to East's king. If East returns the ♠J, South is safe; but East should wonder why South didn't play a low spade from dummy, making it impossible for East to continue spades. Only one answer appeals: South is afraid of a shift and wants to make a spade continuation attractive. So East shifts to the ◇J, and South goes down.

Try this last example yourself.

Dlr: East
Vul: N-S

		♠ K J 10 7 4	
		♡ K Q 10 6 2	
		◇ K	
		♣ 9 2	

♠ 9 2
♡ A 3
◇ Q 10 8 5 2
♣ A J 7 3

WEST	NORTH	EAST	SOUTH
		pass	pass
1◇	2◇[1]	pass	3♠
pass	4♠	all pass	

1.   Michaels.

You lead a low diamond. Dummy's king wins, and South continues with a heart to his jack. How do you defend?

You must hope for two club tricks and a trump, but you need not play East for the ♣K. If declarer had the ♠A, he'd have come to his hand at the second trick to take a club discard on the ◊A. Lead a trump so your partner can shift to a club.

```
                    ♠ K J 10 7 4
                    ♡ K Q 10 6 2
                    ◊ K
                    ♣ 9 2
        ♠ 9 2                           ♠ A 6
        ♡ A 3              N            ♡ 8 7 5 4
        ◊ Q 10 8 5 2    W     E         ◊ J 9 3
        ♣ A J 7 3          S            ♣ Q 8 5 4
                    ♠ Q 8 5 3
                    ♡ J 9
                    ◊ A 7 6 4
                    ♣ K 10 6
```

Dlr: North
Vul: Both

```
                    ♠ Q J 10 5
                    ♡ K J 5
                    ◊ 10 8
                    ♣ A K 5 2
        ♠ 3 2                 N
        ♡ A 10 8 4 2     W         E
        ◊ 7 5 3               S
        ♣ J 9 3
```

TIP 9

ASSUME YOUR PART-NER KNOWS WHAT HE'S DOING

WEST	NORTH	EAST	SOUTH
	1♣	pass	1♠
pass	2♠	pass	2NT
pass	4♠	all pass	

You lead the ◊7: eight, nine, king. Declarer leads a trump, which East's king wins. He shifts to the ♡9, and South plays the three. East must hold the ♠A, since South didn't try a finesse. If the ♡9 is a singleton, you must take the ace and give East a ruff; if he has a doubleton, you must duck the first heart to keep communication. What about it?

South's bidding suggests about 11 points with weak spades and balanced distribution. He's not likely to have four hearts, since with 4-4 in the majors he'd respond 1♡. But if you trust your partner, it is clear to duck the first heart: if East had a singleton heart, he'd cash the ♠A before leading it, giving you no option.

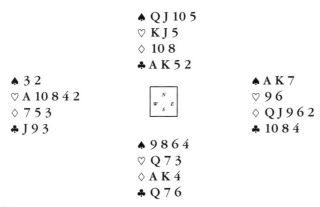

```
                    ♠ Q J 10 5
                    ♡ K J 5
                    ◇ 10 8
                    ♣ A K 5 2
♠ 3 2                              ♠ A K 7
♡ A 10 8 4 2                       ♡ 9 6
◇ 7 5 3                            ◇ Q J 9 6 2
♣ J 9 3                            ♣ 10 8 4
                    ♠ 9 8 6 4
                    ♡ Q 7 3
                    ◇ A K 4
                    ♣ Q 7 6
```

Trying to play tight defense with an undependable partner is like fighting a dragon with one arm tied behind you. If you can't trust your partner, the only choice is to end the partnership.

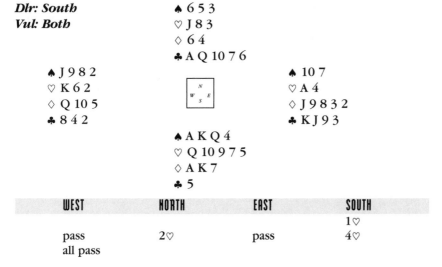

Dlr: South
Vul: Both

```
                    ♠ 6 5 3
                    ♡ J 8 3
                    ◇ 6 4
                    ♣ A Q 10 7 6
♠ J 9 8 2                          ♠ 10 7
♡ K 6 2                            ♡ A 4
◇ Q 10 5                           ◇ J 9 8 3 2
♣ 8 4 2                            ♣ K J 9 3
                    ♠ A K Q 4
                    ♡ Q 10 9 7 5
                    ◇ A K 7
                    ♣ 5
```

WEST	NORTH	EAST	SOUTH
			1♡
pass	2♡	pass	4♡
all pass			

West chooses a trump lead, and East takes the ace and returns a trump to the king. West should lead a third trump. Unless East knew there was nothing to fear from dummy's club suit, he would shift to a diamond at the second trick.

Dlr: East
Vul: None
Matchpoints

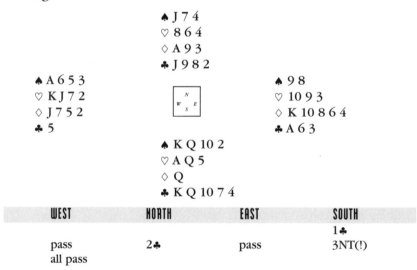

```
                    ♠ Q 10 5
                    ♡ K 9 6 3
                    ◇ Q 8 2
                    ♣ J 9 3
  ♠ A 6 2                          ♠ K J 9 7 3
  ♡ 8 4             ┌─────┐        ♡ J 2
  ◇ J 7 6 4 3       │ N   │        ◇ A 10 5
  ♣ 10 8 5          │W   E│        ♣ A 7 2
                    │  S  │
                    └─────┘
                    ♠ 8 4
                    ♡ A Q 10 7 5
                    ◇ K 9
                    ♣ K Q 6 4
```

WEST	NORTH	EAST	SOUTH
		1♠	2♡
2♠	3♡	all pass	

West decides it's not urgent to lay down the ♠A and leads the ◇4. Dummy plays low, and East takes the ace. East should infer that West has the ♠A and shift to a low spade to collect the defenders' spade tricks; with three or four low spades, West would see no reason to avoid a spade lead.

It's better to trust your partner's defense than to trust declarer's bidding.

```
                    ♠ J 7 4
                    ♡ 8 6 4
                    ◇ A 9 3
                    ♣ J 9 8 2
  ♠ A 6 5 3                        ♠ 9 8
  ♡ K J 7 2         ┌─────┐        ♡ 10 9 3
  ◇ J 7 5 2         │ N   │        ◇ K 10 8 6 4
  ♣ 5               │W   E│        ♣ A 6 3
                    │  S  │
                    └─────┘
                    ♠ K Q 10 2
                    ♡ A Q 5
                    ◇ Q
                    ♣ K Q 10 7 4
```

WEST	NORTH	EAST	SOUTH
			1♣
pass	2♣	pass	3NT(!)
all pass			

After South's bizarre 3NT bid, West leads the ♡2. South wins with the queen and leads the ♣K. East ducks, and South leads another club. West throws a spade. South knows West had four hearts and one club. Since West's opening lead would have been a spade if he had five spades, his shape must be 4-4-4-1. So East shifts to the ◇K, pinning South's stiff queen, and South goes down two (deservedly) when a routine heart return would let him steal off with nine tricks.

Try this one yourself.

Dlr: South
Vul: N-S

♠ 7 5
♡ A Q 7 3
◇ 6 5 3 2
♣ K 7 2

♠ A J 9 2
♡ 10 4
◇ J 10 9 8 4
♣ 8 3

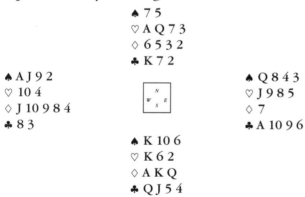

WEST	NORTH	EAST	SOUTH
			1NT[1]
pass	2♣	pass	2◇
pass	3NT	all pass	

1.   16-18 HCP.

You lead the ◇J: two, seven, queen. South then leads a club to the king. East takes the ace and shifts to the ♠3: ten, jack, five. How do you continue?

You should lead another diamond. East is marked with four spades to an honor; but if he had the ♠K, he should lead it and then a low spade to take you off a guess.

                    ♠ 7 5
                    ♡ A Q 7 3
                    ◇ 6 5 3 2
                    ♣ K 7 2
♠ A J 9 2   ♠ Q 8 4 3
♡ 10 4   ♡ J 9 8 5
◇ J 10 9 8 4   ◇ 7
♣ 8 3   ♣ A 10 9 6
                    ♠ K 10 6
                    ♡ K 6 2
                    ◇ A K Q
                    ♣ Q J 5 4

If you cash the ♠A next, you hand South his ninth trick — and rectify the count for a heart-club squeeze against East that gives South an overtrick. But if you exit passively, eight tricks are all South can muster.

Dlr: North
Vul: N-S

♠ 6
♡ A Q 8 3
◇ J 7 4
♣ A Q 10 6 3

♠ A 9 7 2
♡ 7 6 2
◇ K Q
♣ J 9 5 4

MAKE THINGS EASY FOR YOUR PARTNER

WEST	NORTH	EAST	SOUTH
	1♣	pass	1♡
pass	2♡	pass	3♡
pass	4♡	all pass	

West leads the ♠Q. How do you defend?

Take the ♠A and shift to the ◇Q. When you lead the ◇K next, West will know why you've led your honors out of order; he'll overtake and give you a ruff for the setting trick.

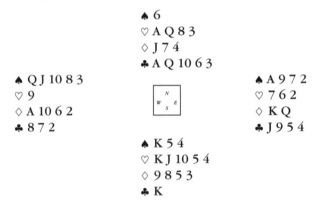

♠ 6
♡ A Q 8 3
◇ J 7 4
♣ A Q 10 6 3

♠ Q J 10 8 3
♡ 9
◇ A 10 6 2
♣ 8 7 2

♠ A 9 7 2
♡ 7 6 2
◇ K Q
♣ J 9 5 4

♠ K 5 4
♡ K J 10 5 4
◇ 9 8 5 3
♣ K

If you lead the ◇K and then the queen, West will play low, waiting for a third diamond, and South will take the rest.

It's common knowledge that most partners need all the help they can get. Even if your partner is Bob Hamman, your duty is to prevent him from making an error.

Dlr: South
Vul: Both

North: ♠ A Q J 10 7 ♡ J 5 ◇ 10 8 4 ♣ J 10 6

West: ♠ 8 3 2 ♡ 7 6 3 2 ◇ J 9 2 ♣ A Q 7

East: ♠ 9 6 4 ♡ 8 ◇ A K 6 5 ♣ 9 5 4 3 2

South: ♠ K 5 ♡ A K Q 10 9 4 ◇ Q 7 3 ♣ K 8

WEST	NORTH	EAST	SOUTH
			1♡
pass	1♠	pass	3♡
pass	4♡	all pass	

West led the ◇2 to East's king, and East next cashed the ace: seven, nine, eight. South won the third diamond and claimed. West was annoyed at East for not finding the club shift, but it was his own fault: for all East knew, South's hand was

♠ K 5 ♡ K Q 10 9 7 6 ◇ J 7 3 ♣ A K.

West should have played the jack on the second diamond, denying the queen.

Dlr: South
Vul: Both
Matchpoints

North: ♠ Q 10 9 ♡ K J 7 ◇ J 9 5 ♣ 8 6 5 4

West: ♠ K 4 3 ♡ A 10 5 3 ◇ 10 ♣ K J 9 7 3

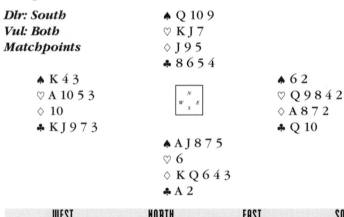

East: ♠ 6 2 ♡ Q 9 8 4 2 ◇ A 8 7 2 ♣ Q 10

South: ♠ A J 8 7 5 ♡ 6 ◇ K Q 6 4 3 ♣ A 2

WEST	NORTH	EAST	SOUTH
			1♠
pass	2♠	pass	3♠
all pass			

The defense started well when West led the ◇10, and East took the ace and returned the ◇2. West ruffed and shifted to the ♣7, forcing out the ace. South next led the ace and another trump; West won, cashed the ♣K and led the ♣J. East threw a heart, and South ruffed and led a heart. West ducked, hoping South might misguess for -200; but South put up the ♡K and made his contract. West couldn't know South had started with five diamonds — and only one heart — but East did. On the third club, East should discard the ♡Q to prevent West from ducking the ace.

Which defender was at fault on the next deal?

Dlr: South   ♠ J 7 5
Vul: Both   ♡ A J 8 6 4
                        ◇ A 10
                        ♣ Q 10 6

♠ A K 10   ♠ Q 8 2
♡ 7 3 2   ┌─────────┐   ♡ K Q 5
◇ Q 8 4 3 2   │ N   │   ◇ 9 7 5
♣ 9 8   │ W   E   │   ♣ 7 5 3 2
                  │   S   │
                  └─────────┘
                        ♠ 9 6 4 3
                        ♡ 10 9
                        ◇ K J 6
                        ♣ A K J 4

WEST	NORTH	EAST	SOUTH
			1♣
pass	1♡	pass	1NT
pass	3NT	all pass	

South won the first diamond with the jack and led the ♡10. East took the queen and returned a diamond: six, deuce, ace. South then led a club to the ace and let the ♡9 ride. East won and. . . led his last diamond. Making four instead of down one.

East was blameless since South's hand could have been

♠ A 6 4   ♡ 10 9 7   ◇ Q J 6   ♣ A K 8 4.

On the second diamond, West must play the queen, denying the king, to prevent East from relying on the diamonds.

Dlr: South   ♠ A K 4
Vul: E-W   ♡ 9 5
Matchpoints   ◇ K Q 10 9 4
                        ♣ J 7 3

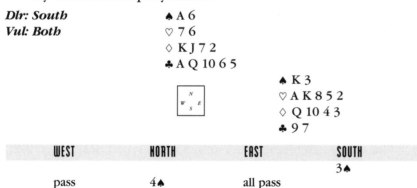

    ♠ 8 3 2   ♠ J 7
    ♡ 8 7 3 2   ♡ 10 6 4
    ◇ A 7 6 3   ◇ J 5 2
    ♣ K Q   ♣ A 10 9 8 4

                 ♠ Q 10 9 6 5
                 ♡ A K Q J
                 ◇ 8
                 ♣ 6 5 2

WEST	NORTH	EAST	SOUTH
			1♠
pass	2◇	pass	2♡
pass	3♠	pass	4♠
all pass			

West led the ♣K, and then the ♣Q. East played low, and the ◇A later won the last trick for the defense. For East to overtake the second club and return a club would cost an overtrick if South had one more heart and one fewer club. East might have reasoned that West would lead a low club at the second trick if he'd started with ♣KQx; but West could make things easy by cashing the ◇A before leading the ♣Q.

Try this last example yourself.

Dlr: South   ♠ A 6
Vul: Both   ♡ 7 6
                   ◇ K J 7 2
                   ♣ A Q 10 6 5

                          ♠ K 3
                          ♡ A K 8 5 2
                          ◇ Q 10 4 3
                          ♣ 9 7

WEST	NORTH	EAST	SOUTH
			3♠
pass	4♠	all pass	

West leads the ♡Q. How do you defend?

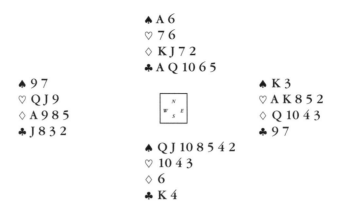

```
                              ♠ A 6
                              ♡ 7 6
                              ◊ K J 7 2
                              ♣ A Q 10 6 5
        ♠ 9 7                                    ♠ K 3
        ♡ Q J 9              ┌─────┐             ♡ A K 8 5 2
        ◊ A 9 8 5            │  N  │             ◊ Q 10 4 3
        ♣ J 8 3 2            │ W E │             ♣ 9 7
                             │  S  │
                              └─────┘
                              ♠ Q J 10 8 5 4 2
                              ♡ 10 4 3
                              ◊ 6
                              ♣ K 4
```

Overtake and cash another heart, then lead a diamond. If you leave West on lead, he may get the bright idea to shift to a club or underlead his ◊A. He can't know you have nothing in clubs, much less a trick in trumps.

Dlr: South
Vul: N-S

```
                              ♠ J 6 5
                              ♡ 7 5
                              ◊ A 3 2
                              ♣ A Q J 7 2
                                                 ♠ K 8 2
                             ┌─────┐             ♡ Q J 9 4
                             │  N  │             ◊ 5 4
                             │ W E │             ♣ K 10 8 4
                             │  S  │
                              └─────┘
```

DON'T GIVE DECLARER AN EASY RIDE

WEST	NORTH	EAST	SOUTH
			1NT
pass	3NT	all pass	

West leads the ◊J. South wins with the queen and leads the ♣3: nine, jack... How do you defend?

Since West can't have much strength, you won't beat the contract by setting up the diamonds or the hearts. The best chance is to deny South dummy's club tricks and hope he runs out of gas. Hence refuse the first club (smoothly, so South won't suspect), which in effect deprives South of an entry to dummy.

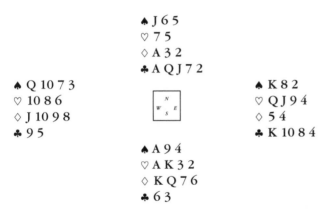

```
                    ♠ J 6 5
                    ♡ 7 5
                    ◇ A 3 2
                    ♣ A Q J 7 2
♠ Q 10 7 3                          ♠ K 8 2
♡ 10 8 6           ┌─────┐         ♡ Q J 9 4
◇ J 10 9 8         │  N  │         ◇ 5 4
♣ 9 5              │W   E│         ♣ K 10 8 4
                   │  S  │
                   └─────┘
                    ♠ A 9 4
                    ♡ A K 3 2
                    ◇ K Q 7 6
                    ♣ 6 3
```

South will return to his hand for another club finesse; but now you win, and South gets only two club tricks and (almost surely) only eight tricks in all. South would make 3NT if you won the first club. He'd win the red-suit return, lead his last club to take dummy's ace and queen, concede a club and score the long club for his ninth trick. (Double dummy, he could always succeed by ducking the first club completely.)

A winning defender is a helpful partner and an unhelpful opponent. When declarer stands at the edge of a cliff, a good defender doesn't mind giving him a shove.

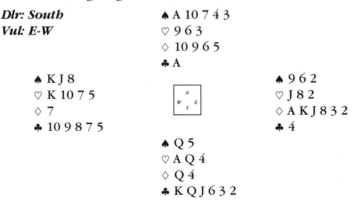

Dlr: South
Vul: E-W

```
                    ♠ A 10 7 4 3
                    ♡ 9 6 3
                    ◇ 10 9 6 5
                    ♣ A
♠ K J 8                            ♠ 9 6 2
♡ K 10 7 5         ┌─────┐         ♡ J 8 2
◇ 7                │  N  │         ◇ A K J 8 3 2
♣ 10 9 8 7 5       │W   E│         ♣ 4
                   │  S  │
                   └─────┘
                    ♠ Q 5
                    ♡ A Q 4
                    ◇ Q 4
                    ♣ K Q J 6 3 2
```

WEST	NORTH	EAST	SOUTH
			1♣
pass	1♠	pass	3♣
pass	3◇	pass	3NT
all pass			

Bob Hamman was West in a Bermuda Bowl. He led a heart against 3NT, and South won with the queen, led a club to dummy's ace and returned a spade to his queen and Hamman's king. Suppose

Hamman returns the ♡K. South wins and cashes the ♣K, and when East shows out, South knows he can take only four club tricks and must therefore hope the spades come in. He cashes two more clubs, leads a spade to the ten — and makes an overtrick.

Hamman foresaw it all. At the third trick, he returned the ♠8, removing one of South's options. South could have got home by finessing, but that seemed a needless risk when the clubs figured to break. So South took the ♠A, came to his ♡A and cashed the ♣K. Down two.

Dlr: North
Vul: Both

	♠ J 10 4	
	♡ A Q J 4	
	◇ A Q 9 8	
	♣ Q 8	

♠ 8		♠ K 9 7 6
♡ 10 7 3 2	N W E S	♡ 9 6 5
◇ 7 6 5 2		◇ J 4 3
♣ A K 9 6		♣ J 10 2

	♠ A Q 5 3 2	
	♡ K 8	
	◇ K 10	
	♣ 7 5 4 3	

WEST	NORTH	EAST	SOUTH
	1NT	pass	3♠
pass	4♠	all pass	

West leads the ♣K, and East takes note of his promising trump holding and signals sneakily with the jack. West then continues with the ace and another club. South fears that if he ruffs low in dummy, East will overruff, and South will go down if West has the ♠K. So South ruffs the third club with the ♠J — and East wins two trump tricks.

When the talk turns to inconveniencing declarer, I always recall a deal the late Lou Bluhm defended in the 1974 Spingold final, a match his team would have lost if Lou hadn't invented a way to beat 3NT.

Dlr: East
Vul: Both

♠ K Q 9 4
♡ Q 5
◇ 9 7 5 3
♣ 9 7 3

♠ 6 3
♡ K 7 6 3
◇ A Q 6 4
♣ 6 4 2

	N	
W		E
	S	

♠ 10 7 5 2
♡ J 9 8 4
◇ 8
♣ K J 10 5

♠ A J 8
♡ A 10 2
◇ K J 10 2
♣ A Q 8

WEST	NORTH	EAST	SOUTH
		pass	1◇
pass	1♠	pass	2NT
pass	3NT	all pass	

Bluhm led the ♡6: five, jack, ace. South then cashed the ♠A, led the ♠8 to the king and returned a diamond to his jack. If the finesse worked, he planned to overtake the ♠J for another finesse.

His finesse did work: Bluhm followed with the ◇6! So South led the ♠J to the queen and tried another diamond. This time East showed out, and Bluhm took South's king and led the ♡K and another heart, forcing out the ten. When Bluhm won the ◇Q, he led a heart to East's nine, and East cashed the ♠10 for the setting trick. At the other table, 3NT made when West took the first diamond.

Try this last deal yourself.

Dlr: South
Vul: Both

♠ K 9 8 4
♡ J 7 6 3
◇ Q 3
♣ A 10 4

♠ 7 2
♡ K Q 10 8 2
◇ K 8 6 2
♣ 9 3

	N	
W		E
	S	

WEST	NORTH	EAST	SOUTH
			1♣
pass	1♡	pass	1♠
pass	3♠	pass	4NT
pass	5◇	pass	6♠
all pass			

You lead the ♡K: three, four, five. What next?

```
                        ♠ K 9 8 4
                        ♡ J 7 6 3
                        ◊ Q 3
                        ♣ A 10 4
        ♠ 7 2                              ♠ 10 5 3
        ♡ K Q 10 8 2      ┌─────┐         ♡ A 9 4
        ◊ K 8 6 2         │  N  │         ◊ J 10 7 4
        ♣ 9 3             │W   E│         ♣ 8 7 5
                          │  S  │
                          └─────┘
                        ♠ A Q J 6
                        ♡ 5
                        ◊ A 9 5
                        ♣ K Q J 6 2
```

The bidding marks South with a singleton heart; but suppose you lead another heart. South ruffs, leads a club to the ten, ruffs a heart, takes the ♠AQ, crosses to the ♣A, draws East's last trump and runs the clubs. He takes twelve tricks: four trumps in dummy, two ruffs in his hand, five clubs and a diamond. A trump shift at the second trick won't work. Dummy plays the nine, and South can still bring off his dummy reversal whether or not East covers with the ten. Only a club switch gives South more problems than he can handle. Did you find it?

TIP 12

DON'T BE A WINNER GRABBER

Dlr: South
Vul: N-S

```
                        ♠ K Q 5 3
                        ♡ J 9 6 4
                        ◊ 7 5
                        ♣ J 6 4
        ♠ A 10 7 2
        ♡ K 5             ┌─────┐
        ◊ Q 10 8 4        │  N  │
        ♣ K 9 3           │W   E│
                          │  S  │
                          └─────┘
```

WEST	NORTH	EAST	SOUTH
			1♡
dbl	2♡	2♠	4♡
all pass			

You lead the ◊4, and East takes the ace and returns the ◊2. South takes the king and leads a spade. How do you defend?

East should have shifted to a club, but you must deal with the situation that exists. If South's hand is

♠ 8   ♡ A Q 10 8 3   ◊ K 9 6   ♣ A Q 8 2

you can grab the ♠A and get a club later. But that hand would be a questionable 4♡ bid, and if East lacked the ♣Q, he'd have been more likely to shift to a club. It's more likely South has a six-card heart suit, and the full deal is something like

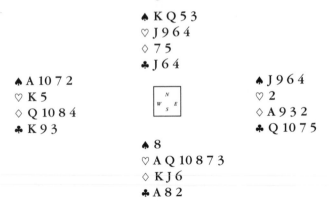

```
                    ♠ K Q 5 3
                    ♡ J 9 6 4
                    ◇ 7 5
                    ♣ J 6 4
  ♠ A 10 7 2                         ♠ J 9 6 4
  ♡ K 5              N              ♡ 2
  ◇ Q 10 8 4      W     E           ◇ A 9 3 2
  ♣ K 9 3            S               ♣ Q 10 7 5
                    ♠ 8
                    ♡ A Q 10 8 7 3
                    ◇ K J 6
                    ♣ A 8 2
```

Count South's tricks. He has five heart tricks, a diamond, a diamond ruff in dummy and a club; and if you grab the ♠A, he'll have two spade tricks and ten in all. If you duck the first spade, he'll lose no spades but two clubs.

A good defender knows when he must go looking for tricks ('active' defense) and when he can sit back and wait for tricks ('passive' defense).

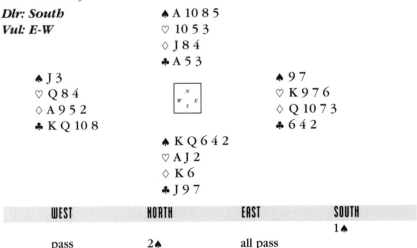

```
Dlr: South          ♠ A 10 8 5
Vul: E-W            ♡ 10 5 3
                    ◇ J 8 4
                    ♣ A 5 3
  ♠ J 3                             ♠ 9 7
  ♡ Q 8 4            N              ♡ K 9 7 6
  ◇ A 9 5 2       W     E           ◇ Q 10 7 3
  ♣ K Q 10 8         S               ♣ 6 4 2
                    ♠ K Q 6 4 2
                    ♡ A J 2
                    ◇ K 6
                    ♣ J 9 7
```

WEST	NORTH	EAST	SOUTH
			1♠
pass	2♠	all pass	

West leads the ♣K, and South takes the ace, draws trumps and leads a diamond to his king. West takes the ace and notes that dummy has no help for South's losers. Hence West need not snatch the ♣Q or break the heart suit; he should simply return a diamond. East wins and returns a club, and West takes two clubs and leads another diamond. South ruffs but must start the hearts himself and lose two hearts. South's play was poor, of course; he could take eight tricks by exiting with a club after drawing trumps, forcing West to break a new suit or concede a ruff-sluff.

Dlr: North
Vul: Both

	♠ K Q 8 3	
	♡ J 9 3	
	◇ A 4 3	
	♣ K Q 4	
♠ A 10 5 2		♠ J 9 7 6
♡ Q 10 2		♡ 6 5
◇ Q J 9 2		◇ K 8 6
♣ 8 7		♣ J 10 6 3
	♠ 4	
	♡ A K 8 7 4	
	◇ 10 7 5	
	♣ A 9 5 2	

WEST	NORTH	EAST	SOUTH
	1NT	pass	3♡
pass	4♡	all pass	

West leads the ◇Q. Dummy's ace wins, and East signals with the eight. South leads a trump to his king and returns a spade toward dummy. The position is similar to the one in the first deal, but this time West should grab the ♠A. The bidding marks South with the ♣A, so all West can do is cash what diamonds he can.

Ducking a winner smoothly can give declarer a losing option.

Dlr: North
Vul: E-W

	♠ A Q 9	
	♡ 6 3	
	◇ K Q 7 2	
	♣ K 8 7 6	
♠ 6 5 2		♠ 4 3
♡ Q 10 8 5		♡ A 7 4 2
◇ 9 5 4		◇ 8 3
♣ Q 3 2		♣ A J 10 9 4
	♠ K J 10 8 7	
	♡ K J 9	
	◇ A J 10 6	
	♣ 5	

WEST	NORTH	EAST	SOUTH
	1◇	pass	1♠
pass	2♠	pass	4♠
all pass			

West leads the ♣2, and South plays low from dummy (he'd do better to offer the king, tempting East to continue clubs). East wins with the nine and shifts to a trump; and South wins in dummy and leads a heart, his jack losing to West's queen. South wins the next trump in dummy and leads another heart — and East must duck again. If South is inspired to put up the king, he'll make an overtrick; but if South finesses with the nine, as most would, West wins with the ten and leads his last trump. South then loses a third heart and goes down.

Try this one yourself.

Dlr: North	♠ K J 7 6		
Vul: None	♡ K 6 4		
Matchpoints	◇ K J 9		
	♣ K 6 4		

♠ 8 2
♡ Q J 10 7 2
◇ A 6 5 3
♣ 5 3

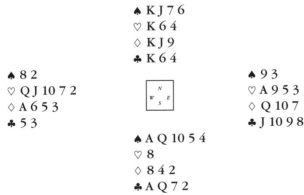

WEST	NORTH	EAST	SOUTH
	1♣	pass	1♠
pass	2♠	pass	4♠
all pass			

You lead the ♡Q, winning, and continue. South ruffs the second heart, takes the ♠KA and leads a diamond. You duck, and dummy's jack loses to your partner's queen. He returns the ♣J, and South wins with the ace and takes the king and queen. He ruffs a club in dummy, as East follows, ruffs the ♡K and leads another diamond. Do you grab your ace or duck? (Quick!)

```
                    ♠ K J 7 6
                    ♡ K 6 4
                    ◇ K J 9
                    ♣ K 6 4
  ♠ 8 2                              ♠ 9 3
  ♡ Q J 10 7 2                       ♡ A 9 5 3
  ◇ A 6 5 3                          ◇ Q 10 7
  ♣ 5 3                              ♣ J 10 9 8
                    ♠ A Q 10 5 4
                    ♡ 8
                    ◇ 8 4 2
                    ♣ A Q 7 2
```

A count of declarer's distribution tells you what to do. He started with five trumps, one heart and four clubs; hence three diamonds. You should duck the second diamond and give him a chance to misguess. South misplayed; he could assure the contract by stripping the clubs and hearts early, then leading a diamond to the jack to endplay East.

TIP 13

DON'T GET HUNG UP ON SUIT PREFERENCE

Dlr: North
Vul: N-S

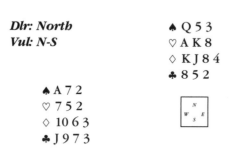

♠ Q 5 3
♡ A K 8
◇ K J 8 4
♣ 8 5 2

♠ A 7 2
♡ 7 5 2
◇ 10 6 3
♣ J 9 7 3

WEST	NORTH	EAST	SOUTH
	1◇	1♠	2♡
pass	3♡	pass	4♡
all pass			

You lead the ♠A. Your partner plays the ten, and South follows with the four. How do you continue?

You should shift to a club. East's ♠10 marks South with the jack, and a spade continuation will give South a club discard on the queen.

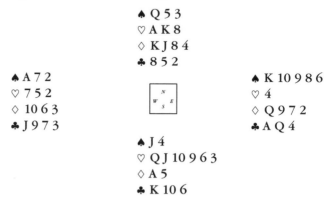

♠ Q 5 3
♡ A K 8
◇ K J 8 4
♣ 8 5 2

♠ A 7 2
♡ 7 5 2
◇ 10 6 3
♣ J 9 7 3

♠ K 10 9 8 6
♡ 4
◇ Q 9 7 2
♣ A Q 4

♠ J 4
♡ Q J 10 9 6 3
◇ A 5
♣ K 10 6

East had to encourage in spades since for all he knew, West had A-x. But West isn't barred from using his brains, and he certainly shouldn't think East's play has anything to do with suit preference. East-West don't need suit preference to defend this deal; an *attitude* signal and good judgment are enough.

A suit-preference signal is the *unmistakable* play of a strikingly high or low card to direct partner's attention to a high- or low-ranking suit. This can be an elegant and useful device. In the deal below, West leads the ♣A against South's 4♡, and East plays the ten.

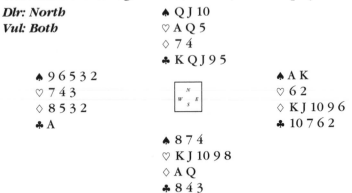

Dlr: North
Vul: Both

```
                    ♠ Q J 10
                    ♡ A Q 5
                    ◇ 7 4
                    ♣ K Q J 9 5
  ♠ 9 6 5 3 2                      ♠ A K
  ♡ 7 4 3          N               ♡ 6 2
  ◇ 8 5 3 2      W   E             ◇ K J 10 9 6
  ♣ A              S               ♣ 10 7 6 2
                    ♠ 8 7 4
                    ♡ K J 10 9 8
                    ◇ A Q
                    ♣ 8 4 3
```

WEST	NORTH	EAST	SOUTH
	1♣	1◇	1♡
pass	2♡	pass	3♡
pass	4♡	all pass	

East's play can be neither an attitude nor a count signal; his dislike for clubs is obvious, and how many clubs he has is irrelevant. So West should interpret East's play as suit preference and shift to a spade. Like all signals, though, suit preference must be your servant and not your master.

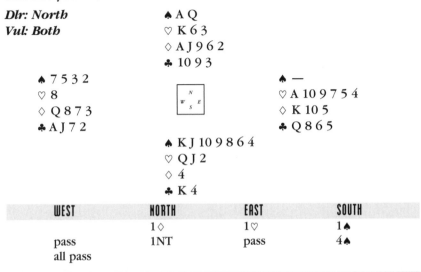

Dlr: North
Vul: Both

```
                    ♠ A Q
                    ♡ K 6 3
                    ◇ A J 9 6 2
                    ♣ 10 9 3
  ♠ 7 5 3 2                       ♠ —
  ♡ 8              N               ♡ A 10 9 7 5 4
  ◇ Q 8 7 3      W   E             ◇ K 10 5
  ♣ A J 7 2        S               ♣ Q 8 6 5
                    ♠ K J 10 9 8 6 4
                    ♡ Q J 2
                    ◇ 4
                    ♣ K 4
```

WEST	NORTH	EAST	SOUTH
	1◇	1♡	1♠
pass	1NT	pass	4♠
all pass			

West leads the ♡8, and East takes the ace and returns the ♡10, suggesting diamond strength. After West ruffs, he must lead a trump. East's diamond tricks, if any, aren't going away. If West shifts to a diamond, South takes the ace, ruffs a diamond, and gets back to dummy twice with high trumps to ruff two more diamonds. He can then draw trumps and return to the ♡K to pitch a club on the good diamond. But a trump lead at the third trick beats the contract by prematurely knocking out one of dummy's entries.

The biggest signaling error is asking the suit-preference signal to bear too heavy a load: interpreting everything as suit preference when the basic attitude signal is adequate.

Dlr: East
Vul: None

	♠ A J 7	
	♡ K 6 4 3	
	◇ K Q 10 7	
	♣ Q 5	
♠ 9 8 4 2		♠ K Q 10
♡ 5		♡ 8 7
◇ 9 6 4 3		◇ A 8
♣ A 9 6 3		♣ K J 10 7 4 2
	♠ 6 5 3	
	♡ A Q J 10 9 2	
	◇ J 5 2	
	♣ 8	

WEST	NORTH	EAST	SOUTH
		1♣	2♡
pass	4♡	all pass	

West leads the ♣A, and East plays the deuce. East's signal says, "Shift... to the logical suit." West should shift to the ♠9, since a diamond shift makes no sense with dummy strong in diamonds.

What if there is no 'logical shift'?

Dlr: North
Vul: Both

	♠ Q 8 2	
	♡ Q 8 5 2	
	◇ K 7 3	
	♣ K 8 2	
♠ A 6 4		♠ K J 10 7 5 3
♡ J 7 4		♡ 9
◇ J 10 6 5		◇ A Q 4
♣ J 10 6		♣ 9 5 4
	♠ 9	
	♡ A K 10 6 3	
	◇ 9 8 2	
	♣ A Q 7 3	

WEST	NORTH	EAST	SOUTH
	pass	2♠	3♡
3♠	4♡	all pass	

West leads the ♠A. East wants a diamond shift, but this time no logical shift is obvious. Since East has several spades from which to choose, though, he can play the jack, an unusually high spade, and expect West to treat it as suit preference.

Here's a final example to try on your own.

Dlr: East ♠ K 10 5 3
Vul: None ♡ K 4
Matchpoints ◇ 8 6 3
    ♣ A K J 10

♠ Q 4
♡ A Q 10 6 3
◇ K 10 9 2
♣ 7 2

WEST	NORTH	EAST	SOUTH
		pass	pass
1♡	dbl	2♡	3♠
pass	4♠	all pass	

You lead the ♡A, and East plays the nine. What next?

Lead another heart. Nothing is illogical about a passive heart continuation even if dummy can win. If East wanted — or could accept — a diamond shift, he'd play his lowest heart.

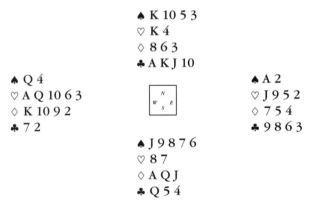

♠ K 10 5 3
♡ K 4
◇ 8 6 3
♣ A K J 10

♠ Q 4   ♠ A 2
♡ A Q 10 6 3   ♡ J 9 5 2
◇ K 10 9 2   ◇ 7 5 4
♣ 7 2   ♣ 9 8 6 3

♠ J 9 8 7 6
♡ 8 7
◇ A Q J
♣ Q 5 4

If you treat the ♡9 as suit preference and lead a diamond, South wins with the queen and may make an overtrick. After a heart exit, though, you'll get a diamond, and South will take ten tricks at most.

Suppose the deal was

                          ♠ K 10 5 3
                          ♡ K 4
                          ◇ 8 6 3
                          ♣ A K J 10

    ♠ Q 4   ♠ 7 2
    ♡ A Q 10 6 3   ┌─────┐   ♡ J 9 5 2
    ◇ K 10 9 2   │ N   │   ◇ A Q 5
    ♣ 7 2   │W   E│   ♣ 9 8 6 3
                          │ S │
                          └─────┘
                          ♠ A J 9 8 6
                          ♡ 8 7
                          ◇ J 7 4
                          ♣ Q 5 4

WEST	NORTH	EAST	SOUTH
		pass	pass
1♡	dbl	2♡	3♠
pass	4♠	all pass	

When West leads the ♡A, East plays the deuce, requesting the logical diamond switch.

TIP 14

LOOK FOR EXTRA TRUMP TRICKS

Dlr: North
Vul: Both

                          ♠ J 10 9 8
                          ♡ 10
                          ◇ A K J 8
                          ♣ A K 6 3

                                              ♠ Q 7 6 4
                          ┌─────┐   ♡ 4
                         │ N   │   ◇ 7 5 4 2
                        │W   E│   ♣ 10 8 5 2
                          │ S │
                          └─────┘

WEST	NORTH	EAST	SOUTH
	1◇	pass	1♠
4♡	4♠	all pass	

West leads the ♡K and then the ♡A, and dummy ruffs with the jack. How do you defend?

The contract is unbeatable unless West has a trump honor; but in that case, your trump holding will improve — provided you discard on the second heart instead of overruffing.

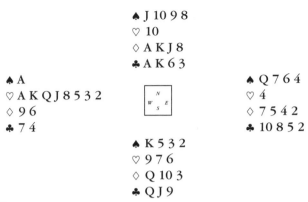

♠ J 10 9 8
♡ 10
◊ A K J 8
♣ A K 6 3

♠ A
♡ A K Q J 8 5 3 2
◊ 9 6
♣ 7 4

♠ Q 7 6 4
♡ 4
◊ 7 5 4 2
♣ 10 8 5 2

♠ K 5 3 2
♡ 9 7 6
◊ Q 10 3
♣ Q J 9

South will let the ♠10 ride next, and West will win and lead a third heart. South must ruff high in dummy again, and you discard again. Now your Q-7-6 of trumps is worth two tricks against dummy's eight and South's king.

Defenders often neglect to win tricks in trumps because they feel declarer's best suit is no place for the defense; but a trump promotion may be the only chance.

Dlr: North
Vul: N-S

♠ 6 4
♡ Q 6 4
◊ K Q 5 4
♣ A Q J 3

♠ K 9 2
♡ 9 2
◊ 9 8 7 3
♣ 10 9 8 7

♠ 8 5
♡ A K J 10 5 3
◊ A 10 2
♣ 4 2

♠ A Q J 10 7 3
♡ 8 7
◊ J 6
♣ K 6 5

WEST	NORTH	EAST	SOUTH
	1♣	1♡	1♠
pass	1NT	pass	3♠
all pass			

West leads a heart, and East takes the ten and ace, and then leads the king. When South ruffs with the queen, West should discard, applying the principle that to overruff with a natural trump winner is seldom correct. (If West overruffs, it's as if South has lost a finesse to the king, which he'd do anyway.) South then leads a club to dummy and returns a trump to his jack. West wins and leads a diamond to the ace; and when East leads a fourth heart, South can't help losing the setting trick to West's ♠9.

Dlr: South
Vul: None

```
              ♠ Q 7 4
              ♡ K Q 9 6
              ◇ K Q 3
              ♣ 9 6 4
♠ J 8 3                          ♠ 10
♡ A 5          ┌─────┐           ♡ J 10 8 7 4 3
◇ 10 4         │  N  │           ◇ 8 7 5 2
♣ A K J 8 7 2  │W   E│           ♣ 5 3
               │  S  │
               └─────┘
              ♠ A K 9 6 5 2
              ♡ 2
              ◇ A J 9 6
              ♣ Q 10
```

WEST	NORTH	EAST	SOUTH
			1♠
2♣	dbl[1]	pass	2♠
pass	4♠	all pass	

1.   Negative.

The trump promotion has a relative: the uppercut.

West cashes two clubs. He can expect to score the ♡A, but the setting trick must come from trumps. If West leads the ♣J next, East may forget to ruff; and even if he does ruff, South can discard his heart, a loser-on-a-loser, instead of overruffing. So West cashes the ♡A at the third trick and continues with a low club. When East uppercuts with the ♠10, South must overruff with an honor, and West's J-8-3 defeats the contract.

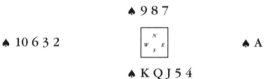

```
              ♠ 9 8 7
♠ 10 6 3 2    ┌─────┐    ♠ A
              │  N  │
              │W   E│
              │  S  │
              └─────┘
              ♠ K Q J 5 4
```

Some trump positions are more obscure. If South leads a trump from dummy, East's ace wins the defenders' only trump trick; but if East gets a ruff with the ace, West's holding is worth a trick.

```
              ♠ 8 6 4
♠ A J 9       ┌─────┐    ♠ K 3
              │  N  │
              │W   E│
              │  S  │
              └─────┘
              ♠ Q 10 7 5 2
```

The defenders' three tricks become four if East gets a ruff with the ♠K.

♠ Q J 5 3

♠ 10   ♠ K 9

♠ A 8 7 6 4 2

Spades are trumps. West has cashed three heart tricks and leads the thirteenth heart. No matter what South does, the defense can win a trump trick.

Dlr: South
Vul: N-S

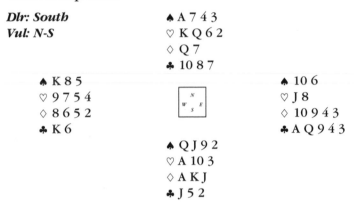

```
              ♠ A 7 4 3
              ♡ K Q 6 2
              ◇ Q 7
              ♣ 10 8 7
♠ K 8 5                        ♠ 10 6
♡ 9 7 5 4                      ♡ J 8
◇ 8 6 5 2                      ◇ 10 9 4 3
♣ K 6                          ♣ A Q 9 4 3
              ♠ Q J 9 2
              ♡ A 10 3
              ◇ A K J
              ♣ J 5 2
```

WEST	NORTH	EAST	SOUTH
			1NT
pass	2♣	dbl	2♠
pass	4♠	all pass	

West leads the ♣K and continues. When East takes the queen and ace, West discards a discouraging low diamond. Since East can see no red-suit tricks on the horizon, he leads another club; and whether South discards, ruffs low or ruffs with an honor, the defense can get a trump.

Try this last example yourself.

Dlr: West
Vul: None

♠ K 10 6 4
♡ 7 3
◇ A K 2
♣ A K J 10

♠ A
♡ K J 9 6 5 4 2
◇ J 3
♣ Q 4 3

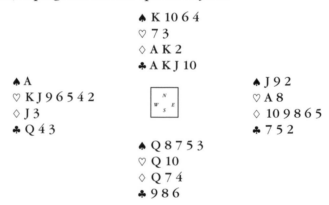

WEST	NORTH	EAST	SOUTH
1♡	dbl	pass	1♠
pass	3♠	pass	4♠
all pass			

You lead a heart, and East produces the ace and returns a heart to your king. South follows with the ten and queen. How do you continue?

Your only chance is to win a second trump trick. Lead another heart, hoping East has the queen or J-9-x:

♠ K 10 6 4
♡ 7 3
◇ A K 2
♣ A K J 10

♠ A
♡ K J 9 6 5 4 2
◇ J 3
♣ Q 4 3

♠ J 9 2
♡ A 8
◇ 10 9 8 6 5
♣ 7 5 2

♠ Q 8 7 5 3
♡ Q 10
◇ Q 7 4
♣ 9 8 6

If dummy discards, East ruffs with the nine, forcing South's queen. When South leads a trump to your ace next, you continue with a fourth heart; and South can't shut out East's ♠J.

Dlr: North
Vul: Both

```
        ♠ A 10 5 2
        ♡ K J 5 3
        ◇ 9 6 4
        ♣ 9 3
                        ♠ 7 4 3
                        ♡ Q 10 7
                        ◇ A K Q 2
                        ♣ 10 6 5
```

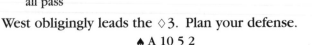

WEST	NORTH	EAST	SOUTH
	pass	pass	1NT
pass	2♣	pass	2♡
pass	3♡	pass	4♡
all pass			

West obligingly leads the ◇3. Plan your defense.

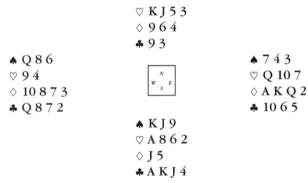

```
              ♠ A 10 5 2
              ♡ K J 5 3
              ◇ 9 6 4
              ♣ 9 3
    ♠ Q 8 6                 ♠ 7 4 3
    ♡ 9 4                   ♡ Q 10 7
    ◇ 10 8 7 3              ◇ A K Q 2
    ♣ Q 8 7 2               ♣ 10 6 5
              ♠ K J 9
              ♡ A 8 6 2
              ◇ J 5
              ♣ A K J 4
```

TIP 15

CONCEAL YOUR HOLDING

Most defenders would take the ◇Q, cash the ace and lead the king, letting nature take its course. South ruffs, cashes the ♡A and loses a finesse with the ♡J. East exits with a club, and South wins, draws trumps and claims, announcing that he will play West for the ♠Q: East, who didn't open the bidding, has shown 11 points and can't hold the queen. As Yogi Berra might say, it takes foresight to look ahead; but an expert East would win the first diamond with the ace and return the queen. When South's jack dropped, East would lead a low diamond next. Late in the play, when the time came for South to guess the ♠Q, he couldn't draw an inference from the bidding and might misguess.

Concealment on defense is an art few players practice. Most players know enough not to signal for declarer's benefit and to false-card in obligatory positions.

♠ A Q 5

♠ K 4   ♠ 10 9 3

♠ J 8 7 6 2

This suit is trumps, and declarer leads low to the queen. East *must* play the nine or ten, leaving declarer to guess whether to lead the jack next time.

Fewer defenders, though, would operate correctly on the deal below.

Dlr: South
Vul: Both

	♠ A Q 10 3	
	♡ J 9 7 3	
	◇ 10 9 7	
	♣ 9 6	
♠ 9 6		♠ K 8 4 2
♡ K		♡ 10 8 2
◇ J 8 6 3		◇ A 5 2
♣ A K J 7 4 3		♣ 10 5 2
	♠ J 7 5	
	♡ A Q 6 5 4	
	◇ K Q 4	
	♣ Q 8	

WEST	NORTH	EAST	SOUTH
			1♡
2♣	2♡	3♣	pass
pass	3♡	all pass	

West cashes two clubs and leads a diamond to East's ace. South wins the next diamond and leads a spade. East plays the nine, suggesting a doubleton, and South tries the queen from dummy. If East takes the king and leads a third diamond, South wins and cashes the ♡A. South reasons that if East held two kings and an ace, he'd have bid 2NT, not 3♣, and that would leave West with a sketchy 2♣ overcall. East should duck the first spade, and South will surely finesse in trumps next. East still gets the ♠K, and South goes down.

When a defender actively thwarts declarer's efforts to get information, it's an 'anti-discovery play'.

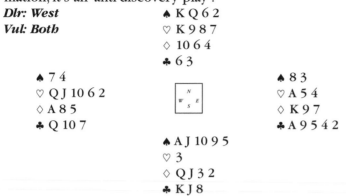

Dlr: West
Vul: Both

	♠ K Q 6 2	
	♡ K 9 8 7	
	◊ 10 6 4	
	♣ 6 3	
♠ 7 4		♠ 8 3
♡ Q J 10 6 2		♡ A 5 4
◊ A 8 5		◊ K 9 7
♣ Q 10 7		♣ A 9 5 4 2
	♠ A J 10 9 5	
	♡ 3	
	◊ Q J 3 2	
	♣ K J 8	

WEST	NORTH	EAST	SOUTH
pass	pass	1◊[1]	1♠
2♡	3♠	all pass	

1.   1♣ would be artificial and strong.

In a Bermuda Bowl, Garozzo and Belladonna were East and West for Italy. Belladonna led the ♡Q and switched to a trump. Declarer, Chagas of Brazil, won in dummy and led a low diamond. Garozzo put up the king(!) and led a low club; he intended to create the idea that he had the ◊AK and therefore lacked the ♣A. Chagas, however, had seen Garozzo defend before. He played the ♣K and wound up making his contract. Well done all around.

Here's a final example for you to try.

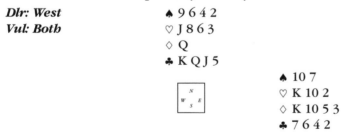

Dlr: West
Vul: Both

	♠ 9 6 4 2	
	♡ J 8 6 3	
	◊ Q	
	♣ K Q J 5	
		♠ 10 7
		♡ K 10 2
		◊ K 10 5 3
		♣ 7 6 4 2

WEST	NORTH	EAST	SOUTH
1◊	pass	2◊	2♠
pass	4♠	all pass	

West leads the ◊4. Plan your defense.

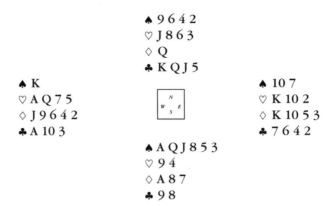

♠ 9 6 4 2
♡ J 8 6 3
◇ Q
♣ K Q J 5

♠ K
♡ A Q 7 5
◇ J 9 6 4 2
♣ A 10 3

♠ 10 7
♡ K 10 2
◇ K 10 5 3
♣ 7 6 4 2

♠ A Q J 8 5 3
♡ 9 4
◇ A 8 7
♣ 9 8

Don't cover with the king; play low! You have nothing to gain by covering — declarer can't get a useful discard from dummy on the ◇ A — and you may give away vital information if you do. South will know you have a heart honor, since West didn't lead a high heart; and if South sees your ◇ K, he'll cash the ♠ A instead of finessing and drop West's king. Play low on the first diamond, and he may go wrong.

PERSONAL GLIMPSES

5

Bridge engages a player's whole personality. Players who are interested in the technical/theoretical side will find endless problems in logic, mathematics, ethics and law. But bridge is also a social, if not always a sociable, pastime: partnership rapport, concentration and will-to-win determine how much you enjoy yourself. In this section, I reflect on some of the personal aspects of our game.

TIP 1

HONOR YOUR PARTNER

Someone asked the late Barry Crane, the best matchpoint player who ever lived, why he found bridge appealing.

"In chess or poker, you're all alone," Crane replied. "I enjoy doing something *with* someone."

Partnership cooperation and trust is bridge's most vital aspect. Partnerships are like marriages: some click, others fail; and the dividing line between success and mediocrity is gossamer-thin. Twenty years ago, I often sat across from a player considered to be my area's best. Ability carried us to some good scores, but we weren't destined for stardom: the chemistry that makes a top partnership just wasn't there, and we drifted on to partners who were more empathetic.

Everything that happens within your partnership affects your score: how much preparation you've had, how you handle bad results, how well you can stay mentally tough. Here's a Top Ten list of my thoughts on partnership procedures.

1. *If you feel the urge to criticize your partner, ask yourself why.*

In my experience, criticism of partner betrays an insecure player. Everyone knows that nothing is gained by telling partner what a dunderhead he is. It won't make him play better; more likely, the thought of hearing more guff will distract him and he'll play worse. To complain over a silly lapse in concentration is especially futile: your partner feels worse than anyone. If he miscounts his aces and gives a wrong Blackwood response, you may as well laugh about it.

Few partners will appreciate even constructive criticism right at the table, when deals remain to be played. The only justification for a brief on-the-spot 'discussion' is to prevent a recurrence of a bidding misunderstanding in the same session. But if your comments are in the least emotional, you do your partnership a disservice.

That brings us back to insecurity: players jump on partner as a face-saving move. If your partner errs, you perceive it as a slight to your own ability — that's how close-knit a bridge partnership is. You feel the urge to humble your partner and make sure everyone knows you're accustomed to a higher standard of play.

Players often lash out at partner because they're upset with themselves.

```
Dlr: North          ♠ J 7 5
Vul: Both           ♡ 6
                    ◇ A Q 9 5
                    ♣ K Q 10 7 5

    ♠ Q 9                          ♠ A 8 3 2
    ♡ A Q 9 7 5 3     ┌─────┐      ♡ J 8 2
    ◇ 10 6 2          │  N  │      ◇ 8 4
    ♣ 6 2             │W   E│      ♣ J 9 8 3
                      │  S  │
                      └─────┘
                    ♠ K 10 6 4
                    ♡ K 10 4
                    ◇ K J 7 3
                    ♣ A 4
```

WEST	NORTH	EAST	SOUTH
	1♣	pass	1♠
pass	2♠	pass	3NT
all pass			

West led the ♡7: six, jack, king. South tried the clubs, but no jack fell; West threw the ◇2. South then led the ♠J from dummy, desperately put up his king when East ducked and ran the diamonds for nine tricks. West castigated East for ducking the spade; but West sensed that he should have thrown the ♡A on the third club. South probably had three hearts (his 3NT suggested four spades, and he hadn't responded 1♡); so West could make sure East knew the hearts were ready to run. West was mad at East because he, West, had slipped, and East had punished him.

Some partnerships use the Keller convention (as in Helen): no colloquy at the table is permitted. None. This approach may be sound in theory, but in practice few players have enough self-discipline to hold it all in. Moreover, a stony silence creates tension and may cause the players to question each other's intelligence. I appreciate *supportive* comments from my partner; it's soothing to hear him say he'd have doubled also after the opponents have made two overtricks.

A sense of humor is indispensible to any partnership that hopes to survive. This deal appeared in a U.S. Team Trials.

Dlr: North
Vul: None

```
                  ♠ Q 10 7 4
                  ♡ J 8 7 6
                  ◇ Q 9 8 6 4
                  ♣ —
♠ —                              ♠ J 8 6 5 3 2
♡ A Q 9 5 2       ┌─────┐        ♡ 10
◇ A               │  N  │        ◇ 10 7 3
♣ Q J 9 8 7 4 2   │W   E│        ♣ 10 5 3
                  │  S  │
                  └─────┘
                  ♠ A K 9
                  ♡ K 4 3
                  ◇ K J 5 2
                  ♣ A K 6
```

WEST	NORTH	EAST	SOUTH
	pass	pass	2NT
3♣	pass	4♠	pass
5♣	pass	pass	dbl
all pass			

According to East-West's system, West's 3♣ was a major-suit take-out, and East duly jumped to 4♠. South passed stoically, but when West corrected to 5♣, South couldn't stand it and got out the chopper. North led a diamond, and West ruffed a couple of hearts in dummy and lost the ♣AK for +550.

In the post-mortem, South observed that a trump opening lead would have beaten the contract. North, of course, protested that he hadn't held a trump, but South was unimpressed.

"A good partner would have found one."

2. *Defensive errors are errors of the partnership.*

A partnership is two players who operate as one. That means that if your partner doesn't play his best, you're partly responsible. Defensive errors are by definition errors of the whole. If your partner misdefends, ask yourself, and ask him, how you might have helped him. (For more on saving partner, see Tip 10 in the section on defense.)

3. *Your partner's dummy play is his business.*

When your partner becomes declarer, your role in the deal is over. Relax. Save your mental energy for the next deal when you may be declarer at a tough contract. Don't watch your partner's progress — or the lack thereof — like a hawk. Don't watch at all. If your partnership is losing points consistently on the deals your partner declares, consider looking for a new partner.

4. *Preserve your partner's supply of mental energy.*

Have you noticed that first-time partnerships often do well? This is no illusion. On your maiden voyage, you're on your best behavior, you usually play a simple system (no disastrous misunderstandings) and you take care not to throw partner curveballs in the bidding and on defense.

Players always do well by letting partner save his supply of mental energy for real problems.

```
Dlr: South          ♠ J 3
Vul: N-S            ♡ A J 6 3
                   ◇ J 6 4 2
                   ♣ J 5 3

♠ Q 10 5 4 2                    ♠ K 9 8
♡ K 8 5            N            ♡ 9 7 4
◇ 9 5 3        W       E        ◇ Q 10 8
♣ A 8             S            ♣ Q 10 7 6

                   ♠ A 7 6
                   ♡ Q 10 2
                   ◇ A K 7
                   ♣ K 9 4 2
```

WEST	NORTH	EAST	SOUTH
			1NT
pass	2♣	pass	2◇
pass	2NT	all pass	

West leads a spade, and South wins the third spade, cashes the ◇AK and runs four hearts with the aid of the finesse. East throws a club and West a diamond. South then tries a club to his king. West takes the ace and cashes a spade, leaving:

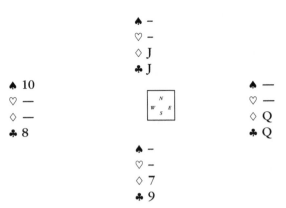

```
              ♠ –
              ♡ –
              ◇ J
              ♣ J
♠ 10                        ♠ —
♡ —          ┌─────┐       ♡ —
◇ —          │ N   │       ◇ Q
♣ 8          │W   E│       ♣ Q
             │  S  │
             └─────┘
              ♠ –
              ♡ –
              ◇ 7
              ♣ 9
```

Since West knows East has the minor-suit queens left, West should lead his club and let East claim. If instead West cashes his ♠10, East must decide which queen to keep. No doubt he should know, but it's inconsiderate of West to make him think about it.

5. **If you're the stronger player in the partnership, don't strain to be declarer. If you're the weaker player, don't try to steer the contract to your partner.**

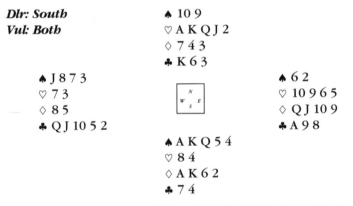

Dlr: South
Vul: Both

```
              ♠ 10 9
              ♡ A K Q J 2
              ◇ 7 4 3
              ♣ K 6 3
♠ J 8 7 3                   ♠ 6 2
♡ 7 3         ┌─────┐      ♡ 10 9 6 5
◇ 8 5         │ N   │      ◇ Q J 10 9
♣ Q J 10 5 2  │W   E│      ♣ A 9 8
              │  S  │
              └─────┘
              ♠ A K Q 5 4
              ♡ 8 4
              ◇ A K 6 2
              ♣ 7 4
```

WEST	NORTH	EAST	SOUTH
			1♠
pass	2♡	pass	3◇
pass	3♡	pass	3♠
pass	4♠	all pass	

South was the more experienced player, and when dummy hit, he said North should have bid 3NT over 3♠. North replied that he hoped South would bid 3NT over 3♡ so he could be declarer. In 4♠, South ruffed the third club and took the three top trumps. He had to start the hearts next; but West ruffed the third heart, and South lost a diamond for down one.

North's 3♡ was fine; South's high reverse to 3◊ promised a strong hand, and North's hearts certainly looked worth rebidding. But 3♡ was wrong if North chose it only to avoid playing the hand; your dummy play can't improve if you're never declarer. As for South, instead of rebidding the spades, he should have raised to 4♡ (cultivating good bidding habits instead of trying to play the hand); even slam in hearts would have a chance.

It's better to play in a laydown contract no matter who is declarer. Even a good South might miss the winning play in 4♠: after South ruffs the third club, he leads a low trump. West takes the jack and leads a fourth club, but South can ruff in dummy, draw trumps and run the hearts.

6. *Distance between partners is desirable.*

More power to those who can play genially and effectively with their spouses. The ideal partnership isn't encumbered by emotional attachments. Detachment and mutual respect is the ideal state.

7. *When you and your partner review your results, check your ego at the door.*

Any aspiring partnership must go over its results, looking for areas that need discussion. (Top partnerships such as Meckstroth-Rodwell spend hundreds of hours reviewing their methods.) The best time is well after the session — ideally, the next day or later — when your objectivity isn't clouded by the result, your mood is dispassionate and you've had time to reflect. (I remember times when, at the table, I was sure my partner had erred; after I thought about it, I realized his play was correct.) In a constructive review, players must set ego aside. They must offer constructive criticism of their partner and of themselves. The goal is not to prove who is the greater player, but to improve the partnership's efficiency.

8. *In the post-mortem, don't neglect your good results.*

Where you do well is every bit as important as where you fall short. Gain confidence from your top boards.

9. *Make your partner feel you're on his side.*

I said earlier that everything that happens can affect your partnership. Little things that may seem inconsequential to you can affect your partner's morale and weaken his will-to-win. At an NABC in the early Eighties, I had a professional date to play with a lovely lady with whom I had done well in the past. It was the last weekend of the tournament, and when we greeted each other, I made the mistake of remarking that I was fatigued from a week's play. We proceeded to turn in a poor session, and afterwards my partner told me she had been disheartened by my comment: she thought, quite understandably, that I wasn't ready to give her my best effort. My comment was especially inappropriate because I was playing pro, but any player owes his partner the courtesy of keeping an upbeat mood.

On another occasion, I had a defensive mix-up with a different partner. He proceeded to ask declarer how we could have beaten the contract — and declarer responded by telling my partner what I could have done differently! I remember being mad enough to chew nails — at declarer, who couldn't have known what my problems were and had no business dissecting them, but mostly at my partner. *Never* appeal to your opponents; it's a letdown for your partner. Instead, let your partner know you're behind him. Display optimism and supportiveness. Keep a smile on your face, and you'll be everyone's favorite partner.

10. The Golden Rule applies.

Treat your partner as you would be treated, and you won't go far wrong.

Even at the social level, bridge is intensely competitive, and bridge players are intelligent, often emotional animals who get as caught up in their game as an NFL linebacker in a playoff game. Since you can't let off steam by tackling your opponents, arguments and bad feeling at the table are regrettable but inevitable. I'm not going to advocate yielding to your baser instincts and being obnoxious to your opponents, but I will offer a different approach to the plaguing problem of rudeness at the table.

TIP 2

DON'T BE CON-TENTIOUS WITH YOUR OPPONENTS

In my younger days, when I was a rising young expert and wanted to make sure everybody knew it, I subscribed to the theory that a fight a day keeps boredom away. I considered a session shot if I didn't get into at least one name-calling set-to. Oh, I could plead that sometimes my antics were marginally justified. The opponents would misdefend, and some self-proclaimed 'authority' would apply the old 'criticize partner before he criticizes you' technique. I'd be so indignant at this defilement of the game that I'd tell my opponent what an idiot he was, and we'd go on from there. I also had the bad habit of grumbling out loud when an opponent made a questionable bid or play that worked — just what he wanted to hear. But a loser denigrates his opponents; a winner refuses to underestimate even the Little Old Ladies and devotes all his energy to trying to beat them.

Now that I'm older and wiser, I've adopted a practical approach to conduct. I commend it to those who constantly contend with their insecurity or suppress a mean streak. My approach is based on two facts:

1. We play bridge because we seek the glow that comes from ego gratification. We like to play well and to win. But *even slight unpleasantness at the table causes tension* that poisons your concentration and keeps you from playing your best. Since even a little tension can distract my focus, I greet the opponents at every table. I want a nice, relaxed feeling of harmony so I can concentrate totally and dispassionately on the game.

2. Most tournament players are technically proficient. A big factor that distinguishes winners is will-to-win. My experience is that it's easier to beat someone who likes you than someone who wants to destroy you. Antagonize your opponents and they'll be determined to send you to the next table with a fishhook in your gills.

Do yourself a favor: court your opponents with good fellowship.

TIP 3

MAINTAIN YOUR FOCUS

One of the incongruous things about bridge is that it often takes more effort to play and defend a one-level contract than a grand slam. In a lifetime, the small potatoes will add up to quite a few bushels.

As West, with neither side vulnerable, you hold

♠ 10   ♡ A 8 4 2   ◇ A Q 6 3   ♣ 8 6 5 3

South's 1NT opening ends the auction, and you lead the ♡2.

```
                    ♠ 8 7 4 2
                    ♡ 10 3
                    ◇ 9 5 2
                    ♣ K Q 10 4
♠ 10
♡ A 8 4 2
◇ A Q 6 3           N
♣ 8 6 5 3        W     E
                    S
```

East produces the ♡Q, and South plays the seven. East shifts to the ♠5. South thinks it over and plays the king. Next comes a club to dummy's king — nine from East — and a diamond: eight, jack. You take the queen. What now?

```
                    ♠ 8 7 4 2
                    ♡ 10 3
                    ◇ 9 5 2
                    ♣ K Q 10 4
♠ 10                                ♠ Q J 9 5 3
♡ A 8 4 2           N               ♡ K Q 6 5
◇ A Q 6 3        W     E             ◇ 8 7
♣ 8 6 5 3           S               ♣ 9 7
                    ♠ A K 6
                    ♡ J 9 7
                    ◇ K J 10 4
                    ♣ A J 2
```

When I was East, West continued with the ♡4 to my king, and we could no longer beat 1NT. We took two more hearts and the ◇A, and declarer claimed. At the fifth trick, West must lead the ♡8 (or the ♡A and then the eight). It's hard to see how West expects to beat 1NT without a spade trick from East as well as four hearts and two diamonds; but then West must find East with two entries. East will take the ♡K and force out South's ♠A; and when West gets in with the ◇A, he can lead the ♡A and then the four, and East will win with the six and run the spades. It was an innocuous deal with only 140 points at stake. Minus 90 points or plus 50? Those small potatoes mount up.

There is an old story about a cattle rancher who sired three boys he hoped would inherit the ranch. With that in mind, he named the place 'Focus' — because that is where the sun's rays meet (sons raise meat). When people ask me how to improve their results, I talk about maintaining focus: they must eliminate avoidable errors. Technical skill and good judgment aren't enough; most errors come from lapses in concentration. A player knows better, but he errs because his mind isn't attuned to the game. Even at the world championship level, events are decided not by who turns in the most brilliancies but by who avoids the most silly errors.

Any player can succumb to a *fixation*: making a hasty, perhaps subconsciously influenced assumption and clinging to it too long. I can offer a personal example: I recall defending a 3NT contract against which my partner led a low club. Dummy hit with ♣10943. I had ♣Q5, and when dummy played low, my queen won. For some reason, my mind told me the opponents would never have bid 3NT without a club stopper — and declarer had the ♣J left. So I shifted to avoid setting up a club trick in dummy, and declarer claimed nine tricks. My partner, who had found a fine lead from A-K-J-x-x, still hasn't got over it.

Focus is a product of two elements: will-to-win (discussed in the next section) and discipline. A single-minded determination to succeed is vital in any pursuit but especially in a mental exercise such as competitive bridge; and a player who can discipline himself to arrange his thinking before he plays — like a golf pro who never deviates from his pre-shot routine — will have an edge. Try these three dummy play problems.

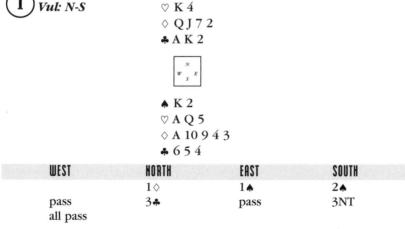

①	Dlr: North Vul: N-S	♠ 10 8 4 3 ♡ K 4 ◇ Q J 7 2 ♣ A K 2
		N *W E* *S*
		♠ K 2 ♡ A Q 5 ◇ A 10 9 4 3 ♣ 6 5 4

WEST	NORTH	EAST	SOUTH
	1◇	1♠	2♠
pass	3♣	pass	3NT
all pass			

West leads the ♠J. Plan the play.

2 *Dlr: South*
Vul: Both

♠ A K 4 3
♡ 7 5
◇ A J 2
♣ A K 5 4

♠ 9 2
♡ A K 6
◇ K 10 5 4 3
♣ Q 7 6

WEST	NORTH	EAST	SOUTH
			1◇
pass	1♠	pass	1NT
pass	3♣	pass	3◇
pass	4NT	pass	5◇
pass	7◇	all pass	

West leads the ◇6. Plan the play.

3 *Dlr: West*
Vul: Both

♠ K Q J 8 7
♡ 3 2
◇ 5 4 3
♣ K 3 2

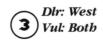

♠ —
♡ A K Q 8 7 4
◇ A 9 6
♣ 7 6 5 4

WEST	NORTH	EAST	SOUTH
2◇	pass	pass	3♡
pass	4♡	all pass	

West leads the ♠A. Plan the play.

SOLUTIONS

Problems that test your concentration are easier on paper but still good practice.

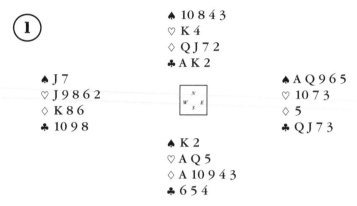

East will duck the first spade — and so must South. Give South the ♠Q instead of the king and it's the same.

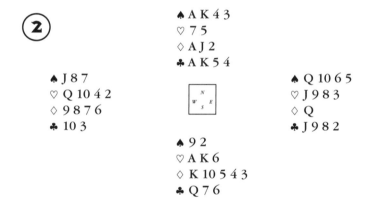

Since the opening lead marks East with the ◇Q, South must play the ace at the first trick. If East followed low, South would finesse against East after ruffing a heart in dummy. As the cards lie, South fails if he plays low from dummy on the first trump: he can't ruff a heart in dummy without setting up a trump trick for West and has no other way to get a thirteenth trick.

(3)

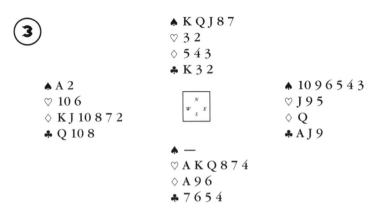

```
                    ♠ K Q J 8 7
                    ♡ 3 2
                    ◇ 5 4 3
                    ♣ K 3 2
♠ A 2                              ♠ 10 9 6 5 4 3
♡ 10 6            ┌─────┐         ♡ J 9 5
◇ K J 10 8 7 2   │  N  │         ◇ Q
♣ Q 10 8         │ W   E│        ♣ A J 9
                 │  S  │
                 └─────┘
                    ♠ —
                    ♡ A K Q 8 7 4
                    ◇ A 9 6
                    ♣ 7 6 5 4
```

South must ruff the ♠A with the ♡7 or ♡8. East is sure to have the ♣A, so South's best chance is to find him with three trumps and toss him in to lead to dummy. After ruffing, South takes the ♡AK and the ◇A, removing East's diamond exit, and leads a low heart. If South ruffs the first spade with the ♡4, an alert East can play his ♡9 and ♡J under the ace and king, avoiding the throw-in.

BE ALL YOU
CAN BE

Dlr: West
Vul: E-W

```
                    ♠ Q 9
                    ♡ 7 4 3
                    ◇ K 9 5
                    ♣ A 9 8 7 5
                 ┌─────┐
                 │  N  │
                 │ W   E│
                 │  S  │
                 └─────┘
                    ♠ A K 10 6
                    ♡ Q J 5
                    ◇ A J 10 8 6 4
                    ♣ —
```

WEST	NORTH	EAST	SOUTH
pass	pass	pass	1◇
pass	1NT	pass	2♠
pass	3◇	pass	4◇
pass	5♣	pass	5◇
all pass			

West leads the ♣J. You play low, ruff in your hand and cash the ace and king of trumps. East shows out, and it seems you're going down. Even if you can cash four spade tricks to pitch two hearts from dummy, the defense may take the ◇Q when they win a heart trick, depriving you of a heart ruff in dummy. Do you concede down one?

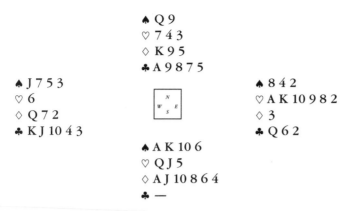

```
                ♠ Q 9
                ♡ 7 4 3
                ◇ K 9 5
                ♣ A 9 8 7 5
♠ J 7 5 3                        ♠ 8 4 2
♡ 6              ┌─────┐         ♡ A K 10 9 8 2
◇ Q 7 2         │N    │         ◇ 3
♣ K J 10 4 3    │W   E│         ♣ Q 6 2
                │  S  │
                └─────┘
                ♠ A K 10 6
                ♡ Q J 5
                ◇ A J 10 8 6 4
                ♣ —
```

In a Bermuda Bowl, Robert Jordan for the U.S. continued with the ♣A, a club ruff, a spade to the queen and a club ruff. He took the ♠AK, ruffed a spade and ruffed a club. West had to follow — and that was eleven tricks!

Natural ability, experience, judgment and concentration contribute to success at bridge, but nobody gets anywhere without desire. Not everyone can have the creativity of a Hamman or the endurance of a Soloway, but what most beginners can achieve is limited only by how much time and effort they're willing to expend. Moreover, I've never known a top player who didn't have a overwhelming drive to be the best.

The will-to-win factor carries over to the play of every single deal: a winning player never gives up on a contract. In a game on OKbridge, the outstanding Internet bridge server, Australian internationalist Margaret Bourke was South on this deal.

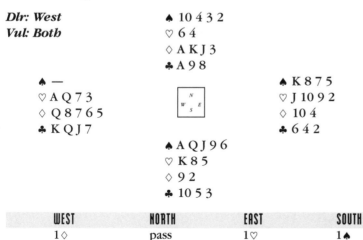

```
Dlr: West        ♠ 10 4 3 2
Vul: Both        ♡ 6 4
                 ◇ A K J 3
                 ♣ A 9 8
♠ —                              ♠ K 8 7 5
♡ A Q 7 3        ┌─────┐         ♡ J 10 9 2
◇ Q 8 7 6 5     │N    │         ◇ 10 4
♣ K Q J 7       │W   E│         ♣ 6 4 2
                │  S  │
                └─────┘
                 ♠ A Q J 9 6
                 ♡ K 8 5
                 ◇ 9 2
                 ♣ 10 5 3
```

WEST	NORTH	EAST	SOUTH
1◇	pass	1♡	1♠
3♠	4◇	pass	4♠
all pass			

West led the ♣K, and Bourke ducked the first trick, a play experts often make instinctively and without knowing exactly why. West then led the ♣J, and Bourke took the ace and led a spade to the queen. West threw a heart.

Declarer had problems. She could finesse the ◇J to get a club discard but couldn't use it without drawing trumps. Then dummy would have no more trumps — three hearts to lose. A simple squeeze against West in clubs and diamonds (or in the red suits) couldn't work because declarer couldn't lose three tricks, rectifying the count to make the squeeze operate. Should South despair and concede down one?

After Bourke's ♠Q held, she returned a diamond to the ace and picked up the trumps. West threw another heart, a diamond and a low club. Declarer next took the winning diamond finesse, leaving this position.

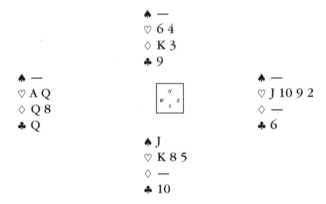

```
              ♠ —
              ♡ 6 4
              ◇ K 3
              ♣ 9
   ♠ —                        ♠ —
   ♡ A Q        N             ♡ J 10 9 2
   ◇ Q 8     W     E          ◇ —
   ♣ Q          S             ♣ 6
              ♠ J
              ♡ K 8 5
              ◇ —
              ♣ 10
```

Declarer threw a heart on the ◇K, ruffed a diamond and exited with a club. West had to concede the last trick to the ♡K: well done! West could have thrown the ♣Q, hoping East had the ten; but as the cards lay, he had no escape.

Dlr: South
Vul: Both

♠ A K J 4
♡ K Q 10 4 3
♢ 6
♣ J 5 3

♠ 8 7 6 2
♡ 8 7 5
♢ J 8 4 3
♣ 8 7

<table>
<tr><td>N</td></tr>
<tr><td>W   E</td></tr>
<tr><td>S</td></tr>
</table>

♠ Q 10 9 5 3
♡ —
♢ A 10 9 7 2
♣ 9 4 2

♠ —
♡ A J 9 6 2
♢ K Q 5
♣ A K Q 10 6

WEST	NORTH	EAST	SOUTH
			1♡
pass	3♡	pass	3♠(!)
pass	4♠	pass	6NT
pass	7NT	dbl	all pass

The bidding left something to be desired, especially East's double, which got him a spade opening lead he didn't want. South took the ♠AK and casually led the ♡4 to his ace and the ♡6 back to the king. He next raced off five rounds of clubs and then cashed the ♡Q, dropping his jack, and the ♡10. And at the twelfth trick, dummy led the ♡3. East had the ♠Q and the ♢A left; and try as he might, he couldn't remember whether South had played the ♡2. When East finally threw the ♠Q, South produced the deuce of hearts, and dummy won the last trick with the ♠J.

Here's a final example for you to try.

Dlr: South
Vul: Both

♠ K Q 7
♡ Q J 5 2
♢ Q J 5 4
♣ Q 9

<table>
<tr><td>N</td></tr>
<tr><td>W   E</td></tr>
<tr><td>S</td></tr>
</table>

♠ J 5 2
♡ 9 8 6 4
♢ A
♣ J 10 8 5 4

WEST	NORTH	EAST	SOUTH
			1♣
pass	1♡	pass	1NT
pass	3NT	all pass	

West leads the ♢10 to your ace. Do you see any hope of beating 3NT?

```
                        ♠ K Q 7
                        ♡ Q J 5 2
                        ◇ Q J 5 4
                        ♣ Q 9
     ♠ A 9 6 4                              ♠ J 5 2
     ♡ A 3              ┌─────┐             ♡ 9 8 6 4
     ◇ 10 9 8 7 3      │  N  │             ◇ A
     ♣ 6 3             │ W E │             ♣ J 10 8 5 4
                        │  S  │
                        └─────┘
                        ♠ 10 8 3
                        ♡ K 10 7
                        ◇ K 6 2
                        ♣ A K 7 2
```

WEST	NORTH	EAST	SOUTH
			1♣
pass	1♡	pass	1NT
pass	3NT	all pass	

The actual East knew South had no more than three spades and also figured the defense was lost unless West held the ♠A. So at the second trick, East shifted to the ♠2. South misguessed by playing the eight, and West's nine forced the queen. When declarer led a heart next, West took the ace and smoothly returned a low spade, giving South a tough guess. Never give up!

Dlr: South
Vul: None

CULTIVATE YOUR TABLE PRESENCE

```
             ♠ K Q 4
             ♡ 6 5
             ◇ A Q 5 4
             ♣ A 8 5 2

                 N
               W   E
                 S

             ♠ A 8 7
             ♡ A 7
             ◇ K 7 3
             ♣ J 9 6 4 3
```

WEST	NORTH	EAST	SOUTH
			1♣
pass	1◇	pass	1NT
pass	3♣	pass	3◇
pass	5♣	all pass	

West leads the ♡Q against your 5♣. You take the ace and lead a low trump: seven, ace, king. "Gosh," says East. "You sure are lucky." How do you continue?

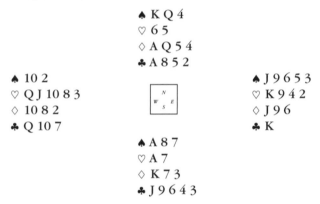

```
              ♠ K Q 4
              ♡ 6 5
              ◇ A Q 5 4
              ♣ A 8 5 2
♠ 10 2                        ♠ J 9 6 5 3
♡ Q J 10 8 3        N         ♡ K 9 4 2
◇ 10 8 2          W   E       ◇ J 9 6
♣ Q 10 7            S         ♣ K
              ♠ A 8 7
              ♡ A 7
              ◇ K 7 3
              ♣ J 9 6 4 3
```

Judging by East's indiscreet comment, he has no more trumps. Instead of leading a second trump and hoping for a 2-2 break, try for a 3-3 diamond break.

Things are always happening at a bridge table: hesitations, remarks and mannerisms. But some of the psychological aspects of the game are becoming extinct: in tournaments, bidding boxes have eliminated vocal inflections from the auction, and in top-level events, screens prevent you from seeing your partner and one opponent. Hence the inference in the deal below might be unavailable in a World Championship — but it is still there in most games.

Dlr: North
Vul: None

```
                    ♠ J 9 4 2
                    ♡ K 10 7
                    ◇ K 6 4
                    ♣ A J 3
     ♠ 10 5                              ♠ Q 8
     ♡ 9 5 3 2         ┌─────┐          ♡ Q 8 4
     ◇ Q 10 9 8        │  N  │          ◇ A J 7 2
     ♣ 9 6 5           │ W E │          ♣ K 8 7 2
                       │  S  │
                       └─────┘
                    ♠ A K 7 6 3
                    ♡ A J 6
                    ◇ 5 3
                    ♣ Q 10 4
```

WEST	NORTH	EAST	SOUTH
	pass	pass[1]	1♠
pass	3♠	pass	4♠
all pass			

1.   After a huddle.

West leads the ◇10, winning the trick, and continues the suit. South ruffs the third diamond, cashes the ♠AK, loses the club finesse, wins the club return and must find the ♡Q. He has seen East play ten points; was East's huddle a 'twelve-point twitch'?

When East huddles before passing, it may be what Mike Lawrence called a 'tell': a legitimate indication. Or East may have been thinking about where to take his wife for dinner. South can draw inferences, but at his own risk (unless it's clear East was deliberately trying to deceive him). Lawrence gave an example of distinguishing between meaningful huddlers and daydreamers. Suppose East huddles. "It's your bid," someone says. If East then passes *immediately*, it's more likely he had a problem. If instead he was daydreaming, he'd examine his hand for at least a moment before passing.

Playing your opponents is an art that won't go out of style.

Dlr: South
Vul: Both

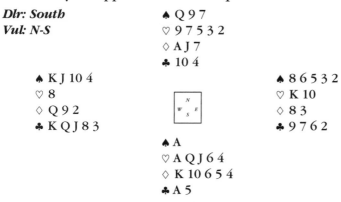

```
              ♠ K 6 4
              ♡ 7 5
              ◇ A Q 10 5 4
              ♣ J 6 5
♠ Q 8 5                          ♠ J 10 7 2
♡ A Q 8 4 3 2      N             ♡ J 9
◇ K 6          W       E         ◇ J 9 8 7 2
♣ 7 2              S             ♣ 9 3
              ♠ A 9 3
              ♡ K 10 6
              ◇ 3
              ♣ A K Q 10 8 4
```

WEST	NORTH	EAST	SOUTH
			1♣
1♡	2◇	pass	3♣
pass	4♣	pass	6♣(!)
all pass			

South's last bid was a complete shot, but he knew West was the type of player who would snatch the ♡A against a slam. After that happened, South made 6♣ by finessing the ◇Q.

On-line bridge is booming. Do you think table presence is possible when your opponent is at a computer a thousand miles away?

Dlr: South
Vul: N-S

```
              ♠ Q 9 7
              ♡ 9 7 5 3 2
              ◇ A J 7
              ♣ 10 4
♠ K J 10 4                       ♠ 8 6 5 3 2
♡ 8              N               ♡ K 10
◇ Q 9 2      W       E           ◇ 8 3
♣ K Q J 8 3      S               ♣ 9 7 6 2
              ♠ A
              ♡ A Q J 6 4
              ◇ K 10 6 5 4
              ♣ A 5
```

WEST	NORTH	EAST	SOUTH
			1♡
dbl	2♡	pass	3◇
pass	4♡	pass	4♠
pass	5◇	pass	6♡
all pass			

I was North, playing on OKbridge, when South and I stretched to 6♡. It would have been a better slam on any lead other than the actual one: the ♣K. South took his ace, thought for a while and led a diamond to dummy's jack. This play produced the three from East, a warm glow in my heart and a rueful comment on the screen from West:

:-(

This was the universal symbol for gloom (turn it sideways!).

South wasn't home yet. He led a trump from dummy and had to take a view when East played the ten. If East had the king left, a finesse would land the slam. If West had the king, South needed to play the ace. Even if the king didn't fall, South would be safe if West had

♠ K J 10 4   ♡ K 8   ◇ Q 9 2   ♣ K Q 10 8

or

♠ K J 10 4   ♡ K 8   ◇ Q 9 8 2   ♣ K Q 8.

since South could shift back to diamonds and get rid of a club from dummy before West would ruff in. South judged to put up the ♡A; but West followed low, and East ruffed the third diamond and returned a club. Down one.

I expect South thought he took the best percentage play. Maybe; but his table presence — or computer presence — was lacking. West's 'comment' was a dead giveaway. When East couldn't beat the ◇J, West obviously thought South was about to wrap up the slam — hence West couldn't have the ♡K.

Some people think the impersonal nature of on-line bridge is an improvement over the table. (For instance, you're free to criticize your partner without fearing he'll bonk you in the nose with the duplicate board.) Whether that's true or not, table presence isn't a defunct art yet. Try this last deal yourself:

Dlr: South
Vul: N-S

♠ K 6 4
♡ A K 7
◇ Q J 2
♣ A Q 6 2

	N	
W		E
	S	

♠ A J 9
♡ J 10 6 4
◇ A 10 9 4
♣ K 7

WEST	NORTH	EAST	SOUTH
			1◇
pass	2♣	pass	2NT
pass	6NT	all pass	

West leads the ♠2. You win with the nine, and West looks unhappy. You lead a heart to the king and let the ◇Q ride, losing to West's king. He returns a heart. How do you play?

East surely has the ♡Q. West already gave away a trick by leading from one queen. Take the ♡A. If the queen doesn't fall, perhaps the run of your winners will squeeze East in clubs and hearts.

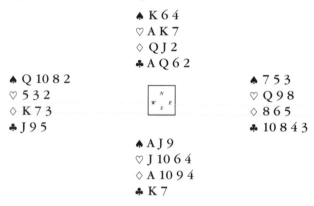

```
                    ♠ K 6 4
                    ♡ A K 7
                    ◇ Q J 2
                    ♣ A Q 6 2
    ♠ Q 10 8 2                        ♠ 7 5 3
    ♡ 5 3 2          N                ♡ Q 9 8
    ◇ K 7 3       W     E             ◇ 8 6 5
    ♣ J 9 5          S                ♣ 10 8 4 3
                    ♠ A J 9
                    ♡ J 10 6 4
                    ◇ A 10 9 4
                    ♣ K 7
```

TIP 6

FOR BRIDGE TEACHERS: CAN BRIDGE BE TAUGHT?

A few years ago, Devyn Press wanted to publish a series of teacher's manuals with companion student texts. I was pleased when I was asked to write the series; it gave me a chance to air my quaint ideas on bridge pedagogy, which I cherish against stern opposition.

Anyone who teaches bridge knows it's no joyride. Besides coping with frustrations such as attrition and limited class time, a teacher must infuse ardor into students who aren't highly motivated. They aren't there so they can get a job or earn a degree; they want to have fun. A teacher who expects his class to absorb gobs of material, especially on bidding, is courting trouble. Is it really possible to turn someone with little or no knowledge of the game into a bridge player in sixteen hours of class time? Of course not. And so I developed my philosophy: *a bridge teacher's role must be to inspire*.

My philosophy was manifested in two ways. First, I embraced an elitist approach: any student with talent would get a chance to develop it. I taught the basics all right, but I refused to pound on them endlessly. Other teachers could give their students an equal chance at mediocrity; not I. The word today — not just in bridge — seems to be, 'Don't demand excellence; settle for less.' So I made 'Expect a lot' my battle cry. Early on, I introduced handling card combinations and inferring the lie of a single suit from the play. I mentioned exceptions (horrors!) to rules. In Intermediate class, I talked about anticipation in the bidding and inference in the play. I blew hard on the spark of a logical thought process. Of course, some of my offerings zoomed past the students like Randy Johnson fastballs. But if one student's eyes lit up as he grasped a point, I knew I'd given a boost to someone with promise — someone who might find bridge a source of intellectual pleasure.

Second, I cut down on dispensing rules. Too many rules obscured the reason for the game's appeal, and my aim was to make it appealing so the students would pursue it on their own. I wanted to show why bridge is so fascinating: it involves problem-solving. Yes, I know players need solid basics; I've written articles on that theme. But for teachers to spend all their precious time on basics is wrong. Work on basics as you must, then get on to something interesting — and hope you impress someone enough to light a fire. *Your role is to inspire*.

You say, "My class struggles with finesses; they'll never draw an inference." Maybe so. But if your students, peering through the mist after ten lessons, still have no idea why you and I find bridge a compelling game, what's the point of pouring on more rules? Any teacher can give his students a rudimentary knowledge of the game. What matters is whether he gives them an incentive to keep playing.

I don't mean to suggest that a teacher should try beginners with compound squeezes, or dote on one student and tell the rest to try gin rummy. The issue is not whether Joe Jones can learn the game in sixteen hours; he can't. It's whether the Joes who have a chance to be bridge players should be fully encouraged. Most courses are fine as far as they go. I simply think at some point a teacher must say, "We've seen lots of rules, but if bridge amounted only to rules, nobody would play. Here's what I mean."

Dlr: East	♠ J 10 7 5	
Vul: None	♡ K 10 5	
	◇ K 6 4	
	♣ A Q 5	

♠ 6 3		♠ Q 9
♡ Q 8 2	N W E S	♡ 9 7 6 3
◇ J 10 9 5 2		◇ A Q 7
♣ 9 7 6		♣ K 8 3 2

♠ A K 8 4 2	
♡ A J 4	
◇ 8 3	
♣ J 10 4	

WEST	NORTH	EAST	SOUTH
		pass	1♠
pass	3♠	pass	4♠
all pass			

South ruffs the third diamond, cashes the top trumps and loses a club finesse. Since East, a passed hand, has played the ◇AQ, ♠Q and ♣K, South knows who has the ♡Q. That's bridge.

The Beginning course I did for Devyn was straightforward; but lessons in the Intermediate and Advanced courses have a section meant to stimulate thinking. Conventions are treated lightly. I know one Advanced course that consists *entirely* of discussions of conventions, but if an 'advanced' player is someone who knows conventions, we all might as well take up Nintendo. An advanced player displays sound technique and judgment, draws inferences and avoids silly errors.

Once I partnered a woman whose interest was keen, but whose game lacked soundness and discipline. I found that someone had taught her a set of artificial responses to 1NT. An early board:

Dlr: North
Vul: Both

```
                    ♠ 6
                    ♡ J 8 3 2
                    ◇ Q 9 4 2
                    ♣ Q J 9 7
♠ A K 4 3                           ♠ 9 7 5 2
♡ 10 6 4          N                 ♡ A K 9
◇ 10 8 7        W   E               ◇ A 5 3
♣ 6 5 2           S                 ♣ 10 4 3
                    ♠ Q J 10 8
                    ♡ Q 7 5
                    ◇ K J 6
                    ♣ A K 8
```

WEST	NORTH	EAST	SOUTH
	pass	pass	1NT
pass	2♠[1]	pass	2NT
pass	3♠[2]	pass	3NT
all pass			

1. Transfer to 2NT.
2. 1-4-4-4 pattern.

It reminded me of Bill Cosby as Dr. Cliff Huxtable, returning from the hardware store with his latest gadget. My partner was so enamored with her toy that she committed us to game with six points! A taste of Blackwood and Stayman is fine, but let the rest go. Conventions do not a good player make. Like my partner in the deal above, students need your help in honing their natural bidding skills. Don't turn them into Dr. Huxtables.

Bridge has been facing a crisis of image: many young people view the game as a sedentary one, like dominoes. Bridge can compete as a leisure activity only if prospective players quickly see its challenges and rewards. A potential player's enthusiasm can't be smothered under a blanket of rules; a teacher's task is to see that it's not.

An average teacher instructs. A better teacher explains. An excellent teacher demonstrates. But an exceptional teacher inspires.

TIP 7

ENJOY THE POST-MORTEM

The game is over, the scores are up, and you and other players are relaxing in the club lounge or at your favorite pizza place, toasting the winners, post-morteming the deals and trading stories of triumphs and setbacks. This is the part of the game I like best: looking back and seeing how I could have done better and what perfect play would have wrought — and enjoying the good fellowship of friends. After all, when all the finesses and squeezes and endplays are done, it's not about your score — it's about the friends you play with and enjoying the good times with them.

Discussing the deals is a route to self-improvement as well as a catharsis. I set many of my syndicated columns in an imaginary club with recurring characters, and quite often I have Unlucky Louie moaning over his latest debacle. Louie, however, never learns anything from his mistakes; he attributes it all to bad luck — despite overwhelming evidence to the contrary.

Dlr: South
Vul: None
Matchpoints

```
                    ♠ Q 10
                    ♡ 4 3 2
                    ◇ 10 9 7 6
                    ♣ A K J 10
  ♠ 9 8 6 5 3                      ♠ K J 7
  ♡ 10 9              N            ♡ K Q J
  ◇ K 4 3 2       W     E          ◇ Q J 8 5
  ♣ 5 4              S             ♣ 9 3 2
                    ♠ A 4 2
                    ♡ A 8 7 6 5
                    ◇ A
                    ♣ Q 8 7 6
```

WEST	NORTH	EAST	SOUTH
			1♡
pass	2♣	pass	3♣
pass	3♡	pass	4♡
all pass			

Most Souths get a spade lead against 4♡. They concede a spade,

BECOMING A BRIDGE EXPERT

ruff a spade in dummy and lose two trumps, making four. Louie, of course, receives the 'killing' trump lead. He ducks, wins the second trump and tries a spade to the ten. East wins with the jack and cashes his high trump, and Louie loses another spade for down one.

After a trump lead, South can duck, win the second trump, cash the ◇A, and get to dummy three times with clubs to ruff diamonds. South then leads another club to dummy. If East doesn't ruff, South throws him in with a trump to lead from the ♠K: making five! But Louie is too busy complaining about his luck to notice this.

Another article of mine included the deal below. Somewhere, I had read a definition of the ultimate compression play — and though I constructed the deal, I wouldn't bet that it never happened to someone in real life.

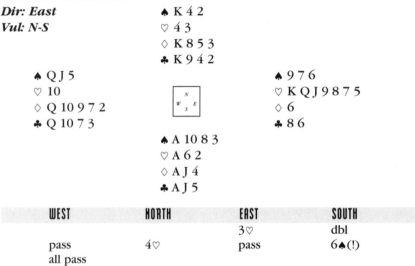

Dir: East
Vul: N-S

```
                    ♠ K 4 2
                    ♡ 4 3
                    ◇ K 8 5 3
                    ♣ K 9 4 2
   ♠ Q J 5                              ♠ 9 7 6
   ♡ 10                                 ♡ K Q J 9 8 7 5
   ◇ Q 10 9 7 2                         ◇ 6
   ♣ Q 10 7 3                           ♣ 8 6
                    ♠ A 10 8 3
                    ♡ A 6 2
                    ◇ A J 4
                    ♣ A J 5
```

WEST	NORTH	EAST	SOUTH
		3♡	dbl
pass	4♡	pass	6♠(!)
all pass			

West leads the ♡10: three, jack, ace. South, looking at about as many losers as winners, cashes the ♠AK and leads a heart from dummy. East plays the seven, South follows with something West assumes can beat a mere seven, and West ruffs. West then leads a club, and South wins with the jack, ruffs his last heart in dummy, comes to the ♣A and takes two more trumps. West can't protect both minors, and South takes four spades, a heart, a heart ruff, three clubs, two diamonds and his twelfth trick in whichever minor West unguards. It's the ultimate compression play: West ruffs his partner's trick with his own natural trump trick, thereby endplaying himself and simultaneously rectifying the count for a squeeze. Can you imagine hearing West tell that story on himself?

Ah, what stories I have heard in post-mortems. Playing in a local duplicate in 1977, I met this deal:

5 · PERSONAL GLIMPSES

Dlr: South
Vul: None

```
                        ♠ 8 6 4
                        ♡ A K
                        ◊ K Q 5 3
                        ♣ 10 6 4 3
  ♠ K 10 7 5 2                              ♠ A 3
  ♡ 10 8 7 3          ┌─────────┐          ♡ J 9 6 5 2
  ◊ A 9 4             │   N     │          ◊ J 10 7 2
  ♣ J                 │ W     E │          ♣ A 2
                      │   S     │
                      └─────────┘
                        ♠ Q J 9
                        ♡ Q 4
                        ◊ 8 6
                        ♣ K Q 9 8 7 5
```

WEST	NORTH	EAST	SOUTH
			1♣(!)
pass	1◊	pass	1NT(!)
pass	3NT	all pass	

I was East. South was a Sweet Old Lady who consistently made mincemeat of me, and West, my partner, was a pupil whose defensive carding I couldn't trust. West led a spade, and I took the ace and returned a spade to the king. West led a third spade. On the bidding, I thought, she could have at most a queen left; but if the South hand were

♠ Q J 9 ♡ Q 7 4 ◊ A 6 ♣ K J 8 7 5

I could beat the contract by discarding the ♣A, creating a sure entry to West's good spades. Well, I didn't beat it; but at Pizza Hut after the game, I had a story to tell that brought down the house.

All I know is, if I had to live my life over, I'd live it over a bridge club.

More Bridge Titles from Master Point Press

Around the World in 80 Hands
by Zia Mahmood with David Burn
256pp., PB   Can $22.95   US $16.95

A Study in Silver *A second collection of bridge stories*
by David Silver
128pp., PB   Can $12.95   US $9.95

Bridge the Silver Way by David Silver and Tim Bourke
192pp., PB   Can $19.95   US $14.95

Bridge: 25 Ways to Compete in the Bidding
by Barbara Seagram and Marc Smith
192pp., PB   Can $1995   US $15.95

Bridge, Zia... and me by Michael Rosenberg
(foreword by Zia Mahmood)
192pp., PB   Can $19.95   US $15.95

Classic Kantar *A collection of bridge humor* by Eddie Kantar
192pp., PB   Can $19.95   US $14.95

Competitive Bidding in the 21st Century by Marshall Miles
254pp.,PB   Can. $22.95   US. $16.95

Countdown to Winning Bridge by Tim Bourke and Marc Smith
92pp., PB   Can $19.95   US $14.95

Easier Done Than Said *Brilliancy at the Bridge Table*
by Prakash K. Paranjape
128pp., PB   Can $15.95   US $12.95

For Love or Money *The Life of a Bridge Journalist*
by Mark Horton and Brian Senior
(foreword by Omar Sharif)
189pp., PB   Can $22.95   US $16.95

I Shot my Bridge Partner by Matthew Granovetter
384pp., PB   Can $19.95   US $14.95

Murder at the Bridge Table by Matthew Granovetter
320pp., PB   Can $19.95   US $14.95

Partnership Bidding *A Workbook* by Mary Paul
96pp., PB   Can $9.95   US $7.95

Playing With The Bridge Legends by Barnet Shenkin
(forewords by Zia and Michael Rosenberg)
192pp., PB   Can $22.95   US $16.95

Saints and Sinners: *The St. Titus Bridge Challenge*
by David Bird & Tim Bourke
192pp., PB   Can $19.95   US $14.95

Tales out of School *'Bridge 101' and other stories* by David Silver
(foreword by Dorothy Hayden Truscott)
128pp., PB   Can $ 12.95   US $9.95

The Bridge Player's Bedside Book edited by Tony Forrester
256pp., HC   Can $27.95   US $19.95

The Complete Book of BOLS Bridge Tips edited by Sally Brock
176pp., PB (photographs)   Can $24.95   US $17.95

There Must Be A Way... *52 challenging bridge hands*
by Andrew Diosy (foreword by Eddie Kantar)
96pp., PB $9.95 US & Can.

You Have to See This... *52 more challenging bridge problems*
by Andrew Diosy and Linda Lee
96pp., PB   Can $12.95   US $9.95

World Class — *Conversations with the Bridge Masters*
by Marc Smith
288pp., PB (photographs)   Can $24.95   US $17.95